Word/Information Processing

Concepts and Procedures

Word/Information Processing
Concepts and Procedures

L. Joyce Arntson
Saddleback College
Irvine, California

Kent Publishing Company
A Division of Wadsworth, Inc.
Boston, Massachusetts

Senior Editor: Richard C. Crews

Production Editor: Nancy Phinney

Text Designer: Glenna Collett

Cover Designer: Skolos, Wedell & Raynor

Kent Publishing Company
A Division of Wadsworth, Inc.

Printed in the United States of America

1 2 3 4 5 6 7 8 9 — 87 86 85 84 83

Library of Congress Cataloging in Publication Data

Arntson, L. Joyce.
    Word/information processing.

    Includes index.
    1. Word processing (Office practice)   I. Title.
HF5548.115.A77   1983   652   82-18020
ISBN 0-534-01346-5

To my husband, Ronald H. Arntson

Without his support, this
and other projects may
never have come to fruition.

Contents

Part V WORD PROCESSING SPECIALIST'S PROCEDURES MANUAL 197

Preface

This book was written for you—the student and the professional worker in the word/information processing industry, a rapidly changing industry with many challenging opportunities. Described throughout are the industry, its changes, and career opportunities. Illustrations and examples presented give a state-of-the-art view of the industry as it operates today. Procedures manuals also presented teach practical and effective use of technology in the creation, production, reproduction, and distribution of documents.

The key to productivity is the combination of knowledgeable, skilled people with technology and procedures. Consequently, this book focuses on this combination and attempts to:

1. Show how word/information processing (WP) relates to management information systems (MIS).
2. Present the broad concepts of word/information processing and its four phases.
3. Apply these concepts through the use of industry-like procedures.

Part I is an industry overview. Chapter 1 presents management information systems (MIS), their four components (administrative support, word processing, data processing, and records management), how these components relate, and how they are integrated.

Chapter 2 presents MIS career opportunities as they relate to AS, WP, DP, and RM. Because of integration of these components and trends toward decentralization, MIS interrelationships are shown.

Chapter 3 describes the development, justification, and components of the WP industry and organizational designs.

Part II presents the input and output phases of WP. Chapter 4 discusses input, the origination of information, the technology available, and related skills. Chapter 5 categorizes and presents technology for output, the production of documents. Print devices and media are some components discussed. Chapter 6 relates technology to production of documents. Seven common types of documents produced in WP are illustrated, in addition to transcription concepts and procedures. Chapter 7 is concerned with output procedures and includes proofreading, critical in document production.

Part III encompasses the reprographic and distribution phases of the WP industry. Explored in Chapter 8 are the reprographic processes, how they relate, and how they can be integrated or improved with the use of WP equipment. Integration of phototypesetting with WP equipment and organizational designs are discussed.

Chapter 9 presents perhaps the most dynamic phase of the WP industry—telecommunications. The future of the industry lies in the integration of different equipment. The speed, accuracy, and reduced costs of telecommunications contribute significantly to productivity. This chapter also includes the science of micrographics, important in cost-effective records management.

A section on future trends in many of the chapters gives readers a glimpse into people aspects and what to expect in various technologies and procedures.

End-of-chapter activities review material in Chapters 1–9. Summaries, key terms, review questions, and case problems help to verify the reader's understanding of the text. A glossary at the end of the text defines commonly used terminology.

To illustrate document origination, a User's Procedures Manual is provided in Part IV for clients of Arnco, Inc., a hypothetical AS and WP service bureau. It demonstrates what a user needs to know to get information produced and distributed through WP, reprographics, and telecommunications. This procedures manual brings global concepts to a practical level for students. The manual emulates industry and is a composite of several actual user's manuals.

An important extension to output chapters, the Word Processing Specialist's Procedures Manual for Arnco, Inc., in Part V assists WP specialists with procedures for transcription, optical character recognition, keyboarding, language arts, and formatting. Formatting is addressed in the style guide, a collection of commonly used documents for clients of four industries—general business, legal, medical, and engineering/technical. These documents illustrate in the creation and production of communications the detail that is required to ensure maximum productivity for users and support staff. Sections on magnetic media retention and filing demonstrate how databasing documents reduces or eliminates paper files. As records management becomes more expensive for organizations, magnetic media databases become more valuable.

Both manuals contain procedural information relating to reprographics. Considerations regarding cost, quality, turnaround time, and binding are included in the User's Manual; logging and clerical considerations are included in the Word Processing Specialist's Procedures Manual. Both procedures manuals also include important distribution procedures and how they relate to the user or WP specialist.

The instructor's manual which accompanies the text provides additional material. Especially important in the instructor's manual are exercises for use with the procedures manuals. Transparencies and lecture notes for class presentations, tests for each chapter, a unit examination for each part, a final examination, and an additional case study for each chapter are also included in the instructor's manual. As you build your future in this exciting industry, I hope this text makes a positive contribution.

L. Joyce Arntson

Acknowledgements

Without the help of many, this book would not have been completed. A thank you is not enough; special mention must be given to:

Phyllis Barnes, for coordinating the production of the manuscript.

My production editor, Nancy Phinney, for producing the book.

My editors, Wayne Barcomb, David McEttrick, and Dick Crews whose many ideas and suggestions are incorporated.

Patsy Emmert, Hazel Francis, Jean Gonzalez, Sue Hein, Barbara Horton, John Moss, Dixie Sandahl, and Margaret Taylor, who contributed ideas and material in the preparation of the manuscript.

Jeffrey Krause for his willingness to share his wealth of knowledge of the WP industry.

John Aufhammer and James McHugh for sharing their vast knowledge of telecommunications.

Ann Cambron, Teri Ciranna, Jo Ann Clemens, Judie Fowler, Sylvia Goldberg, Jane Hestor, and Carol Taylor for typing away many hours on the manuscript.

Special thanks to artists George Kyle and Diane Marlin.

Special appreciation goes to the vendors who gave so generously of illustration materials.

For their helpful suggestions the reviewers of the text are also acknowledged:
    Joylne Ghanatabadi, Des Moines Area Community College
    A. Goodfriend, Queensborough Community College
    Linda Henson, Jefferson College
    Grace Heringer, Syline College
    Mina M. Johnson, San Francisco State University
    Marjorie A. Turner, Lake City Community College
    Kathleen P. Wagoner, Ball State University
    Mary Weidman, Cerritos College

About the Author

L. Joyce Arntson is Professor of Business Science at Saddleback College North Campus. She has an M.B.A. from California State University, Long Beach. She was born and grew up in Houston, Texas, but began her career in the word processing industry in southern California where she has lived for 17 years.

She speaks nationally and has written and conducted seminars for many organizations. Her areas of expertise are management information systems including telecommunications, design and implementation of word processing systems, productivity, procedures, records management and retention systems, and training of management and support staff.

She has written a number of articles that have been published in word processing journals as well as audiovisual publications. As a consultant and specialist in business and word processing education, she has developed complete programs for several colleges and schools either in a teaching capacity or as a consultant.

As an active participant in the International Information/Word Processing Association, she has chaired the Educators' Advisory Council and is presently the national chairperson of the telecommunications task force.

Part I
****
AN INDUSTRY OVERVIEW

Chapter 1

****

Management Information Systems

Chapter Objectives

After reading this chapter and completing the end-of-chapter activities, the student will be able to:

1. Define management information systems (MIS).

2. Describe the components of MIS—administrative support, word/information processing, data processing, and records management—and their interrelationships.

What Is a Management Information System?

management information system

Do you work or have you worked in an office that is highly efficient, cost effective, and well organized? Is it an organization where a system has been established that will make executives more effective? Is paperwork produced without restarts and retypes? Are there procedures that prevent duplication of effort and establish backup support? Is information readily available when needed for effective decision making?

If this sounds like a place you know, the chances are that a **management information system** (MIS) has been implemented. A MIS is a method of organizing and producing information that uses well-designed procedures and sophisticated equipment to assist the management in operating the business in a cost effective and efficient way.

Such a system helps to solve the major problems for many businesses—high costs of operation, low productivity, poor communications, insufficient time, lack of information, and employee dissatisfaction.

Consider the cost of people working in an organization. Frequently, 70 percent of an organization's budget is salaries and associated benefits for employees (Figure 1.2). If these employees can be assisted by technology that provides a tool to be more productive, the business will benefit. If a system is designed with streamlined procedures that further assist in getting the job done, communications have probably improved considerably. In order to achieve cost effectiveness, maximum productivity, and good communications, an organization must be structured in such a way that people are employed and trained to work in an area of their interest at their maximum capacity. Executives can administer most effectively with a system designed to make necessary information for decision making readily available and easily accessible. All of these results are likely in organizations with MIS. A business organization with

Figure 1.1. Data General Corporation's approach to a management information system using the ECLIPSE MV/Family. Courtesy of Data General Corporation and Bob O'Shaughnessy, Copyright 1981, Bob O'Shaughnessy.

Figure 1.2. Personnel costs compared to total costs of the office. (*Source: Office of the Future,* 1976, Stanford Research Institute, guideline series.)

wise leadership designs a MIS that will assist executives and extend their efforts. Goals to balance the work load and narrow the peaks and valleys are important. The system should provide for:

1. Delegation of all routine tasks to support staff.
2. Manipulation, storage, and retrieval of information.
3. Preparation, reproduction, and distribution of documents.
4. Immediate retrieval of records from both permanent and temporary files.
5. Support personnel to assist in nondelegable duties.

Managers and executives operate or manage the business. Professionals and technologists provide the expertise required to operate the functions of the organization. Examples of professionals and technologists are accountants, programmers, and engineers. Other people—support staff—trained in handling specific kinds of tasks assist or support them. It is important that executives spend their time doing what they are charged to do and that only they can do—manage. They should not perform routine or clerical duties to be optimally productive.

The functions required to accomplish these goals may be divided into four parts: *administrative support* (AS), *word/information processing* (WP), *data processing* (DP), and *records management* (RM). With the development of technology, the design of systems and procedures, and the rise of trained personnel, each of these four parts has grown into a field of its own. Even so, they still relate to one another. Not only does each of the parts represent a method of cost reduction and increase in productivity, but each represents career opportunities that promote employee satisfaction. Used appropriately, these tasks make available greater time and information to do business on a productive and cost effective basis.

1. Management Information Systems

This book's primary focus is on WP and its integration with the other components in the MIS. In order to understand WP and its relationship to MIS, it is necessary to look at the whole and at each of its components, AS, WP, DP, and RM (Figure 1.3).

Administrative Support

administrative support

Administrative support (AS) is the assistance given to management and the professional staff in carrying out office duties. The individual working in an AS capacity is usually called an administrative secretary or administrative assistant. This support involves nontyping and nontechnical tasks such as locating and compiling information, opening and sorting mail, ordering and stocking office supplies, scheduling conferences and appointments, calculating and preparing fiscal data, proofreading, greeting and directing visitors, composing routine documents, answering telephones, and planning itineraries as well as other routine tasks that can be delegated.

These delegable tasks contribute significantly to the appeal of the position and the cost effectiveness of the job. Secretaries want more challenging work. When administrative secretaries assume more responsibility, executives can better allocate their time and do more sophisticated work, and the job of the AS staff becomes more challenging. Much work is being done to develop the administrative secretary job descriptions more fully because of the tremendous organizational savings possible. Consider five middle managers earning $25,000 a year plus benefits and spending one hour per day doing such clerical tasks as copying, a common practice. This costs the organization over $15,000 annually. If the administrative secretary were doing the work at half the salary cost, the company would save almost $8,000 in direct salary costs alone. Also, consider what the savings would be if administrative secretaries were trained to do some of the routine or delegable tasks managers presently do.

There are at least three ways that organizations have set up the work environment of AS staff—one-to-one, one-to-several, and several-to-several. Depending on the size of the organization and the design of the personnel structure, the duties of the AS staff vary. There seem to be at least three levels of AS staff—receptionist/clerks, administrative secretaries or assistants, and senior administrative secretaries or assistants. These are differentiated and described more fully in Chapter 2. In small companies an administrative secretary may also have receptionist responsibilities, whereas large organizations most frequently need one or more receptionists as well as administrative secretaries or assistants. The executive involved as well as the

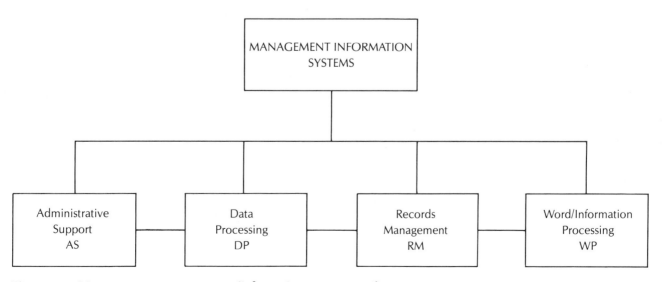

Figure 1.3. Management support system (information management).

traditionalism of the organization often affects whether each executive has a secretary or shares one or several with other executives.

One-to-One

There still is and may always be a one-to-one relationship with one executive supported by one administrative secretary. Although it takes a busy executive with many delegable tasks to justify the cost of a one-to-one administrative support relationship, many do exist. The administrative secretary is really an extension of the executive, helping to stretch his or her efforts.

One-to-Several

More common in organizations using a systems approach to management support is the one-to-several relationship, where the administrative secretary provides direct assistance to several executives. Here one administrative secretary is located close to the offices of the several executives he or she supports. In many cases, this design offers good support at less cost. The work of several executives is kept moving. Peaks and valleys of the secretarial work load may be more even. However, developing priorities becomes important since there are several executives being assisted. Whose work comes first? Which is most important?

Several-to-Several

Another environment for the administrative secretary is that of a team of AS specialists providing assistance to a number of executives. In this environment, the AS center functions in a manner similar to a WP center where several secretaries assist several executives. The administrative secretaries have primary or direct responsibilities to one or more executives and secondary or backup support responsibilities to the other executives whom the AS team assists. This organizational model ensures that every executive has someone who is responsible for providing direct or primary

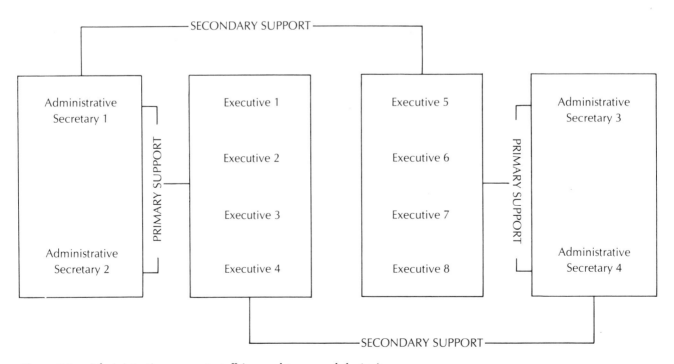

Figure 1.4. Administrative support staff (several-to-several design).

support. When an administrative secretary with primary support responsibilities is absent, there is someone available for secondary or backup support of those executives.

Administrative Support with Typing Duties

The three models of AS discussed in the previous sections have separated typing duties from AS tasks, and WP has been responsible for document production. However, some executives and MIS experts are again including typing in the AS staff's duties, primarily because of the significant reduction in the cost of WP equipment. Some consider the most cost effective model is to separate AS tasks from WP tasks because the more a person specializes in a specific area, the more skilled the employee becomes.

The rationale for combining the tasks can, however, also be justified. Some executives simply like to work with one secretary. A more substantial reason is that this model provides a higher level of individual support to the executive. The executive and secretary can work as a team. The secretary can assist in the preparation of documents and may directly apply an awareness of meetings and conversations to a document being produced. Content errors may be caught by the secretary as a matter of course in working through the document.

Let us suppose that you assume duties of answering telephone calls, copying documents, and compiling data formerly done by your employer who earns $25,000 per year plus benefits. Your task which previously cost $260 will cost $125. Indeed, if secretaries can provide a greater level of support to executives by absorbing more of their routine responsibilities and enabling executives to do more of the tasks that only they can do, perhaps in the long run this model is as cost efficient, if not more so, than an AS system that does not include typing.

Let us analyze this. Suppose you work for Arnco, Inc., for $1,000 per month plus benefits as an administrative secretary with typing or WP duties. If your duties are evenly divided between AS and WP, you are paid $500 per month for each type of work. If you have WP equipment to assist you in your duties you can produce at least three times the documents or $1500 worth. However, it costs your organization only your salary, $500, plus the cost of the equipment, say, $275 per month. Thus, the organization pays $775 for $1500 worth of document production work.

However, let us recognize that the key to success in the design of a system is what works for that organization. There are no ironclad absolutes; flexibility is very important in a system design.

Word/Information Processing

word/information processing

What is this thing called **word/information processing** (WP)? It can be many things to many people. To some, it is simply a faster method of typing by using a WP system. To others, it has become a systematized way of performing the office tasks or perhaps a portion of them. To many, WP is a method of producing, copying, and distributing information using advanced technology, sophisticated procedures, and highly skilled personnel. Basically, WP is a method of producing information from the author in an appropriate format as cost effectively as possible by using equipment and procedures designed for this purpose. Then, if it is necessary, the document is revised, copied, and telecommunicated to a recipient via electronic transmission over telephone lines.

Since its beginning, WP has been in a constant state of evolution. Today, with an industry that includes more advanced technology than it did a decade ago, word and data processing technology is becoming more integrated with the processing of

Figure 1.5. The Xerox 9700, an intelligent printer/copier, simultaneously produces computer-generated text, business forms, and a wide variety of graphics at a speed of up to two pages a second. It also duplexes, produces microfiche, and communicates with word processing equipment. Courtesy of Xerox Corporation.

information. The name word/information processing more closely describes the industry as it has developed.

A word processing system has vastly improved, for example, the flow of paperwork for the U.S. Supreme Court, which hands down hundreds of pages of opinions in one day. Since as many as fifteen rewrites are required to compose an opinion acceptable to a majority of the judges, a large savings will occur in the drafting and revision of opinions.[1]

The basic functions of a WP system are to provide a way to produce, copy, store, and distribute easily the paperwork on which a business operates. The paperwork required is often an ocean so vast that it threatens to drown some poorly organized executives and their businesses.

WP technology is rapidly advancing. WP equipment not only permits the typewritten characters to be captured for future revision and modification but also to be used in the creation of similar documents. This library or database of stored documents saves time for the author because he or she does not have to write an entire new document, and the secretary does not have to retype the entire document.

A variety of forms can be produced from stored files or lists of information after only one keyboarding. The stored information can also be sorted either alphabetically or numerically. These capabilities are significant. For example, a list of employees may be keyboarded with their titles, departments, and building locations. From the one keyboarding, an alphabetical list may be produced of all employees or of any department selected. The employees in the Harris-Addington Building, for example, may be listed sequentially by room number. Ways to reproduce the information are limited mainly by the imagination of the executive and support staff.

WP equipment also easily produces repetitive correspondence. Many organizations send numerous letters with essentially the same message to different recipients. The improvement in time savings, due to easy revision techniques and personalized mass production is significant. Math functions are also available. Finally,

---

[1]"Word Processing: The High Court Affirms High Tech," *Business Week,* April 12, 1982, p. 108c.

telecommunications **telecommunications** (electronic transmission of the document) using WP equipment assures timely receipt.

Vendors, that is, equipment manufacturers, say more sophisticated equipment is ready for marketing. However, the enormous job of educating managers and office staff is taking time. Little by little, communication improvements are occurring as we learn to apply the equipment available. More advanced equipment will be released by vendors when the market is profitable, that is, when managers and staff are able to integrate this equipment into their offices.

To use the new equipment most effectively, WP managers and supervisors write detailed procedures for handling the office functions. In fact, the procedures are as essential as the automated equipment in promoting efficiency, productivity, and standardization.

To review, some important advantages of WP are:

1. Increased efficiency for executives and support staff.
2. Higher quality documents.
3. Greater utilization of equipment.
4. Improved utilization of employee talents and abilities.
5. Increased productivity.
6. Electronic libraries of documents from which to create new documents.
7. Availability of information, alphabetical and numerical.
8. Timely receipt of the document.

Data Processing

data processing

Data processing (DP) is the entry, processing, control, and storage of data, which is often of a numerical nature. Since its birth in the 1950s, DP has become more and more sophisticated.

The computer has several components—terminal, logic system, output device, software, and media. A terminal can be a work station used to input or keyboard data, or to access, use, or print stored data. A terminal with both keyboarding and printing characteristics is called an input/output (I/O) terminal (Figure 1.7). The logic

Figure 1.6. Fast and direct communications are provided through telecommunications. Courtesy of Wang Laboratories, Inc.

Figure 1.7. The Apple II Plus personal computer system includes components for input, output, storage, as well as software for increasing capabilities. Courtesy of Apple Computer, Inc.

central processing unit (CPU) system or brain of the computer is in the **central processing unit (CPU)**. The CPU controls the storage of data on the computer. The memory inside the computer can take several forms, such as a drum, chip, disc, or bubble. The present trend in small, powerful, yet less costly devices is toward the chip.

A computer also needs an output device, such as a printer or screen. Programs or software are the instructions that make the computer perform desired tasks. The software may have to be written as new tasks are defined; some is commercially available that has universal appeal. Software that can be purchased may be called *media* canned. **Media** are the device on which the data and software are stored. Forms of media include magnetic tape, diskettes, and rigid disc technologies.

Computers and their terminals have become smaller, faster, and less expensive. Originally, business and industry used computers for financial applications; today they are used for both financial and technical applications. It is estimated that as much as 30 percent of the entire United States work force uses DP for its daily work. In fact, today computers in the form of microprocessors are being installed in homes for personal use.

The DP cycle has three elements: input, processing, and output. The equipment *hardware* used in DP, called **hardware**, consists of input equipment, output equipment, and the central processing unit.

Input

input **Input** means to enter data to be stored on media for manipulation, updating, and printing. The methods of inputting are keypunching cards or paper tape and reading

Figure 1.8. Components of Data General Corporation ECLIPSE MV/8000—display terminals, CPU, storage, and printer—with access to storage of over 4 billion characters of information. Courtesy of Data General Corporation and Bob O'Shaughnessy. Copyright 1981, Bob O'Shaughnessy.

them into the computer, or keyboarding data into the central processing unit with a typewriter-like terminal.

Central Processing Unit

processing

The CPU is the logic and controller and handles the storage of the system; this is the **processing** of the data. The logic capabilities are those such as arithmetic or comparison. The controller unit makes sure the computer does what it is told; that is, that it follows the instructions of the computer programs, or software. However, unique programs for special applications are sometimes necessary for the computer to perform certain functions. The CPU also controls the massive storage capacity of the computer. The storage capability makes it possible to store much more on media in a fraction of the space it takes to file paper in cabinets that take up expensive floor space.

There are many languages of DP systems—Fortran, COBOL, BASIC, PL11, RPG, and APL are only a few. These languages represent different ways that the software is written.

Output

output
cathode ray tube

Data may be **output** or shown for reading on either a **cathode ray tube** (CRT) or gas plasma screen that looks much like a television screen, printed on paper at the terminal, or printed by a separate line printer that is controlled by the terminal and used for high-speed printing. Printers are available with a variety of speeds and quality.

Figure 1.9. This Xerox 820 information processor can be used as a desktop computer and/or word processor with the appropriate software. Courtesy of Xerox Corp.

Interfacing Data Processing and Word Processing

There are similarities between DP and WP. They both have input, output, media, and processing or logic. With DP, input is via keypunched cards, paper tape, or typing into a terminal; with WP, input is by typing onto a word processing keyboard from dictation, long hand, revised typed copy, and so forth. Output for both DP and WP may be on paper or on the CRT screen itself. Media for DP may be diskettes, tapes, or hard discs; media for WP may be tapes, magnetic cards, diskettes or hard discs. Both DP equipment and WP equipment contain logic for carrying out the machine functions. WP and DP technologies are converging. WP equipment is talking to DP equipment through cables connecting them or over telephone lines. Data keyboarded on WP equipment is being stored in the computer. WP equipment is reproducing numerical data from the computer in documents.

Many DP systems can also perform WP functions and vice versa. In fact, it is possible to save money on equipment by acquiring a terminal that can work with WP equipment as well as with the computer. The computer often assists the WP equipment with document functions such as **photocomposition** and **computer output microfilm (COM)**. Photocomposition is the setting up and printing of text in a variety of type styles and type sizes. COM is the technical creation by computer command of microfilm directly from text stored in the computer.

photocomposition
computer output
microfilm (COM)

As WP equipment continues to evolve, it will be more DP-oriented. As office automation is more universally implemented, the computer will play the central role.

Records Management

hard copy

An important reason for the development of an organization's records management is the cost of storing **hard copy**. (In industry, hard copy is the name used for paper copies.) Consider the cost of the floor space where a file cabinet is set and used, let alone its purchase price. A space approximately three feet by five feet is needed for

Figure 1.10. Comp Set phototypesetter. Courtesy of AM Varityper, a Division of AM International, Inc.

Figure 1.11. The merging of micrographic and computer technologies—computer output microforms (COM) and computer assisted retrieval (CAR)—makes millions of documents available at the touch of a key. Courtesy of Eastman Kodak Company.

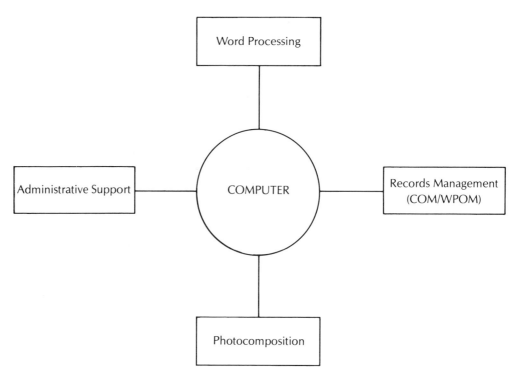

Figure 1.12. The computer plays the central role in office automation.

one file cabinet; this is fifteen square feet. How much does a square foot of office space cost? If it is $1.00 per month, as it is in some large cities, it costs $15 per month for each file cabinet, that is, for floor space for only one file cabinet. How many does the average organization have? If as many as one hundred are used, this is the price of one support staff's salary. When the number of file cabinets in an organization is multiplied by $15, it is easy to see why organizations are looking more and more toward electronic filing systems.

Consider the following:

> Fifteen hundred trillion pieces of paper are filed in the nation's offices and storerooms and this number is growing at the rate of 62 million file drawers each year. Studies have revealed the following:
>
> 1. Of the nation's papers, 35 percent could be destroyed and not be missed. This would save $500 million annually or $20 per cubic foot.
>
> 2. Another 20 percent is equally useless but these papers are interfiled with useful records. The cost to weed them out would be greater than retaining them.
>
> 3. Of the remaining papers, 95 percent are useful for five years or less. About 50 percent can be kept in low-cost storage rather than office space. *Only 1 percent must be kept permanently.*[2]
>
> 4. It costs an average of 7 cents to index and file one paper—$1,343.75 for a single five-drawer cabinet.[3]

records management   **Records management** (RM) is the systematized method of indexing, storing, and maintaining a retrieval system for permanent documents. Because of government regulations and threat of lawsuits as well as good business practice, more and more documents are being stored. How can we store only that which is essential and retrieve it quickly, easily, and economically? Around these goals are built some very effective file retention systems to provide the information needed by managers. The

[2]H. B. Maynard, ed., *The Handbook of Business Administration* (New York: McGraw-Hill, Inc., 1967).
[3]3M Company study, December, 1981.

documents on file may be on paper, micrographics, or WP or computer media. Many organizations file their permanent documents that they have generated on WP or computer media. What about documents received that need to be retained on a permanent basis? A good method of permanent retention is to file them on micrographics, that is, on **microfilm** or **microfiche**. Microfilm is photographed text in miniature form on small reels of film.

microfilm
microfiche

Microfiche, or fiche, is typically a 105 mm by 148 mm sheet of film containing rows of images in a grid pattern. Chapter 9 presents more detail about this process.

Retention is a major consideration in a RM program. The government dictates retention of some documents, the organization's policies may establish some retention, and individual managers may specify a certain retention. Integrating all these requirements and dealing with the volume and costs may be quite a challenge.

Some organizations are trying to establish a records management program with less paper. An example of such an office is Micronet, Inc., in Washington, D.C. In fact, its goal is to be a totally paperless office, using instead WP and DP media and microfiche for storage. Micronet suggests that an average savings of one million dollars in filing costs over a ten-year period is likely.

Employees at Micronet, Inc., use a telephone, a centralized dictation system, a terminal to access their computer, and a microfiche reader/terminal. All documents are generated via dictation to the endless loop system where the material is transcribed by a WP specialist using a WP system and is stored on a magnetic diskette. If a copy is to be mailed, it is printed. Otherwise, it is stored, and, if important, transferred to the computer's active storage file. This permits reference for anyone who desires it. After ninety days all stored documents are reviewed. Those that are no longer needed are erased. All others are electronically converted to microfiche via the computer output microfilm (COM) process. In addition, all incoming documents are recorded on microfiche before delivery to the recipient. Thus, the entire system

Figure 1.13. Microforms. Courtesy of 3M Micrographic Products Division.

revolves around the reliable, retrievable technology of microfiche with little need for paper.

The important thing is that an organized system does exist that will store all incoming, outgoing, and internal documents for easy access and retrieval. The successful records system requires an indexing method which promotes this easy retrieval of information and cost effective storage. The system not only serves the executive as a source of reference, but also provides access to an established database. A **database** is a collection of existing documents, from which parts may be used for new documents. The essential elements of a system are **integrated technologies** (different types of equipment working together) that are effective and economical to use, procedures to make the system work, and people trained to use and administer the system.

database
integrated
technologies

Future Trends

Alvin Toffler identifies the first movement of labor as an agricultural one and the second, the industrial revolution, as a movement of people into the factory. His third wave heralds an information explosion in the office at an accelerated pace that threatens to leave behind masses of people who are not knowledgeable about data technology, its integration into the office, and its implementation. The world becomes a small place indeed with the swift spread of a global telecommunications network.

The challenge for people will be to cope with the rapid pace. Some people have extreme difficulty with change; many would prefer to have no change. People in existing positions fear that they may lose recognition or promotions if they do not keep up with the technology. Even so, the office of the future will be an interesting one with technological solutions for some of our current problems.

Administrative Support

Work stations for management and AS are likely to involve multifunction, multimedia terminals. Tying executives into the automated office system will give them direct access to reports, files, correspondence, and budget, as well as to other information. They will have better control of their time through calendar reminder and follow-up functions. Communications among executive offices and branches will be accelerated. Calculation capabilities will be a helpful tool in the performance of the job. The terminals will also make the administrative secretary's job of calendaring and scheduling easier. Instead of making many telephone calls to determine personnel availability for a meeting, an AS secretary may find accessing their calendars in the system's memory quite simple. Reminder systems, or tickler follow-up files, will be convenient. Message taking will become second nature due to the knowledge of people's whereabouts which will be keyed in before they leave their offices. Personal databases will cut down significantly on composition time for the author and typing time for the secretary when text can be pulled from an already stored document.

Word Processing

More and more companies will be testing and implementing WP. WP systems will replace regular electric typewriters. WP operations will tie in with other departments in the information network such as DP, photocomposition, and micrographics. This will create extensive and complex information systems. Greater sophistication and capabilities will provide for a higher level of task performance. WP technology will take on many more DP capabilities. Standardization as well as telecommunications will permit more compatible integration. Faster and higher quality printers will produce larger quantities of work with a high level of quality.

Data Processing

It is said that business will change as much or more in the decade of the 1980s as it did from 1930 to 1980. Computers will play a major role in this change. By the middle of the decade, 70 percent of the work force will rely on computers for daily work.

The computer is making a monumental amount of information available through stored databases. Existing today and available is a range of data from what was printed on any given date in *The New York Times* to the many theses from the major universities to what an individual needs to do to incorporate a business, complete with all the forms.

In fact, there is a concern by the professions that their businesses will become do-it-yourself operations. Doctors can subscribe to a diagnostic service and can key in the symptoms of a patient and get a preliminary diagnosis. What implications does this have for individuals? Will we key in our temperatures, and other problems and have a diagnosis and medication prescribed? That may be a bit extreme but, on the other hand, it is not impossible. The legal profession also has concerns. If an attorney performs the activities necessary to incorporate a business, he charges several hundred dollars. If, however, an individual can key into a legal database and see the instructions and forms to complete, and then simply have an attorney review them, the cost to the individual is much less—and so is the attorney's income.

These vast storehouses of data are also helping the professions. To research a case via a computer takes far less time than to go through volumes of books. If an attorney is working on a case where a dog bites an individual and needs to know the legal precedents, the database can be quickly searched for the dog bite cases and their decisions for a given time, region, and so forth. To be sure, the computer databases existing today are only the tip of the iceberg compared to what is anticipated throughout the decade.

With extensive development of microprocessors and computers, people will need them on and off the job to work, play, and shop. An important question may be whether the computer is a mainframe, minicomputer, or microcomputer. The energy crunch and the hardware development will work together to expand this area.

Records Management

The combination and integration of technologies seems to be the direction of the decade for records management. There will be an increased emphasis on multi-function equipment and a total systems approach.

Retrieval for computer assisted micrographics is expected to continue its present rate of growth. These microforms will be generated from WP equipment telecommunicated to the computer and from computer terminals.

Facsimile is expected to be able to transmit microfilm electronically via telephone lines in the same way as hard copy is transmitted now.

Summary

A management information system (MIS) is a management tool that enables the executive to lower the cost of operations, increase productivity, improve communications, and make needed information available for decision making. It also provides additional career paths for employees. It is a systematized procedure using sophisticated technology and highly trained personnel for administering the office paper flow, information and records management. The four components of MIS are administrative support (AS), word/information processing (WP), data processing (DP), and records management (RM).

AS staff have the responsibilities of greeting and directing visitors, answering telephones, filing, sorting, opening, and distributing the mail, composing routine correspondence, scheduling meetings and appointments, planning itineraries, and other delegable tasks that will assist the executive.

WP is a systematized method of producing, copying, and distributing documents using advanced technology, sophisticated procedures, and highly skilled personnel. WP significantly increases the cost effectiveness of the paper flow.

DP is the entry, processing, control, and storage of data. The computer is often used in conjunction with WP equipment to interrelate the information functions in the office further.

RM is the systematized indexing, storing, and retrieving of documents. The increase in numbers of records as well as the cost of retrieval and storage have contributed to the expansion of this field.

Key Terms

Administrative support (AS)
Cathode ray tube (CRT)
Central processing unit (CPU)
Computer output microfilm (COM)
Database
Data processing (DP)
Hard copy
Hardware
Input
Integrated technologies
Management information system (MIS)
Media
Microfiche
Microfilm
Output
Photocomposition
Processing
Records management (RM)
Telecommunications
Word/information processing (WP)

Self-Check Questions

Completion

1. A _____ is a method of organizing people using well-designed _____ and sophisticated _____ to assist the management in operating the business in a cost effective way.
2. _____ is defined as assisting management to carry out the duties of the office.
3. There are at least three ways organizations have set up the work environment of AS staff. They are _____, _____, and _____.
4. _____ can be defined as a systematized method of producing, copying, and distributing documents using advanced technology, sophisticated procedures, and highly skilled personnel.
5. _____ and _____ are as important as the automated equipment in a WP system.
6. The DP cycle has three elements. These are _____, _____, and _____.
7. Computer programs are also called _____.
8. _____ is a systematized method of indexing, storing, and retrieving permanent documents.
9. Five applications that could be performed on an administrative terminal by a manager are _____, _____, _____, _____, and _____.
10. Six applications that could be performed more easily and quickly on an administrative terminal by an administrative secretary are _____, _____, _____, _____, _____, and _____.

Matching
Write the correct definition letter in the space provided in front of the corresponding term.

Terms	Definitions
_____ 1. Administrative Support (AS)	a. Entry, processing, control, and storage of data to a computer.
_____ 2. Central Processing Unit (CPU)	b. Individual who works with users as they generate documents that must be permanently indexed and stored in the system.
_____ 3. Database	c. Electronic transmission of data between WP and DP equipment via telephone lines, hardwired cables, microwaves, and satellites.

_____ 4. Data Processing (DP)

_____ 5. Integrated Technologies

_____ 6. Media

_____ 7. Microfiche

_____ 8. Records Management (RM)

_____ 9. Telecommunications

_____ 10. Word Processing (WP)

d. People assigned to assist management in performing the nontyping duties of the office.

e. Library of stored documents from which new and different documents can be created.

f. Photographed text on sheets of film which has rows of images in a grid pattern.

g. Devices used for the recording or storing of data for dictation, computer, or WP equipment.

h. Systematized method of indexing, setting up, storing, and maintaining a retrieval system for permanent documents.

i. Systematized method of producing, copying, and distributing documents using technology, procedures, and trained people.

j. Unit which controls the storage, logic, and manipulation of the data on a computer and shared logic WP system.

k. Different types of equipment tied together through telecommunications to perform a function.

Exercises

Exercise 1.1. Visit individually or as a class a large organization. Write a report which focuses on:
1. The MIS.
2. The extent to which AS, WP, DP, and RM are used and the organizational design of each.

Exercise 1.2. Interview two managers of departments or organizations that have implemented a MIS. Discuss the operation of the organization before and after implementation. Write a report comparing their responses.

Exercise 1.3. In an automated office reference book or journal, read two articles discussing the implementation of a management information system. Compare and contrast the two in a short report.

Case Problem

Mr. Brown is launching a business to provide consulting services for organizations that wish to implement or expand MIS. His staff consists of two consultants, Ms. Cole, a specialist in DP, and Ms. Jurado, a specialist in RM. Mr. Brown's area of expertise is WP and its integration with all the components of MIS.

He wants to be sure he practices what he preaches. Thus, he wants his own organization to be set up in an appropriate style. What should he consider and how should he proceed?

Chapter 2

****

Career Opportunities in Management Information Systems

Chapter Objectives

After reading this chapter and completing the end-of-chapter activities, the student will be able to:

1. List and describe career choices in administrative support, word/information processing, data processing, and records management.

2. Describe career paths in all the components in management information systems.

3. Describe the basic duties of positions in each career path.

Introduction

In all the phases of WP there a great need for people, highly trained and interested in this new and exciting industry. If we look one step beyond WP into the total spectrum of information management, there are many, many opportunities. Information management includes AS, WP, DP, and RM; each of these components needs knowledgeable individuals. Also, there are various levels of positions—entry, experienced, and managerial.

Not only is there a variety of jobs in public and private industry in MIS, but the vendors of the technology and the systems design consultants also offer many challenging employment opportunities. Because some companies have combinations of the various MIS components in one position, it may be necessary to look at the job descriptions of all components to get a composite picture of what such a position would involve.

Professional organizations are an important resource for general information as well as career opportunities. These organizations provide an arena for people to meet and informally discuss openings in the job market. There are a number of organizations related to the various components of MIS. AS has many, including the Professional Secretaries International and the National Legal Secretaries Association. WP has the International Information/Word Processing Association (IWP), the National Association for Word Processing Specialists, and the Word Processing Society. DP has the Data Processing Management Association. RM has the Association of Records Managers and Administrators.

In the next few pages, let us look at each component and investigate career opportunities in each.

International Information/Word Processing Association

is a member of this Association which is dedicated to the purpose of contributing to the progress of information management through the development and exchange of ideas, methods and techniques pertaining to the processing of information in the office environment and to enhancing the recognition and professional status of those engaged in the field.

DATE OF ADMISSION

Lorraine M. Lear
EXECUTIVE DIRECTOR

Figure 2.1. International Information/Word Processing Association membership form. (Reprinted with the permission of the International Information/Word Processing Association.)

Administrative Support Career Opportunities

administrative support staff

The most numerous job opening for the 1980s is that of secretary. This has many implications. More opportunities and choices are developing. Salaries are increasing. Career paths leading from secretary are developing. The **administrative support staff** frequently is comprised of receptionists, administrative secretaries, senior administrative secretaries, supervisors, and managers. The career paths in AS and WP create the ability to grow vertically into new jobs or to move laterally between AS and WP. Some companies combine the two while others specialize.

The qualifications for AS include flexibility, self-direction, detail conciousness, and the ability to work with interruptions and under stress. Since the focus of this book is on WP, duties of the AS staff will be treated more fully here to enable those who may apply for combination positions to know all of the duties.

Receptionist

In the office of the 1980s, the reason we mechanize what we can is so we can afford to personalize what we should. Receptionist duties are important to personalize. Many organizations need receptionists not only at the main entrance to the facility, but also for various departments and divisions. The individual who functions as a receptionist should be someone who enjoys meeting the public. A receptionist appreciates the challenges of addressing each new person and of responding to each appropriately. Directing guests to the proper individual or department in the organization is an important function which requires extensive knowledge of the organization.

The directing of guests to the appropriate individual implies the use of another important skill—an ability to use the telephone, a very important instrument which

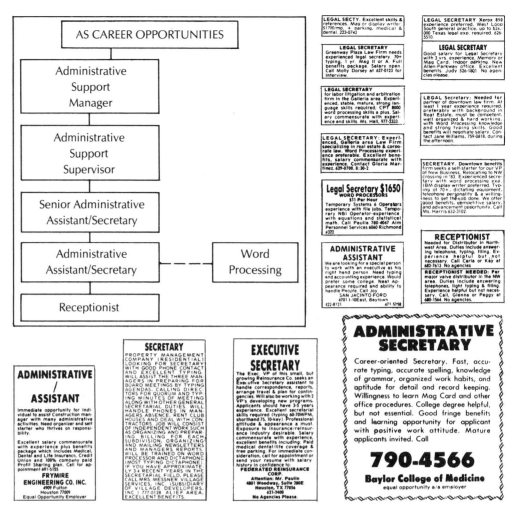

Figure 2.2. Advertisements for administrative support staff.

should be treated with respect. It is a tool of the trade that can make or lose a lot of business.

Miscellaneous duties are often delegated to an individual serving as receptionist for the organization. These duties normally are of a routine nature and can be started and stopped easily since the first responsibility is to the organization's callers. Much office support of a repetitive nature, such as the ordering of supplies, can also be performed by this individual.

Administrative Secretary

The administrative secretary is one who provides administrative assistance to an executive. The need for administrative secretaries is crucial. Management must have competent assistance; AS is necessary to provide for the functions of the executive's office—to ensure that deadlines are met and that business goes on. Many telephone and personnel inquiries can be handled by the administrative secretary. An individual who is familiar with the responsibilities of the office and the needs of the organization can perform some of the routine administrative tasks of the executive. Any efforts that save the executive time are cost effective. It makes sense to use a $15,000 support staff employee to perform the delegable tasks of a $35,000 executive. Direct support to the executive may include varied duties of a complex nature that require the exercise of judgment, such as arranging for and scheduling appointments and events, answering telephones, composing routine documents, photocopying, processing documents, filing, managing records, handling mail, and proofreading. Administrative secretaries may also act as a liaison between WP staff and the executives.

Senior Administrative Secretary

The senior administrative secretary is that person who has developed his or her skill level to a high degree. These secretaries often work in the areas of public relations, data compilation, and origination of routine documents on a higher level. Senior administrative secretaries frequently assist by researching topics for reports and presentations and by creating presentation materials as well. Composing and editing many of the documents in the work flow may be included in the challenging work day. The task of followthrough on departmental activities is an important concern. Completing delegated projects with appropriate directions from the manager is another facet of the complex nature of the position, which requires initiative and judgment.

Administrative Support Supervisor

The supervisor who coordinates a group of AS secretaries provides direction, training, and motivation. Complete training is essential and must include cross-training to provide backup during absences and peak loads. Selection, hiring, and evaluation are important parts of the supervisory role. By coordinating the evaluation and the training process, employees become most valuable.

Day-to-day operations of the support staff are directed by the AS supervisor. He or she may also serve as a liaison between the executive and the rest of the information management group.

The AS supervisor may handle special projects and confidential assignments which require both a knowledge of company policy and an ability to deal with all levels of personnel, including top management.

Administrative Support Manager

In large organizations there may be several AS centers. The manager is responsible for the administration, design, and overall monitoring of these centers. Selection, promotion, and evaluation of the supervisors and support staff are primary responsibilities.

Word Processing Career Opportunities

WP has a varied and multilevel career path. The WP staff consists of a WP specialist (from trainee to senior levels), technician, editor-proofreader, supervisor, and manager. The work may involve a centralized or production environment, a custom environment, or a combination or specialized production environment. These environments are fully discussed in Chapter 3. Qualifications for WP positions include flexibility, technical aptitude or machine affinity, logic application, the ability to work in a cooperative team environment, and the ability to handle interruptions and stress.

Opportunities with vendors are increasing in both marketing and training areas. Similarly, with the growth of the industry, the need for consultants increases.

Word Processing Trainee

word processing trainee

A **word processing trainee** is one who will be trained for an entry level position in the production of documents. Duties include routine transcription, keyboarding of text, and basic machine operations.

Word Processing Specialist

word processing specialist

A **word processing specialist** is skilled in the operation of WP system and transcriber. Fully utilizing the capabilities of the system, the WP specialist is able to format, keyboard, retrieve, revise, assemble, produce and telecommunicate documents.

Word Processing Technician

word processing technician

The **word processing technician**, a senior level WP staff member, works with minimum supervision in the document preparation process. The most complex and technical documents which require analysis of projects are assigned to this individual. Often confidential documents may be done by the senior WP technician. The individual holding this position is responsible for establishing and updating procedures, including electronic media files, for the operation of the organization. Proofreading is often coupled with editing in this senior level position. Training of new staff may also be included in the responsibilities of this position.

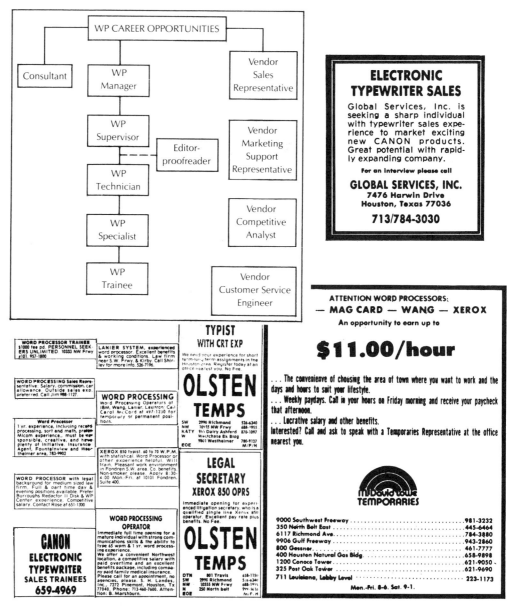

Figure 2.3. Advertisements for word processing specialists.

Editor-Proofreader

editor-proofreader

The **editor-proofreader** plays an important role in the production of documents by providing editorial assistance as the documents are being created and/or produced. Duties include proofreading the spelling and reviewing text content for consistency in format, appropriate use of grammar, capitalization, and punctuation.

Word Processing Supervisor

word processing supervisor

The **word processing supervisor** operates the center and monitors the work flow, as well as trains, motivates, and evaluates WP staff. The WP supervisor also acts as liaison with management and other information management departments. The analysis of production data and monitoring of quality control are important facets of this position.

Word Processing Manager

word processing manager

In large organizations there may be several WP centers. The **word processing manager** is responsible for administration, design, and overall monitoring of these centers, as well as design and implementation of future systems. Selection, guidance, promotion, and evaluation of the supervisors and WP staff are primary responsibilities. Budgeting and coordination of services are key duties of this position. A strong background in technology is important, but an ability to deal with people is even more important.

Vendor Positions and Consultants

consultant
vendor

Many career opportunities are available for those working as **consultants** or with **vendors**. Consultants are experts retained for assistance in designing, implementing, and maintaining a WP environment. Vendors are the manufacturers of WP equipment and supplies. People skills are primary in these positions. Marketing skills are also important for consultants and vendor sales representatives. With the projected 30 percent growth in the WP industry by 1985, sales representatives will make many sales. Very important to sales representatives are vendor service engineers or **marketing support representatives**, who train customers to use and apply equipment to their particular environment.

marketing support representative

Many opportunities may be available in training. Consultants often find that one of the greatest needs of their clients is greater training of personnel. Another area in which consultants seem to help considerably is the development of procedures and the writing of procedures manuals, which is another kind of training.

vendor competitive analyst

Vendor competitive analysts analyze equipment sold by other vendors so that they can brief sales representatives on how to sell against other vendors.

A very important and wide open field is that of customer service. Because a large part of a vendor's success is dependent on service, the demand for customer service engineers for all MIS technologies is very great.

Data Processing Career Opportunities

Career opportunities in DP are growing at a phenomenal rate. Computerization has created new, better-paying positions in place of many routine clerical jobs. However, computers are machines; it is the people who use them who generate the vast amount of data. Let us look at the most common positions these people fill as they work with the computer.

Data Entry Clerk and Keypunch Operator

data entry clerk
keypunch operator

Data entry clerks and **keypunch operators** keyboard, verify, and edit data to be entered into the computer. Keypunch operators prepare data for entry by punching

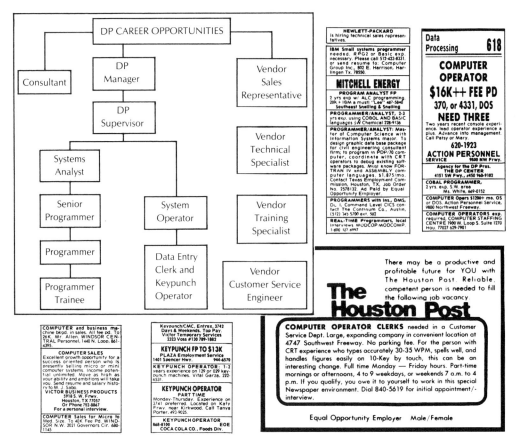

Figure 2.4. Advertisements for computer operators.

it on cards. Data entry clerks enter the data either directly into the computer or on cards, magnetic tapes, or discs.

Systems Operator

systems operator
peripheral equipment

A **systems operator** loads the input into the computer, starts it, operates **peripheral equipment** connected to the computer, and unloads it. The peripheral equipment may include such devices as printers or media units.

Programmer Trainee

A programmer trainee does basic design and debugs elementary programs. The programs are written in a computer language according to problem descriptions and specifications of systems analysts.

Programmer

programmer

A **programmer** designs, writes, and debugs program instructions to a computer. A programmer may specialize in scientific applications programming, business applications programming, or systems programming.

Senior Programmer

A senior programmer designs and develops advanced programs for special problems. Developing these programs often requires considerable interaction with the organization's management. This position may also include responsibility for confidential applications.

2. Career Opportunities in Management Information Systems

Systems Analyst

systems analyst

The **systems analyst** analyzes and designs information systems to solve user information needs. A close working relationship with managers, accountants, and various specialists within the organization, in order to determine their information needs, is necessary.

Supervisor

supervisor

The job of **supervisor** requires technical and supervisory skills. It involves work flow, working with other departments as liaison, and personnel considerations.

Manager

manager

In large organizations there may be such extensive DP facilities that there are several supervisors. The **manager** is responsible for administration, design, and overall monitoring of DP. Selection, promotion, and evaluation of the supervisors and DP staff are primary responsibilities.

Vendor Positions and Consultants

Career opportunities are available with vendors for people with technical expertise. These companies employ many people. Sales representatives, technical experts, trainers, and consultants enjoy working with people in conjunction with technical hardware. Marketing skills are important for consultants and sales representatives. Technical experts and trainers need to be able to relate equipment capabilities to people.

Consultants may specialize in computer services for a particular industry, such as insurance. They may design and implement systems and procedures, install equipment, or develop programs for specific needs.

Service engineers for computer equipment maintenance are highly sought-after personnel. These are definitely positions with good opportunities and much potential.

Figure 2.5. Control Data Corporation's test technician checks the memory module of a CYBER 170 Series 800 system. Courtesy of Control Data Corporation.

**Records
Management
Career
Opportunities**

RM is the application of technologies and procedures to the accumulation of reliable information. The voluminous amount of information available today has created a need for a documented information retrieval system. The people who work in such a system have career paths that include the following positions:

Clerk

clerk

A **clerk** in a RM center has the varied duties of taking file requests, refiling, creating lists, and maintaining records. A senior clerk may also work with filming micrographics.

Information Specialist

information specialist

The **information specialist** works with users as they generate documents to be entered into the system. The indexing system must show the new documents, and the new documents must reflect the numbering or coding of the indexing systems.

Systems Analyst

systems analyst

The **systems analyst** is responsible for analyzing user needs and designing and implementing documented information retrieval systems.

Records Management Manager

*records management
manager*

The **records management manager** is responsible for the design of the RM center, liaison with users, and the work flow of the center. Personnel selection, training, motivation, and evaluation are primary responsibilities of this position.

Future Trends

The key to successful implementation of anything is people. If we are to implement the automated office successfully, it must be accomplished on an evolutionary basis rather than on the revolutionary basis of the last decade. The problem of implementation will not be technology so much as the human resistance to change.

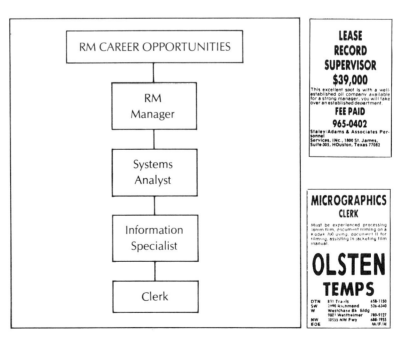

Figure 2.6. Advertisements for records management specialist.

Figure 2.7. This word processing specialist using Lanier word processing equipment is working at home. Courtesy of Lanier Business Products, Inc.

Many more office workers will be needed in the 1980s. However, the fear is that the supply of qualified people is decreasing rather than increasing. Skill level requirements continue to increase as technology automates many entry level jobs. For example, people will need basic keyboarding skills since most typing, drafting, editing, and verifying is likely to be done in front of a screen from a computer terminal or WP work station. This may promote the demise of the traditional 8 to 5 office workday as the new technology makes it possible to do many kinds of office work in the home or elsewhere. Needless to say, the office will still exist, but a significant difference in work habits may develop. People must be able to function in a technology-driven society.

The desire and the ability to cope with the pace of technological change will be mandatory. The change in the personnel organization may be interesting. Where today we have many specialists in departments such as DP, WP, and records management, future offices may be directed by an information systems manager with the specialists reporting to him or her. Not only the availability of technology, but the economics of the world will contribute to technology's dominance.

Decision making by task forces seems to point the way to implementation and administration of the latest technological opportunities. Because of increased awareness on the part of the users, a high level of demand will be placed on systems. Libraries, for example, will look to computer databases rather than to books.

flextime   Employment in this decade may be marked by a shorter work week. Many U.S. workers may be on flextime in the 1980s. **Flextime** is a work schedule that is outside the ordinary 8:00 A.M. to 5:00 P.M. time frame. For example, a ten-hour, four-day work week, a 4:00 P.M. to midnight shift, or a weekends only schedule may be convenient for an employee and helpful to the organization.

Figure 2.8. A business professional uses this personal information system to create, modify, store, and retrieve text, graphics and records and to distribute documents via telecommunications. The hand-held control device, at right, and four main function keys permit the operator to perform a wide range of tasks with no special skills. The two-page display is a very helpful feature. Courtesy of Xerox Corporation.

Figure 2.9. Clerical production work station (dedicated). The height adjustable table with easy-access mechanism permits a 5-inch range of adjustment to suit individual physical characteristics, once the operator has adjusted the chair to proper sitting height. A manuscript holder positions reference materials in front of the operator for tasks that are document driven, while VDT viewing angle can be precisely controlled by the machine support tray. The printer support table and specialized storage components, including a center hanger bar, are located within close proximity of the operator, to promote economy of motion.

offload the principal

Increased training will be needed to meet industry's complex technological needs. Both professional and support staffs will need to learn to use the equipment more effectively.

A continuing shortage of professional and support personnel will necessitate a more extensive leveling of tasks. For example, entry level tasks must be delegated to trained personnel. The administrative secretary will be trained to **offload the principal** to a greater degree and to take on more of the kinds of functions the manager may delegate.

Executives must learn to do a more effective job of allocating time to tasks only they can perform. The WP manager will, of necessity, become more and more immersed in integrated systems.

ergonomics

Ergonomics, sometimes referred to as the study of the relationship of work performance to equipment, seems to command more and more attention as the people part of the automated office is emphasized. Manufacturers exhibit concern for the effect of their products on people as they produce more people-oriented, friendly machines. The CRT is pleasing to the eye, the noise level is reduced, and the design is more aesthetically pleasing. The functions of the equipment are also easier to learn.

Summary

Career opportunities abound in MIS. Professional organizations provide information and leads. Positions exist in the public and private sector as well as in the organizations of vendors of the technology. Knowledge of technology continues to be an important requirement. The most prevalent position available for the 1980s is that of secretary; this fact will create more opportunities and choices. Positions on all levels are challenging, interesting, and numerous.

Although technology will continue to play an important role, more emphasis will also be placed on the people aspect throughout the 1980s. The possibility of fewer trained personnel will require better organization of training and task assignment.

Key Terms

Administrative support staff	Marketing support representative	Systems analyst (RM)
Clerk	Manager	Systems operator
Consultant	Offload the principal	Vendor
Data entry clerk	Peripheral equipment	Vendor competitive analyst
Editor-proofreader	Programmer	Word processing manager
Ergonomics	Records management manager	Word processing specialist
Flextime	Supervisor	Word processing supervisor
Information specialist	Systems analyst (DP)	Word processing technician
Keypunch operator		Word processing trainee

Self-Check Questions

Completion

1. Careers in MIS are multilevel. Besides public and private industry, the _____ provide many challenging opportunities.
2. An _____ is one who provides administrative assistance to an executive.
3. An _____ is responsible for the administration, design, and overall monitoring of the AS centers.
4. In a WP center, the most complex and technical documents are assigned to the _____.
5. The _____ monitors work flow and trains, motivates, and evaluates personnel.
6. A _____ trains customers to use equipment for their applications.
7. A source for general information as well as job openings is the _____.
8. A _____ does basic design and debugs elementary programs.
9. In DP, a _____ analyzes and designs information systems to solve user information needs.
10. In RM, _____ work with users as they generate documents to be entered into the system.

True/False

1. There are many career opportunities in AS, but few in other MIS fields.
2. Most career opportunities are at the senior management level.
3. Keypunch operators are no longer needed.
4. The ability to work cooperatively with people is extremely important.
5. Keyboarding skills are becoming essential.
6. Service engineers are in plentiful supply.
7. There is not much variety in career opportunities.
8. A career path exists for all MIS fields.
9. Many dollars will be made by sales personnel in the MIS industry in the next decade.
10. Professional organizations offer assistance in employment information.

Exercises

Exercise 2.1.   Contact the local professional organizations in your field. Write a brief paper discussing the organizations, their headquarters, purposes, and the local chapters or affiliations.

Exercise 2.2.   With information gathered from newspapers, employment agencies, and professional organizations, list and describe three current job openings in your field.

Case Problem

Mrs. Carol Muench is interested in going back to work now that the children are much older. Her husband is a systems consultant for a major computer vendor. She is, therefore, aware of and interested in the implications of MIS. Carol has not worked for ten years, however, and she knows many changes have occurred since she last worked as an administrative secretary. Where does she begin? Is training advisable? Training in what aspect of MIS? What is step one?

Chapter 3

✳✳

Word Processing

Chapter Objectives

After reading Chapter 3 and completing the end-of-chapter activities, the student will be able to:

1. *Describe the development of word/information processing.*
2. *Identify the four phases of word/information processing.*
3. *Discuss the components of word/information processing and their importance.*
4. *Describe the three organizational designs for word/information processing and their advantages and disadvantages.*
5. *Discuss justification for implementation of word/information processing.*

Development of Word Processing

electronic typing system

MTST

WP, as an industry, is beginning to come of age. Many developments have occurred in the field since IBM introduced the first WP machine in 1964, the Magnetic Tape Selectric Typewriter (MTST) (Figure 3.1). In 1965 in Germany, an IBM employee, Ulrich Steinhilper, coined the term *textverarbeitung,* which can be translated as word processing. He designed a cost effective system for the specialization of typing tasks that we know today as centralized WP. This system allowed specialized, highly trained employees using sophisticated **electronic typing systems** (typewriters with special correction, revision, print, and information manipulation capabilities) and following specific procedures, to produce much more information with higher document quality in less time with fewer interruptions. The equipment used in this setting was the **MTST** in conjunction with dictation and transcription equipment.

The MTST was, in fact, the first WP electronic typing system. The machines that were the forerunners of WP were the Robo Typer and the Auto-Typist. Their media were paper. As the typewriter keys were depressed, a hole was punched in the paper. The rolls of paper were then played back automatically, very similar to a player piano.

The MTST, still to be found in a few organizations, though limited in capabilities for revision, insertion, and deletion, proved to be a giant step from a conventional typewriter. It was the first of many text-editing electronic typing systems with magnetic media that could be reused. Since 1964, IBM and many other vendors have marketed more sophisticated equipment. Considerable improvements have also oc-

Figure 3.1. Magnetic Tape Selectric Typewriter (MTST). Courtesy of IBM Corporation.

Figure 3.2. The IBM 5520 Administrative System used in a centralized environment. Courtesy of IBM Corporation.

Figure 3.3. Magnetic cards. Courtesy of BASF Systems Corporation, Computer Products Division.

Figure 3.4. Magnetic Card Selectric Typewriter II (Mag Card II or MCST II). Courtesy of IBM Corporation.

Figure 3.5. The Xerox 800 operates from magnetic cassette tapes or cards. Courtesy of Xerox Corp.

curred in the development and capacity of the storage media. The media of the MTST are a 16 mm tape of varying lengths, housed in a cartridge. The typical length is 100-foot, which holds 24,000 characters.

magnetic card

From this magnetic tape, IBM revolutionized WP media with the **magnetic card** (Figure 3.3). The magnetic card is an erasable and reusable 3½ inch by 7⅜ inch magnetic film card which eliminates the difficulties of searching through a tape for a specific page. It stores approximately one page of information and permits moving a portion of text to another position. Sections of a document can be significantly increased by adding magnetic cards with text recorded on them at the appropriate places.

The Magnetic Card Selectric Typewriter (Mag Card I or MCST), introduced by IBM in 1969, was the first machine to use magnetic cards. This machine has greater revision and assembly capabilities than the MTST. The IBM Mag Card II (Figure 3.4), Redactron, Xerox 800 (Figure 3.5), and A.B. Dick Magna I and II have even greater capabilities and also use magnetic cards. Magnetic cards hold varying amounts of

track

data; IBM or A.B. Dick cards have a capacity of 50 **tracks** or lines with 100 characters each, Xerox cards have 72 tracks with 150 characters each, and Redactron cards store 64 tracks with 160 characters per line. IBM and several other vendors still use cards in their equipment today.

A revolution appeared on the horizon in 1971 when the Mag Card I was modified with a communications option. A Communicating Mag Card I (CMC) could talk to another through telecommunications. Even more revolutionary, perhaps, was the capability of a CMC to telecommunicate with a computer. This meant that data could be stored in massive amounts in the computer and many capabilities of the computer could be used. The advent of the IBM Mag Card II, formally called the Magnetic Card Selectric Typewriter II and also referred to as MCST II, really launched WP. It used not only the versatile magnetic card, but also contained a memory, a device that makes it possible to insert, delete, and change text easily by automatically adjusting for needed space or closing gaps.

Cassette tapes much like those used in tape recorders were also introduced as an alternative to the MTST tape media. These cassette tapes hold 25 to 60 pages. Both cards and cassette tapes are being replaced more and more by discs (or diskettes, as many vendors call them). In 1973, Vydec was the first system to be marketed with a diskette. Discs or diskettes, in general, hold 60 to 500 pages, are automatically indexed so the WP specialist knows where each document is located, and are much easier to handle.

Not only have the media improved significantly, but features of the various machines permit far greater capabilities and ease of operation.

In 1972, Lexitron and 3M/Linolex introduced the first video display units. These are cathode ray tube (CRT) or TV screenlike devices. Today, new models of most brands, which number in excess of 100, have CRT devices. In addition to easy keyboarding and revision of textual materials, equipment manufacturers are now focusing on many different capabilities—alphabetical/numerical file/sort, telecommunications, and high speed printout. Also in 1972, Comptek Research marketed the first shared-logic, multikeyboard computer system dedicated to WP tasks. A **shared**

shared logic

logic, multikeyboard WP system is a configuration of more than one work station where the logic capabilities of the system can be shared.

WP today has come a very long way. The equipment is much more sophisticated, the people involved in the operation and management are far more knowledgeable, and the procedures required to ensure the productivity of the staff using the equipment are more and more encompassing.

Figure 3.6. Magnetic cassette tapes used in word processing equipment. Courtesy of BASF Systems Corporation, Computer Products Division.

Figure 3.7. Vydec, manufacturer of first system to be marketed with a diskette, offers the Vydec 4000 with communications capabilities. Courtesy of Vydec, Inc.

Figure 3.8. Word processing diskettes. Courtesy of American Word Processing Company.

Figure 3.9. Lexitron, manufacturer of first video display units, continues to successfully market word processing equipment. Courtesy of Lexitron Corporation.

Figure 3.10. Magna SL word processor with shared logic. Courtesy of A. B. Dick Company.

The Four Phases of Word Processing

throughput

It is estimated that over half of the communications of any business are written. The types of documents or correspondence that must be created in every organization include letters, memos, reports, proposals, and specifications, to name but a few. Figure 3.11 shows the Exxon Corporation's 1975 study of the time cycle of the production and delivery of a document and a *flowchart* (sequence of tasks from beginning to end) of the document from origination to distribution. This study is an important one in that it breaks down the phases of the time cycle or **throughput** of a document to input, output, reprographics, and distribution. Thus, we arrive at the four phases of WP.

Documents must be authored or originated. In fact, this first step in producing a document is its creation. The method by which it is transmitted to the person who will produce or type it is usually called the input. The different ways a document may be originally input are longhand, shorthand, machine dictation, and optical character recognition (OCR). These methods are further discussed in Chapter 4.

The typing or production of the document is the second or output phase. Many factors need to be considered in the output of a document. Is it a rough draft? Final? What format should be used? Type style? Which WP system is most appropriate for this type of work? Perhaps the most outstanding opportunities today for exercising creativity are found in the output phase of WP, which is fully discussed in Chapters 5 through 7.

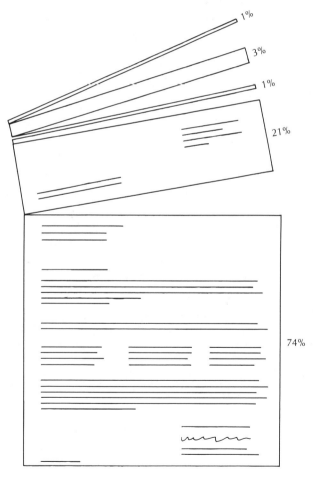

Figure 3.11. The Exxon Corporation study of the time cycle of a document identifies the four phases of word processing.

Certainly no one will deny that the business world is a paper mill in which everyone needs copies of documents. A large variety of equipment and processes may be selected for the reproduction or duplication of documents. The reproduction or copy processing of documents is the third phase of WP. A name coined for this phase is image processing. Chapter 8 more fully discusses image processing.

The fourth phase is distribution, where the document is distributed to the recipient and filed. It has two major categories—physical distribution and electronic distribution. As you will notice in the Exxon study, 74 percent of the time cycle of the document is consumed in this phase. Therefore, the distribution phase is a very important one. Many of the newest automated functions being marketed, such as telecommunications and micrographics, are in this area. They are discussed in Chapter 9.

The Equilateral Triangle—Personnel, Equipment, and Procedures

An organization has three equally important components to consider in the operation of the office—its *personnel*, the *equipment* used to do the work, and the *procedures* established for the performance and flow of the work. The challenge is to combine equipment and procedures successfully to make work flow more smoothly and to make people more productive. No matter how advanced the technology and how sophisticated the procedures, systems fail without well-trained, dedicated, and skilled personnel. The personnel can do a better job faster and more efficiently if they have the benefit of automated, electronic equipment. However, the equipment must be integrated into a system of procedures for consistency and uniformity in the processing of documents being keyboarded, as well as in the administrative support given the executives.

Personnel

In all system designs, the people involved are the most important component. The success and productivity of the system depends on them. WP has opened career avenues not previously available to people who do secretarial and clerical work in offices. It has given them the potential for choosing the type of work they wish to do. For example, you may be a person who prefers to work with equipment and on your own as much as possible. You are just as happy if you do not constantly have to deal with people. Perhaps you enjoy being creative in the preparation of documents. If this sounds attractive, the WP center in an organization may be for you. On the other hand, if you would like the creativity of document preparation but also want people contact, many organizations will provide this for you in their WP centers because their procedures are designed for direct contact between the originator and the WP specialist.

Perhaps you like contact with people and minimum typing; if so, you may be the perfect administrative secretary. The important thing is that you can choose your area of interest, a factor many people appreciate. The employment projections for the next decade show that you will continue to have this flexibility of choice.

How are the positions for both AS and WP staff structured for the people who hold them? AS staff and those who do a combination of administrative and correspondence tasks usually work seven to eight hours during the regular business day. WP staff frequently have a choice of times to work as well as numbers of hours available to work because organizations are creating systems that operate over an extended business day; some work in shifts around the clock, in order to produce more documents in a given period of time. The WP equipment is used longer each day, thus stretching the equipment dollars.

Figure 3.12. Three equally important components in an office—personnel, equipment, and procedures.

Equipment

There are many kinds of equipment used in the WP cycle—dictation equipment, WP systems, duplicating equipment, telecommunications, and micrographic equipment. These are discussed extensively throughout the coming chapters. This technology and the consequent increase in productivity make it possible for the secretarial support staff to render better and more efficient service to the executives of an organization.

Procedures

No matter how sophisticated and workable the equipment, or how well-trained the personnel, thorough procedures are required for success. We have seen that automated equipment can make the secretarial support staff more productive. Staff members who operate in the administrative or WP capacity also need to use uniform procedures for standardization and ease in company operations for highest produc-

procedures manual tivity. **Procedures manuals** must outline procedures for both the executive and the support staff and indicate the way in which information for that organization will be created, produced, duplicated, stored, and distributed. Most organizations have at least two manuals, one for the user and one for the support staff. The executive is a user of the system. A user's procedures manual should provide the data necessary to input a document into the system and to get back a draft or finished product, to submit requests for revisions of material already typed, to make requests for special projects, and so forth. All the services of an organization should be explained for easy reference by the user. Part IV is a User's Manual.

turnaround time

The WP specialists need a complete procedures manual to use on a daily basis to produce the documents required. This manual may include how priorities will be established on documents needing to be produced; how long **turnaround time** (the time the work takes to be completed) will be; what format will be used for various documents; samples of standard formats; type styles; color of typing ribbon or ink; how long the media (magnetic card, cassette, or diskette) on which the documents are typed will be retained; what form of document origination (machine dictated or handwritten material, for example) will be accepted. The manual for the WP specialist will contain considerable detail regarding the typing and recording techniques for various documents, revision procedures, standardized document procedures, filing of copies, and the recorded media. It may also show how documents are logged, stored, and distributed.

Part V is a Word Processing Specialist's Procedures Manual. Notice the wide range of information provided. No matter what the design of the organization, good procedures result in clearer communication, more efficiency, less confusion and conflict, and better equipment usage.

Organizational Design

There probably are no two organizations that have implemented a WP system with exactly the same structure or design. There is no right WP system design; the primary factor is that the system fits the organization. However, there are three major systems or designs into which we can loosely place most organizations' WP structures.

feasibility study

Organizational design is not dependent on equipment. Equipment should be selected that best performs the applications of the organization. There is no one equipment configuration that must be used. All types of equipment should be considered, and a **feasibility study** which will show the administrative information and document needs of an organization should be made. This will help to determine the right equipment for a given situation. The appropriate configuration with the right equipment will provide a successful WP system. A major consideration that can never be overemphasized is compatibility of equipment. Selecting equipment manufactured by different vendors limits the WP staff. Since the media of one manufacturer cannot be used in another's equipment, dividing long documents between staff using different equipment is complicated. With a variety of equipment, training and procedures become more difficult.

Centralized Design or Production Centers

centralized design

A **centralized design** or production center (Figure 3.13) is responsible for the production of documents created by many executives. These documents range from simple to complex, from straight copy to highly technical reports and statistical data. A WP center can have one or more specialists.

WP systems, transcription equipment, information processors, telecommunications equipment, and highly sophisticated procedures are used for most, if not all, of the document preparation for the organization. The centralized design or production center is task-oriented rather than executive-oriented. The key to its success is specialization. WP specialists are concerned only with document production, so they become experts in this area. The more someone specializes in a certain area, the faster and better he or she will perform that specific type of work and the more cost effective it will be.

Some managers feel the centralized production center is the most cost effective in terms of individual or group performance, implementation, and maintenance. Less space, an expensive item today, is used for a group of stations in a center than for the same number of individual work stations. Equipment is used steadily and, therefore, is more easily cost justified. The centralized structure has also been promoted as the most efficient WP configuration. It may be implemented for an entire organization or for just a single department. In fact, in some organizations, some departments are so large they seem to operate like minicompanies.

For some companies, one drawback of this design is that a complete reorganization of the secretarial support staff and facilities is often required for implementation. Both executives and secretaries often object to restructuring, saying that it is depersonalizing. In addition, executives often display resistance to working with a group of people rather than with just one secretary. Some secretaries prefer to work for just one executive. The key decision seems to be the willingness to pay for these preferences.

AS can also be clustered in a center environment. The center's tasks might include answering the telephone; opening, sorting, and delivering mail; research; filing; scheduling appointments; coordinating meetings; and answering routine correspondence. The staff is employed to do specific tasks for one or more executives rather than to support or work for a specific executive. Since AS secretaries in this

Figure 3.13. This well-designed centralized word processing environment focuses on the people who use word processing and office information systems. Courtesy of Wang Laboratories, Inc.

configuration work with all phases of general office duties except typing, they become more proficient.

Let us take a look at typical interactions among the three groups involved in a centralized design or production center:

1. The user (the executive).
2. The administrative secretary in an AS Center.
3. The WP specialist in a WP center.

The executive arrives at the office and greets the administrative secretary who works in the AS center for him and two other executives. As she hands him the telephone message she has just taken, he hands her a cassette tape from his portable dictation unit and asks her to send it to the WP center for transcription. She calls his attention to an important piece of correspondence, which she determined has a high priority when she sorted the mail earlier and suggests today as a deadline. She has made two appointments and canceled one on today's calendar, which she clears with him. He asks her to set up travel arrangements for tomorrow's trip to the Cleveland office and sits down to review the mail. He picks up the telephone and dictates into the central dictation system a document needed to satisfy the correspondence with today's deadline. As he concludes his dictation, the WP specialist comes in to discuss an alternative deadline on a long report usually due this date each month. After one is agreed upon, the executive is off to a meeting with the board of directors. He remembers to let the AS center know he is gone so that his telephone can be answered.

Decentralized Design or Custom Support

decentralized design

Decentralized design, also called custom or distributed support, is a design in which the secretary has a WP system and other high production equipment to produce documents, but also performs administrative tasks for the department. The decentralized design or custom support system is a work group that is executive- or function-oriented. The staff is employed to support one or more specific executives engaged in the dealings of one entity, department, or division. The executive and the administrative WP specialist or secretary are located near one another for ease in handling work flow. This may be thought of as the traditional office structure equipped with advanced technology and sophisticated work flow procedures. It provides for significant increases in productivity. Frequently, the one-to-one relationship between the executive and the secretary is preserved. By not severing that relationship, a higher degree of performance may be maintained inasmuch as the secretary is familiar with the executive's terminology and nomenclature, as well as the working structure. A reorganization of the secretarial support staff usually will not be required; this is often a great benefit to companies who are happy with the personnel design as it exists.

satellite design

Another form of decentralized design or custom support is the assignment of one WP specialist to a department. That specialist works in the department and for only that department. This is also called a **satellite design.** The reporting structure of the WP specialist may be divided under the satellite design. The specialist may be evaluated by the department executive as well as the WP manager. Frequently, the WP manager is given this authority in order to establish and maintain standardization of documents, equipment, and procedures throughout the organization. A word of caution, however; in certain facilities it is not advisable to decentralize because of equipment expense. For example, high performance printers, which may be too expensive to install at each work center, will need to be in a centralized location. In

Figure 3.14. This team illustrating a decentralized word processing environment is using the Wang Alliance 250, a user-friendly system which integrates data processing, word processing, audio processing, image processing, human concerns, and networks. Courtesy of Wang Laboratories, Inc.

addition, backup support to help in the case of absenteeism is more likely needed in a decentralized system than in a centralized one.

Let us take a look at the typical interaction between the participants in a decentralized design or custom support:

1. The user (the executive).
2. The administrative/WP specialist secretary.

The executive arrives at the office and greets the secretary who performs a combination of administrative and correspondence functions. She hands him a cassette tape from her portable dictation unit and asks him to make an extra copy when transcribing for the file as he hands her a telephone message he has just taken for her. He has made two appointments and canceled one on today's calendar, which he clears with her. She asks him to schedule tomorrow's travel arrangements to the Cleveland office. She then goes into her office and begins to dictate a document she will need to have him transcribe before noon. After dictating the document, they discuss format before she leaves for a board of directors meeting.

Combination or Specialized Production System

specialized production

The combination or **specialized production** system design is a combination of the centralized and decentralized systems. Executives have secretarial support staff who operate in a decentralized manner, that is, do both administrative and correspondence tasks. They also have a WP center that is built into the design of the organization as a production center. A large amount of documentation, especially long documents that will need considerable revision, is done by this center since the secretarial support staff, performing the combination of administrative tasks and document creation for the executive, do only short jobs—letters, memos, and so forth.

This is probably the most supportive design for executives, but it is also the most expensive in terms of numbers of secretarial support. However, if the time spent by the executive on tasks that can be delegated to secretarial support staff can be significantly reduced, the dollar savings may be greatest with this design.

A good example of an organization that may employ the combination or specialized production system is that of a law office. In most law offices, the attorney has a secretary who performs administrative tasks and keyboards short documents. However, long documents, such as contracts, briefs, and pleadings, are done by the production center. Both the secretary and the production center provide the attorney with a very high level of support, and neither the administrative nor light typing requirements have to be sacrificed while the long documents are produced or vice versa.

Let us take a look at a typical interaction among the three participants in this design, combination or specialized production:

1. The user (the executive).
2. The administrative/WP specialist or secretary.
3. The WP specialist.

The executive arrives at the office and greets the administrative/WP specialist, who hands the executive a telephone message just taken and also calls attention to a document received in the mail with a deadline of today. The executive hands the secretary a cassette tape from the portable dictation unit and asks that it be transcribed since there are only short letters and memos on it. The secretary has made two appointments and canceled one on today's calendar, which is cleared with the executive. The executive goes into his office and sits down to review the mail. He picks up the telephone and dictates into the central dictation system a document needed to satisfy today's deadline. The central dictation unit is wired to the central stations of the WP center. All long documents such as this one are processed in this area. As he concludes his dictation, the WP specialist from the production center comes in to discuss alternative deadlines with him on a new type of report. After one is selected, the executive leaves for a meeting with the board of directors, after letting the secretary know he is gone so that the telephones can be answered.

Justification of Word Processing

An organization has a great deal to consider in the operation of its office functions. The costs of running an office are increasing. SRI, International reports that office expenses used to account for 20 to 30 percent of a company's expenditures; today, they amount to approximately 50 to 60 percent. Dartnell Institute of Business Research (1982)[1] found the cost of a one-page business letter in 1982 to be $7.11; in 1952, the same letter cost about $1.15. Business is faced with the problem of holding costs down in order to keep profits up.

In addition, an executive must deal with a great deal more information in today's business world. Some have termed this information overload. Two examples of the ever-growing flood of printed matter are:

1. Approximately 7,000 new books are published in the U.S. annually.
2. American business now deals with 325 billion documents with 72 billion added each year.[2]

---

[1]SRI, International.
[2]Personal communication with Arlene Gamble, Manager Technical Services, American Productivity Center.

The costs involved in dealing with all this paper are staggering. The Commission on Federal Paperwork reported to President Carter in 1980 that the government spends over $100 billion a year processing paperwork. The nation's ten thousand largest firms spend $10 to $12 billion per year and the five million small businesses spend an average of $3000 each on government paperwork. This has created a tremendous increase in the number of office personnel or secretarial support staff needed, and the number is expected to increase at least through the 1980s. Salaries for this staff continue to rise at the rate of 10 percent or more per year. Training of the office staff costs a company annually more than $1000 per replaced or added person.

What is the answer to these increased paperwork demands and their related costs? Should an organization continue to hire more and more secretarial support staff? Is overtime the answer even though many studies show a marked decrease in productivity during overtime?

Perhaps WP provides part of the solution. In the 1980s, WP is more easily justified than ever before. Seventy percent or more of the budget of many organizations goes to pay salaries.

People are the most expensive commodity a business can buy. If a system can stretch the capabilities and production of the people involved in an organization, justification becomes easy. Studies made show that one WP specialist in a centralized environment can frequently do the work of three clerk-typists. Thus, a centralized environment, where an emphasis is put on the production of documents rather than the usual variety of office tasks, seems to be the most cost effective of all configurations thus far analyzed and studied by industry. Dividing or at least designing a system for specializing and isolating administrative and document creation tasks leads to greater productivity, as workers are able to concentrate their efforts on specific tasks with fewer interruptions. Frequently, fewer people can do the work, so several things may occur. The office staff may be gradually reduced as people leave. The executives may find that the delegation of their more routine administrative work to the administrative secretary frees them to do more of the work which requires their special expertise. Often there are opportunities to complete those extra tasks that are difficult to get to.

The custom work station or decentralized environment has not been as thoroughly analyzed and studied as the centralized system. Because of lack of analysis, a three-to-one cost savings for this design cannot be substantiated. It is thought, though, that perhaps even greater indirect savings can be realized with a decentralized WP environment. These indirect savings occur in the stretching of executives' time and efforts. For example, executives commonly perform clerical tasks for approximately one hour per day that a secretary could do. To create the time for the secretary to do these tasks, other tasks need to be eliminated or aid provided to speed up the process for some jobs. This aid can be a WP system. Thus, the executive can do more management-related tasks. At the executive's salary level, the savings indirectly related to the decentralized design may be far more significant even than the three to one shown for centralized systems.

A very important benefit to both the company and the office staff is the professionalism that has come to be associated with WP. Job titles, career paths, and salaries are indicators of this professionalism.

WP has provided for the office what has been effective in factories for many years —mechanization through equipment, specialization for higher productivity, and professionalism. A particular bonus for secretarial support staff is that organizations are creating career paths for the office staff as management support systems are designed.

Summary

WP emerged in 1964 and its sophistication continues to increase. The four phases of WP are input, output, reprographics, and distribution.

The three equally important components of WP are personnel, equipment, and procedures. People can do a more productive, cost effective job with appropriate technology used with sophisticated procedures.

Three common organizational designs are centralized or production centers, custom or decentralized support, and combination or specialized production systems. No design is correct; the one that fits the organization is appropriate. A summary of these three designs follows.

Centralized or Production System—Task Oriented

1. Specialization frequently provides better performance.
2. Automated equipment and sophisticated procedures provide faster turn-around time.
3. Cross-training permits absences with easier and smoother work flow.
4. Career opportunities arise through the design at the senior and junior levels. Also, the ability to change jobs laterally is more available.
5. Documents can be stored on magnetic media for later revision and use, if desired.

Decentralized or Custom Support System— Executive-Oriented

1. Existing secretarial staff can do more work faster.
2. Because technology encourages greater productivity, existing staff have time to assist the executive in delegated work or to do work for other executives.
3. It eliminates the need for reorganization of the secretarial support staff of a company, as is required with a centralized system.
4. It provides for documents to be stored on magnetic media for later use if desired.

Combination or Specialized Production System— Task- and Executive-Oriented

1. It frees existing secretarial support staff from time-consuming production of long documents to be more responsive to the executive's administrative needs.
2. WP specialists can provide higher quality documents.
3. There are additional career opportunities within the organization for secretarial support staff.
4. Turnaround time for documents is faster.
5. More work can be done with fewer people than with the decentralized system.

WP has provided an answer in many cases to increased paperwork demands. The equipment is justified by increased production, better utilization of staff, and the employment of fewer people.

Key Terms

Centralized design	MTST	Throughput
Decentralized design	Procedures manual	Track
Electronic typing system	Satellite design	Turnaround time
Feasibility study	Shared logic	
Magnetic card	Specialized production	

3. Word Processing

Completion

1. The executive is also called the _____ of the system.
2. The organizational design proposed by Ulrich Steinhilper for the original concept of WP is _____ .
3. The forms of media used in the past two decades are _____ , _____ , and _____ .
4. Three basic reasons used to justify WP are _____ , _____ , and _____ .
5. The four phases of WP are _____ , _____ , _____ , and _____ .
6. The largest expenditure of time in the document cycle is in the _____ phase.
7. No matter how sophisticated the equipment and the procedures, without _____ the system will fail.
8. Procedures manuals are beneficial to both _____ and _____ .
9. The organizational design most supportive to the executive is the _____ .
10. The system design with the fewest changes in personnel structure is the _____ .

Matching

Write the correct definition letter in the space provided in front of the corresponding term.

Terms	*Definitions*
_____ 1. Cathode Ray Tube (CRT)	a. A vacuum tube which focuses electrons on a visual screen for viewing text in WP and/or DP.
	b. The devices used for the recording or storing of data for dictation, computer, or WP equipment.
_____ 2. Decentralized Center	c. The first WP electronic typing system, Magnetic Tape Selectric Typewriter.
_____ 3. Magnetic Card	d. Magnetic film card that is erasable and reuseable and holds from 50 to 100 lines of text.
	e. A measurement equivalent to one line of stored text.
_____ 4. Media	f. Organizational design wherein the WP specialist works in the physical location of a given department exclusively for that department.
_____ 5. MTST	g. WP system that has more than one work station, all of which share one or more resources, such as logic, media, and printer.
_____ 6. Satellite Design	h. Time that elapses between the submission of a document for completion and its return to the originator.
_____ 7. Shared Logic	i. Multiterminal WP system in which each terminal shares the capabilities, storage, and peripherals of the system's central processing unit.
_____ 8. Track	j. Cycle of a document from origination through output, reprographics, and distribution.
_____ 9. Throughput	k. Organizational design whereby an individual performs administrative secretarial duties with the aid of WP equipment; also, a design which may assign WP specialists to individual departments.
_____ 10. Turnaround Time	

Exercises

Exercise 3.1. Visit an organization which has implemented WP. Make a report which focuses on:

1. Type of system design.
2. Type of equipment used for each of the four phases of WP.
3. How sophisticated each phase of WP is at that company.
4. Whether or not a procedures manual is used.
5. Cost per page of correspondence, if such data are available.

6. Job titles of the secretarial support staff.
7. Salary range of secretarial support staff positions.

Exercise 3.2. Read two articles in current periodicals about:

1. Implementation of WP. Summarize the articles, showing similarities and differences of implementation.
2. Current employment opportunities in WP. Summarize the articles. Describe your personal interest in the profession.

Case Problem

Horton, Ltd., is experiencing considerable difficulties this year in its office functions. The secretarial support staff is having many problems. Deadlines never seem to be met. There is consistently a large amount of overtime. The quality of the work is poor because of the extreme pressure of the situation. Morale is low due to overload and uneven balance of work. Executives simply are not as effective as they might be because they frequently have inadequate support and have to do many tasks a good support person might do for them. Temporary services personnel can only do so much due to their lack of knowledge about Horton, Ltd.'s specific procedures. In fact, there are no complete procedures manuals.

The president, Mr. Hughes, approached the administrative office manager, Mr. Koepp, and suggested that Mr. Koepp investigate WP and present a WP system design for his consideration.

Mr. Koepp, in an effort to do a thorough job on his assignment, contacted various vendors and looked at equipment. The International Information/Word Processing Association held its national Syntopican meeting at this time. Mr. Koepp sat in on several seminars. He began to see the scope of his assignment, and he was able to begin to consider possible alternatives for the design of a system. He met at the conference Ms. Hester, a WP consultant. The following week he contacted Ms. Hester and asked her if she could design the most appropriate system for Horton, Ltd., and implement it. She accepted the job, and at the first meeting, which included a familiarization with Horton, Ltd., she was given the following information:

1. The company is an engineering, design, and construction company and has a large volume of correspondence—both internal and external—as well as specifications, proposals, and reports that must be produced.
2. The secretarial support staff members have been employed at Horton, Ltd., for some time and are firmly entrenched in their jobs as secretaries on a one-to-one basis with the executives.
3. The executives need an undetermined amount of additional AS.
4. No one seems to know much about WP.
5. The costs of the office seem to be rising astronomically.

What kind of system design should Ms. Hester recommend? How should she go about approaching this assignment?

Part II

****

THE INPUT AND
OUTPUT PHASES
OF WORD PROCESSING

Chapter 4

****

Input—The Origination of Information

Chapter Objectives

After reading this chapter and answering the end-of-chapter questions, the student will be able to:

1. Define input.

2. List the four methods of input and their advantages and disadvantages.

3. List the categories of dictation equipment and the types of units in each category.

4. List the features common to all dictation equipment.

5. List the advantages and disadvantages of each type of dictation unit.

6. List the types of input media and their advantages and disadvantages.

7. Describe the key points of effective dictation.

Input Defined

In Chapter 3, we discussed the four phases of WP—input, output, reprographics, and distribution. Let us focus here on input—the first step in the creation of a document. Input is the origination and transmission of the information to the WP specialist who will keyboard, print, and store it on magnetic media. The person authoring the document starts with an idea and builds the idea into a form of business communication; the person doing the authoring may be called an **originator**. This originator may be an executive administering an organization, a salesperson creating the necessary paperwork in the generation of sales, an administrative secretary, or one of many other people who will originate documents.

originator

Anyone and everyone creates documents of some kind—personally and/or professionally. You will, no doubt, find yourself in the role of an originator at some time, and you will need to know how to transform ideas into written documents. Another important reason for learning about document origination is that you may be transcribing documents someone else has authored. It is easier to transcribe if you have had some experience as an originator.

Methods

You may work as an administrative secretary for an executive who says, "Write a letter to John Smith and ask him for the latest figures he has on the tolerance factors of a thermocoupler." Your task is to originate a document to be given to a WP specialist for transcribing. How might you transmit this information? There are four possibilities—dictating it into a machine, dictating it to a stenographer who takes shorthand, writing it out in longhand, or typing it in rough draft form using optical character recognition (OCR). The average speed for the four methods of originating are as follows:

Method	Input Rate	Transcribing Rate
Longhand	8–15 wpm	10–20 wpm
Shorthand	30+ wpm[1]	15 wpm
Machine dictation	60–80+ wpm	20–25 wpm
OCR	30+ wpm	—[2]

[1]Average of authoring and taking.
[2]Text input from OCR requires revision only; the industry generally recognizes 30 wpm as a good rate of revision. Since time relates directly to cost, it is an important consideration.

Let us take a look at each of these input techniques.

Machine Dictation

machine dictation

Machine dictation is the process of moving the idea of the originator through the spoken word into a machine which records it on magnetic media (Figure 4.1). Magnetic media are media—cassette, belt, or disk—that can be recorded over again and again.

Dictating into a machine has several advantages over the other methods. The first is *speed*. You can dictate into a machine at least five times faster than you can write in longhand. An originator dictates at 60–80 or more words per minute using machine dictation or dictation to a stenographer writing shorthand. Originators write at the rate of eight to fifteen words per minute using longhand.

Transcription is also faster from the spoken word than from longhand or shorthand notes. On the average, a person can type from longhand at approximately ten to twenty words per minute, from shorthand notes at approximately fifteen words per minute, and from machine dictation at about twenty to twenty-five words per minute. The primary reason for the substantial increase is that no deciphering of handwriting or written notes is required. Another important reason is that the WP specialist does not have to look up from the keyboard to read shorthand or longhand notes.

The second advantage of machine dictation is *efficiency*. Machine dictation is at least twice as efficient as shorthand, since dictating to a machine requires the time of just one person, whereas shorthand requires the time of two, thereby reducing the efficiency by one-half. Originators are finding that when machine dictation and transcription are used they can still have the advantage of a secretary to correct their grammar and punctuation without tying up the time of two people to record the message.

The third advantage of machine dictation is *convenience*. An originator can pick up a microphone and work on a project at almost any time and place he might choose, at 10:00 A.M. or at 10:00 P.M. He would not have this flexibility in dictating to a stenographer. Any trained transcriber can transcribe dictation from a machine, but a stenographer may have difficulty reading someone else's shorthand notes. The stenographer may even have difficulty reading his or her own cold shorthand notes.

The fourth advantage of machine dictation is *economy*. Although the equipment requires an initial investment, the time it saves more than makes up for this expenditure. In most organizations labor accounts for 70% or more of the budget. A good way

Figure 4.1. This executive uses the Lanier standard cassette desk-top dictating unit. Courtesy of Lanier Business Products, Inc.

to save money often is to save time. Let us look at the typical time and cost savings of an executive who makes $30,000 per year (24¢ per minute). The typical business letter is 175 words long and takes the originator an average of two to three minutes to dictate versus an average of fifteen minutes to write it out in longhand. The twelve-minute savings is equal to approximately $2.88. Multiply this by the number of letters created per day in an organization, and the savings become substantial.

Machine dictation is becoming more popular in today's business offices. A study by Dartnell Institute of Business Research[3] shows that nearly 54 percent of today's executives at one time or another use machine dictation. This provides for more inexpensive correspondence. It costs $5.32 to produce an average business letter with machine dictation compared to $7.11 with face-to-face dictation. When dictation units are used in conjunction with WP systems, cost savings are more substantial. When corrections or author changes have to be made, only the revised portions have to be retyped—hence, additional time and costs are saved. Originators are also using machine dictation, particularly with portable units, for notetaking. For example, an executive on the way to the office may have some important thoughts that he or she would like to record for reference.

Another use of machine dictation is communicating verbally rather than on paper. An executive going away on vacation may leave for a secretary or assistant a number of directions about projects to be followed up.

Machine dictation is also being used for some unusual purposes. For example, police call in from the call box on their beat or from a telephone to dictate crime reports. Automobile service technicians dictate the parts order for a customer's repair work; this results in faster delivery of parts and produces automatic accounting

[3]Dartnell Target Survey, "1982 Cost of a Business Letter Breaks $7.00 Barrier," Dartnell Institute of Business Research.

Figure 4.2. Electronic recording system using standard cassettes can be used in the court room and in the conference room. Courtesy of Lanier Business Products, Inc.

information. Doctors dictate their patient reports while they are completing the examination rather than having to write the reports later. Group meetings may need to have minutes taken for the record and later follow-up (Figure 4.2).

Shorthand

There may always be those executives who prefer to dictate to a stenographer. Shorthand is a system of symbols or abbreviations used by stenographers to write, edit, and transcribe the spoken word. Shorthand of one kind or another goes back several thousand years. Many forms of shorthand have been used over the centuries. Today secretaries or stenographers may take shorthand not only manually with the pen and tablet, but also with a shorthand machine. Court reporters taking verbatim dictation in a legal setting will most frequently use machine shorthand.

Whether manual or machine shorthand is used, this method is at least double the speed of longhand. The one-to-one working relationship between the executive and the stenographer is often valued by both parties. The executive appreciates having someone to correct the grammar and enjoys the status symbol of having a secretary. The secretary sometimes likes working for only one individual. However, shorthand is costly for several reasons. As stated earlier, Dartnell in its 1982 target survey showed the cost of a letter originated by face-to-face dictation to be $7.11 as compared to $5.32 by machine dictation. The fact that the time of two people is required is significant. Transcribing from machine dictation is faster than transcribing from shorthand notes. Dictation is one more interruption in a day already filled with interruptions for the secretary. And, as we have said before, cold shorthand notes are often difficult to transcribe.

Longhand

Since people are all different, there are some who prefer to write out in longhand the document to be given to a WP specialist for typing. Even though it is the slowest method of originating a document, since most people write only eight to fifteen words a minute, longhand is the most commonly used method of input. Indeed, it is estimated that 60 to 70 percent of input into WP centers is via longhand, despite the costs involved. Many originators feel they can do a better job if they can see their words on paper as they create the document. To be sure, some highly technical documents do merit the use of this method of input. However, an important factor in transmitting a document to a WP specialist for output is that of legibility of handwriting. Since some handwriting is difficult to read, the transcription process may be slow.

Optical Character Recognition

optical character recognition

An excellent method of input gaining more and more acceptance is that of **optical character recognition (OCR).** This is a process of handwriting or typing a document on a single-element typewriter using characters that will be recognized when read or scanned through an OCR reader/scanner (Figure 4.3). The handwritten or typed characters are captured and transferred to the media of the WP system and can, therefore, be revised as necessary.

OCR operates on the principle of light reflection; that is, OCR readers recognize the contrast between a handwritten or printed character and the white background of the paper. Recognition is based on an identical match to characters stored in its memory. Entire pages and documents are read by the OCR reader/scanner and stored on media by the WP system. Legal firms are an example of users who may want the documents keyboarded by all secretaries to be recorded on the WP system. If the user company acquires an OCR reader/scanner and uses OCR recognizable

Figure 4.3. Optical character recognition (OCR) provides significant opportunity for increased productivity. Courtesy of Hendrix, Inc.

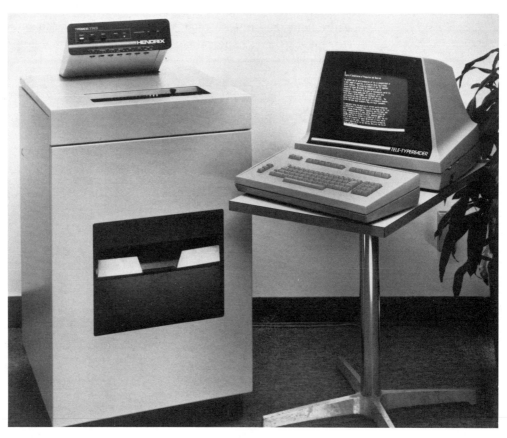

elements or print wheels for all typewriters being used by the secretaries, the documents typed by these individuals are easily put into the system. The secretary never needs to rekey the page and the WP specialist needs only to revise the document. This cooperative effort between the AS and the WP specialists results in a cost and time efficient system.

The OCR system provides for easy revision of a document. Let us take a look at the work flow (Figure 4.4):

1. The originator composes at the typewriter or has the administrative secretary do initial rough drafts. An OCR-recognizable element is used on the typewriter to keyboard the document.

2. The document, now in typewritten form, is revised with a red felt tip pen. Since the OCR reader/scanner is blind to red ink, it will not pick up these revisions when the document is read or scanned through the OCR reader/scanner.

3. Through telecommunications, the document is read through the reader/scanner onto the media of a WP system.

4. The WP specialist then makes any revisions on the media that were noted in red ink on the original and returns the revised document to the originator for further review and signature. Since the document is stored on media, it can be revised as many times as necessary.

The User's Procedures Manual in Part IV gives an example of a practical way to keyboard, edit, and scan using OCR.

Several types of OCR scanners are being marketed. Some recognize only one type style, while others recognize several. A few recognize handwriting. There are units which handle a wide variety of applications on all kinds and sizes of forms, containing data generated by hand as well as by typewriters and printers. Speed of recognition and transfer to the media is an important consideration in selecting an OCR reader/scanner. Another especially important concern is reliability; a number of characters may not be recognized by the reader/scanner and must be revised or inserted by the WP specialist after transfer to the media of the WP system. Equations

Figure 4.4. Work flow using an OCR system.

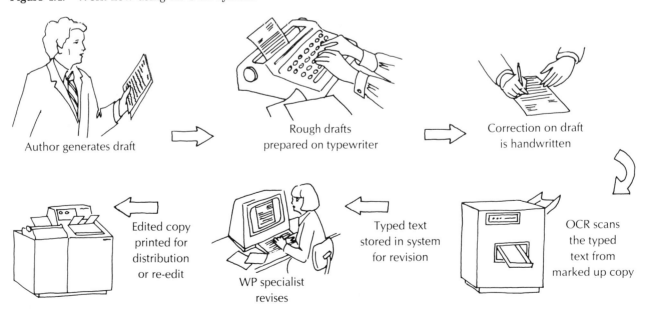

Author generates draft

Rough drafts prepared on typewriter

Correction on draft is handwritten

OCR scans the typed text from marked up copy

Typed text stored in system for revision

WP specialist revises

Edited copy printed for distribution or re-edit

can be a drawback to the use of OCR as some reader/scanners are unable to recognize them.

There is an additional benefit to using an OCR system in conjunction with a WP system: media conversion. Currently, there is little compatibility of equipment manufactured by different vendors. A document started on one type of equipment must be completed on that type of equipment. Some users have difficult procedures as well as personnel problems with cross-training WP specialists on equipment when there is a mixture of brands. OCR can bridge the gap between brands of equipment. A document keyboarded and stored on one manufacturer's WP system can be printed using an OCR element or print wheel on hard copy (paper). The hard copy can then be read into a different manufacturer's OCR reader/scanner and stored on that manufacturer's media via that brand of WP system. The paper is the medium through which the document is transferred from one WP system to the other.

The many uses of OCR make it a viable technology in the information processing industry. In fact, the use of OCR seems to double annually, primarily because of its relative ease of use and flexibility. Some organizations have eliminated the need for rekeyboarding completely with the use of OCR. If all administrative secretaries typing text to be read into the WP system use an OCR-recognizable element to keyboard all documents, any revisions to the document are then made on the WP system. OCR also provides a method for expediting rush and overflow jobs.

OCR also works well with computers and phototypesetters. Information can be read into computer storage, or text can be read into a phototypesetter that will convert it to the size and typeface desired.

The important things to consider in deciding upon the method of input—machine dictation, shorthand, OCR, longhand—are what works best for the originator and which method is the most cost-effective. As a WP specialist, you will encounter all these means of inputting information. By knowing all the methods, you will be able to deal with each as it appears.

Machine Dictation Equipment

dictating device
recording unit

Machine dictation equipment usually has three components:

1. **Dictating device**—the microphone or telephone for the originator to speak into while dictating.
2. **Recording unit**—the unit that houses the device that records the spoken word.
3. Media—the material on which the recording of a document is stored. There are inscribed media (physically cut or scratched as they record) and magnetic media (erasable and reusable). Inscribed plastic belts are infrequently used in offices today. The common types of magnetic media that have been marketed are:
   a. Cassettes, standard, microcassettes, and minicassettes (Figures 4.5, 4.6, and 4.7).
   b. Belts.
   c. Discs.
   d. Endless loop.

Media

discrete media

Discrete Media. The first three forms of media (cassettes, belts, and discs) are **discrete media.** These are media that are individually distinct and can be physically handled, that is, removed from the dictation unit and inserted into a transcribing machine for transcription. Discrete media must be used when the dictation must be stored since the other type of media, endless loop, is continuously recycled and reused and, therefore, not able to be stored.

Figure 4.5. Standard cassettes as dictation/transcription media. Courtesy of BASF Systems Corporation, Computer Products Division.

Figure 4.6. Lanier's portable dictation unit uses microcassettes. Courtesy of Lanier Business Products, Inc.

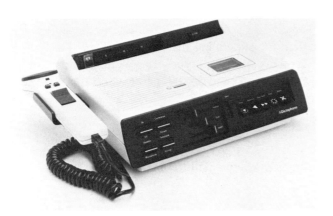

Figure 4.7. Dictamaster desktop dictation/transcription unit uses minicassettes as media. Courtesy of Dictaphone Corporation.

The recording time of common types of discrete media may be of interest:

Media Type	Each Side (in minutes)	Total Time (in minutes)
Minicassette	15, 20, 25, 30, 50	30, 40, 50, 60, 100
Microcassette	30, 60	60, 120
Standard cassette	15, 30, 45, 60	30, 60, 90, 120
Belt		10–20
Disc		6

Belts are used on older dictation equipment still employed in some offices. Discs are used on IBM 6:5 dictation equipment. Each disc has a six minute recording capacity; the cartridge that houses the discs in the dictation unit holds up to fifty discs. Therefore, a cartridge full of discs has a recording time of 300 minutes or five hours. Hence, the name 6:5 represents recording time of six minutes to five hours.

There are three sizes of cassettes: standard, microcassettes, and minicassettes. The largest of the three is the standard cassette. The minicassette is only fractionally larger than the microcassette.

Advantages of discrete media:

1. Dictation can be distributed among several transcribers for faster completion of the work.
2. Dictation is not limited to a specific amount of media.
3. Flexibility: if an organization has compatible input equipment, all dictation can be transcribed in the WP center using the same transcription equipment.
4. Information can be permanently stored.
5. Rush or confidential documents can be expedited or isolated easily on different pieces of media.

Disadvantages of discrete media:

1. The media may need to be monitored, even with automatic media changers, to be sure they are replenished when dictation time has run out.
2. Storage space is needed for the unused and stored media.

endless loop

Endless Loop.   The **endless loop** is a nonremovable tape that flows in a continuous circle or loop and is housed in a tank or case for protection (Figure 4.8); it is never handled as it is a sealed system. As the tape is recycled, it is erased for reuse. Total recording time for endless loop media ranges from 90 to 240 minutes.

Advantages of endless loop media:

1. There is simultaneous recording and transcribing—transcription is possible only seconds after dictation—a feature especially beneficial for rush projects.
2. There are no unused media to store, since new dictation is recorded over old dictation, which has been erased.
3. There is less monitoring because there is no need to replenish the supply of media.

Figure 4.8.   Dictaphone's endless loop system. Courtesy of Dictaphone Corporation.

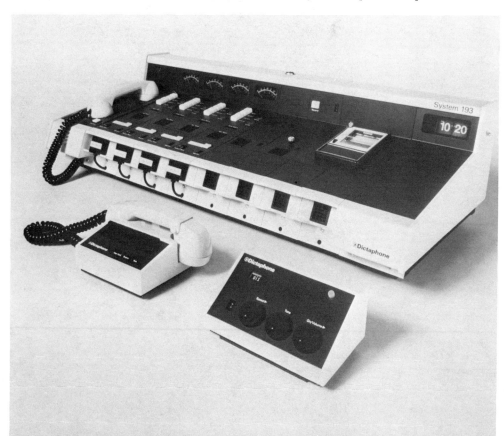

Figure 4.9. Norelco's minicassette portable with electronic indexing. Courtesy of Philips Business Systems, Inc.

Disadvantages of endless loop media:

1. Information cannot be permanently stored.
2. On endless loop systems which have only one tank, only one originator can dictate at a time.
3. Distribution of dictation from one tank is generally limited to one WP specialist for transcription. If two transcribers transcribe from one tank, no recording may be done at that time.

Input Equipment

Input equipment is used to record and play back dictation, and give the transcribers end-of-dictation and other special instructions. It can be categorized as

1. Portable units.
2. Desk-top units.
3. Centralized dictation units.

Portable Units. Portable units (Figure 4.9) are small, lightweight, battery-operated units with built-in microphones and are used for dictating from the field, in remote locations, or in an automobile. The media used in portable units are compatible with those units that may be used in an office. Therefore, they can be transcribed on the same desk-top transcribing unit as used for dictation input from desk-top or centralized units.

Sony is marketing a portable unit called the Typecorder (Figure 4.10) that is a combination keyboarding/dictating unit small enough to fit inside a briefcase. The originator can choose to dictate or keyboard a document with the unit. The microcas-

Figure 4.10. The Sony Typecorder provides the executive with the alternative of dictating or keyboarding a document to be finalized by a word processing specialist. Courtesy of Sony Office Products, Sony Corporation of America.

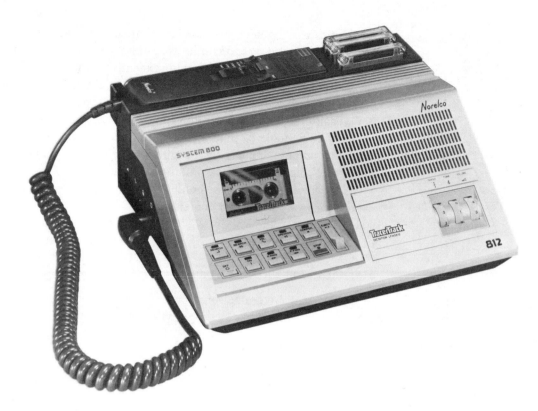

Figure 4.11. Norelco's TracerTrack microprocessor controlled desk-top unit for dictation and transcription. Courtesy of Philips Business Systems, Inc.

sette stores either the dictation or keyboarded text or both. It can then be transcribed by a WP specialist using either the Typecorder as a transcription unit or another compatible transcriber. Or, the originator's text can be printed directly with Sony's Compact Printer or with one of many compatible print devices available. Keyboarded text can also be telecommunicated to compatible word processors where it can be revised, stored, or printed.

Desk-top Units. Desk-top units (Figure 4.11) are stationary units used in the office. They are larger than portable units and have more controls for special instructions to the transcriber. Some desk-top dictation units can also be used as transcribing units simply by unplugging the microphone and plugging in a foot pedal. Desk-top units are used in offices where there are not a large number of originators or in very large organizations where the central system is used for light-to-moderate dictation and supplemented with desk-top units for heavy dictation. Desk-top units fit nicely into a decentralized or custom WP environment. They can also be used to record conferences.

Centralized Units. Centralized units are permanently installed dictation systems and are used in organizations with a large number of originators. Even though prices range from under $1,000 to over $20,000, this is the most cost effective dictation equipment system for many large organizations. All that needs to be provided to an originator is a microphone or a telephone wired into the central dictation system. Centralized systems fit nicely into an organization with a centralized WP system and are ideal for unattended operation at night or over the weekend. All the dictation is wired into the WP center and one or more specialists transcribe the documents. Some companies use the telephone system connected to the centralized dictation system. This allows originators to call in from any telephone anywhere in the world. This is especially good for companies with executives who travel.

Centralized units may utilize discrete media with an automatic media changer for continuous dictation capabilities (Figure 4.12). The changer automatically ejects individual cassettes or disks after they have been recorded. A discrete media system with an automatic media changer offers the flexibility of more transcribers being able to transcribe simultaneously by distributing the media among them. Frequently, it may provide a longer continuous dictation availability.

Companies may also use endless loop media. The length of continuous dictation capabilities and the need for storage of input media, as well as the number of transcribers that the system wishes to have transcribe at one time, generally determine whether an organization uses a discrete media or endless loop system.

Monitoring the Dictation System

Some systems have electronic capabilities for measuring the amount of dictation, measuring a transcriber's productivity, and keeping track of documents. Summaries are available on a screen (Figure 4.13) on the supervisor's unit or printed as hard copy and show such information as:

1. Documents by originator dictating and the department or WP specialist transcribing.
2. Time document was dictated and completed and by whom.
3. Status of the document.
4. Productivity of WP staff.
5. Chargeback to originators and/or departments.

Figure 4.12. Dictaphone's Thought Center Multiple Cassette, an automatic media changer. Courtesy of Dictaphone Corporation.

4. **Input—The Origination of Information**

Figure 4.13. Lanier's monitor allows you to "see" what is in the system. Courtesy of Lanier Business Products, Inc.

Equipment Features

All dictation units have some similar features. These are record, playback or review, fast forward, rewind, and special instructions or cueing.

There are some features that differ from brand to brand of dictation equipment. These are:

1. Indexing feature.
2. Digital counter.
3. Voice operated relay (VOR).
4. Automatic backspace.
5. Security device.
6. Automatic gain control.
7. Lockout.

Let us look at each of these features:

indexing feature

The **indexing feature** is used to show the transcriber the total length of dictation, the number of documents, and the beginning and end of each document, thereby showing its length. Some machines use paper strips on which the originator marks the end of one document before beginning another; others use an electronic display to show the end of a document or its length as well as the number of documents ready for transcription. The electronic display uses light emitting diodes (LED) to give these indications.

digital counter

The **digital counter** (also called an odometer or a scanner) is used to access a particular portion of the document. The dictator or transcriber can back up or fast forward to a specific location to review it.

voice operated relay

The **voice operated relay** (VOR) is especially helpful to the inexperienced dictator; it stops the media and prevents silence for long periods of time while the dictator is not speaking.

automatic backspace

An **automatic backspace** that allows the WP specialist instant review of the past several words can be very helpful.

lockout

Lockout, which provides privacy from eavesdropping on another dictator, is a major feature for some users. Another security device prevents unauthorized review of prior dictation.

automatic gain control

The **automatic gain control** automatically adjusts the volume during dictation or transcription.

Principles of Effective Dictation

We have established in this chapter the advantages of machine dictation. Now, how do you create documents effectively using the "mighty mike?"

Time management experts say that dictation is most effectively done in an uninterrupted period that allows ample time to do a good and complete job. Another suggestion is that you dictate every day so that it is easy to keep up with correspondence and other documents.

Let us consider, step by step, the process of machine dictation.

Setting the Dictation Environment

Much time will be saved and better documents will likely result if the originator arranges his thoughts and working area before he begins to dictate. Consider these suggestions:

1. Establish priorities among the documents. Begin with the most important one.
2. Gather all of the necessary files and data before you start to dictate.
3. Set the environment for uninterrupted dictation by isolating yourself from visitors, telephone calls, and so forth.
4. Make dictation logical and complete by outlining key points or underscoring items in a document you are answering before you begin.

Using Effective Dictation Techniques

You can save the WP specialist a great deal of time and effort by supplying the needed information at the appropriate time. Consider the following procedures for effective dictation.

Before Dictating.

1. Identify yourself—name, department, telephone or office number.
2. Specify what kind of document you are dictating, approximate length, format, stationery, number of copies, final or draft.
3. Number the documents as you dictate them and refer to them by the numbers.
4. Give the time frame for each document—rush or routine, priority, day and time each completed document is required.

While Dictating.

1. Speak at a normal rate and in a conversational tone. Visualize the recipient, as you frequently do when you are talking on the telephone.
2. Observe good letter-writing techniques and English usage by using complete sentences, correct grammar, and punctuation. Be natural in your dictation; say

what you mean in a straightforward manner. As a rule, devote one sentence to each idea.

3. Dictate addresses slowly, including zip codes. Spell out technical terms and all names, except for very common ones.
4. Use good etiquette. Put yourself in the place of the transcriber listening to you. Do not cough into the microphone or telephone handset; do not chew gum, smoke, put your hand over your mouth, or rattle objects while dictating.
5. Indicate paragraphs, format changes, and unusual punctuation (especially colons, semicolons, parentheses, and quotation marks).
6. Dictate thoughts in sentences or in phrases, rather than pausing after every word or two.
7. Check your voice level indicator to be sure that you are speaking loud enough for the transcriber to hear.
8. Alert the transcriber if you have forgotten to give information or have given out-of-sequence instructions.

After Dictating.

1. Specify the end of the document and who will sign it, if it will not be you.
2. List enclosures to go with the document.
3. Specify whether it will be necessary to store either temporarily or permanently the input media on which you have dictated the document if you are not using an endless loop system.
4. Specify the period the document must be stored on the output media. This may be for a temporary period, just until you get the document signed and in the mail, or permanently.
5. Review the dictation by playing it back, especially if you need a first-time final. Is your dictation complete? Is your message easy to understand? Did you use good dictation procedures?

Important Skills in Document Creation

The Team Approach

Administrative Secretarial Support. A time- and cost-conscious executive will establish procedures that give all secretarial support staff as much challenge as possible and that will free the executive from tasks someone else can do. This will allow him or her to concentrate on executive tasks and will provide for maximum utilization of people.

As an administrative secretary, you might do the following to help your boss in document creation:

1. Sort mail and other documents to be dictated into two categories—rush and routine.
2. Highlight important points by underlining them.
3. Establish priorities among mail which requires a response.
4. Attach relevant files or materials for reference.
5. Compose and draft responses to routine correspondence.
6. Develop standard paragraphs for repetitive use.

Word Processing Support. Dictation is only half the task. The WP specialist at the other end of the line also has an important job. The efforts expended to make the job easier and more pleasant may determine the success of the team. You might do the following to promote a good working relationship:

1. Use the name of the WP specialist if you know who will be doing the transcription.
2. Be courteous; use "Please" and "Thank You" when appropriate.
3. Speak in a conversational tone, as though you were talking on the telephone.
4. Be conscious of your voice. Is it too high or too low? Is it too loud or too soft? This is especially important if you do not have automatic gain control, which eliminates the need for you or your WP specialist to readjust the volume while dictating or transcribing on your dictation unit.
5. Use the special cueing feature for giving instructions to make the WP specialist's job easier.
6. Review your dictation periodically to be sure your voice is recording properly.
7. Be constantly aware of the environment in which you are dictating. Do not make distracting noises. Turn pages quietly. Reduce the noise level around you as much as possible.

User Procedures

To be a user in a company with a sophisticated system of producing paperwork can be a challenge if you are not accustomed to working in such an environment. Procedures are absolutely necessary to make the system run as effectively as it is designed to.

A User's Procedures Manual is provided in Part IV. Review it carefully to see how to create the paperwork you need.

This manual serves client users of Arnco, Inc., which provides AS and WP services. It is important to know what the organization providing the services can and cannot do. Job descriptions of the personnel may also be helpful to provide information on who is doing the work and how. Certainly the equipment they have and how they handle supplies for the production of documents is important. Section 1.5 of this manual demonstrates the work flow so that users can see where they fit in. To place a request, a Job Request Form must be completed as shown in Figure 2 of the manual. All the information requested is important if the job is to be done correctly. Each client company of Arnco, Inc. has already set up standard formats with Arnco, and documents will be produced according to these formats. Priorities, overtime, confidential documents, and rushes are all important. The manual tells about the types of documents produced and how they should be submitted, whether in longhand, OCR, or machine dictation. The manual also covers the areas of reprographics and distribution. This coverage will help users in these phases of the document cycle.

Section 2 of the manual is a Guide to Effective Dictation. It includes a Technical Reference Section which provides help with the Greek alphabet, a phonetic alphabet for use when the originator is trying to enunciate clearly and wants to use an example of an alphabetical character, signs and symbols, elements and symbols, and examples of technical abbreviations.

Any automated system is only as successful as its users. WP staffs are usually very interested in helping users work with the system effectively.

Future Trends

Much research and development is being conducted presently which makes the future of input devices look bright. Let us take a look at some of those on the horizon:

Voice Mail

voice mail
voice messaging

Voice mail or store-and-forward **voice messaging** is intended to automate the delivery of messages over telephone lines; it is not voice recognition. It combines three elements of communications equipment—telephone, computer, and a recording device. Voice mail will primarily serve one-way, brief communications, will be accessible from any location, and will be deliverable to any other telephone.

To initiate a voice mail transaction, the user calls the computer on a touch-tone telephone. Through the use of the pad on the telephone, the user can request a transmission, identify the recipient's telephone number, and designate priority of the message. The message is then spoken to the computer. The analog voice signal is digitized so it can be forwarded and then is converted back to analog for the person at the other end.

Voice Recognition

voice recognition

Voice recognition is the voice-actuated recording on media of the spoken word. As its level of development increases, voice recognition will decrease the amount of actual keyboarding required on terminals and WP equipment. Instead, an originator will pick up the telephone, and his words will be recorded as he talks. Documents will be stored on computer media for permanent use because of the cost efficiency over paper. Voice recognition may be used with the computer for such entries as sales orders, information input, and credit authorizations. Almost everyone, regardless of training, can use a voice recognition system since speech is the most common, most natural form of communication. This method is faster since it is possible to talk more rapidly than type or push buttons. Computers can talk as well as listen; they can give current order status on information requested by customers and can handle hundreds of telephone calls each day.

Although voice input of text and instructions is not now commercially feasible, it is in the research and development phase. Machines have been developed which translate voice input into digital form to be output on a printing device, but the error rate is still unacceptable.

A day will come, perhaps in the 1980s, that voice input will assist the labor intensive keyboard devices.

OCR

The OCR marketplace will double every three years during the 1980s, with significant cost reductions. Later in the decade OCR equipment will include facsimile and software for many applications and will become input devices for electronic mail networks.

Operational requirements for scanning will be considerably lessened. Paper color and weight will not be important. Characters scanned from hard copy will not be rejected so easily; as long as something is visible to the naked eye, the reader/scanner will accept it. Any typewriter using any type style will be acceptable. Graphics will also be scanned. Substantial improvements over current recognition capabilities will be attained by the latter part of the decade.

OCR will be a method of capturing and inputting into automated systems information from various sources. This information will be revised without requiring equipment changes.

Summary

Input is the origination and transmission of the document to the WP specialist. The individual who creates and transmits the document to the WP specialist to produce is the originator.

The methods of transmitting a document are machine dictation, longhand, shorthand, and OCR.

The three components of machine dictation units are the dictating device, the recording unit, and the media. Media that can be physically handled and permanently stored are discrete media; common types of discrete media are cassettes, belts, and discs. Endless loop media are continuously recycled and reused nonremovable tape media housed in a case for protection.

Categories of input equipment include portable units, desk-top units, and centralized dictation units. Systems for monitoring the work flow and measuring productivity are available for use by the supervisor of a centralized or production center.

The key points of document creation by machine dictation include:

1. Preparation for effective dictation
   a. Know how to operate dictation equipment properly.
   b. Decide upon your objectives and organize your thoughts.
   c. Set a proper dictation environment.
   d. Have everything you need handy.
   e. Establish document priorities.
   f. Underline or outline key points to which you will respond.
   g. Implement teamwork procedures for maximum people utilization.
2. Dictation procedures
   a. Identify yourself, department, document number, priority, and time frame.
   b. Give document format, copies, copy recipients, stationery.
   c. Specify punctuation, unusual spelling, format changes, and paragraphs.
   d. Give special instructions when necessary.
   e. Specify the end of the document and, if appropriate, who will sign it and his or her title.
   f. List enclosures.
   g. Specify storage of input media if applicable and retention of output media.

As a user, it is important to know how the WP system is set up and how to use it for all phases of document production. A system is only as good as the procedures that drive it. A user's procedures manual is essential.

The future promises many technological developments that will reduce the labor-intensive functions performed today, such as dictation and keyboarding, which are two separate tasks. Voice recognition will allow voice actuation to replace keyboarding. WP systems can then be used as editing tools.

OCR, which scans different input such as graphics, has a bright future. Its integration with facsimile and other equipment ensures its place in the electronic office.

Voice mail, soon to be as commonly used as the telephone, promises increased productivity. Its capabilities for storing and forwarding messages reduce telephone tag and provide a personal touch since the recipient of a call hears the message spoken by the caller.

Key Terms

Automatic backspace	Indexing feature	Recording unit
Automatic gain control	Lockout	Voice mail
Dictating device	Machine dictation	Voice messaging
Digital counter	Optical character	Voice operated relay (VOR)
Discrete media	recognition (OCR)	Voice recognition
Endless loop	Originator	

Self-Check Questions

Completion

1. The process by which people generate their ideas for communication to others is called _____.

2. The person who originates the document is called an _____.

3. The four methods of input are _____, _____, _____, and _____.
4. The most commonly used method of input is _____.
5. The least expensive form of input is _____.
6. The most expensive form of input is _____.
7. The method of input from which it is easiest to type is _____.
8. The transcription feature that eliminates the need for adjusting the volume of dictation is the _____.
9. The three major categories of input equipment are _____, _____, and _____.

Short Answer
1. What benefits would an originator derive from outlining key points before beginning to dictate?
2. What would be the result if an originator did not gather the necessary files and data before beginning to dictate?
3. What might happen if the originator did not tell the transcriptionist the type of stationery and format to be used until the end of the document?
4. What possible errors in the document might occur if an originator were interrupted while dictating?
5. Is it important to play back dictation before giving it to the WP specialist for transcription?
6. List at least four things an administrative secretary might do to help an executive with document creation.
7. Why would VOR be important for an inexperienced originator?
8. Name two possible results that may occur if the originator does not establish priorities for the documents before beginning to dictate if endless loop media are used.
9. If the originator forgets to give an instruction on the format of the document until the dictating is half finished, what action is appropriate?
10. Some originators are unsure of their use of grammar and just want "to get something down on paper" to work on further. Is it more cost effective to write the document out in longhand, revise it as necessary, and then dictate it, or is it better to dictate the document and revise it after it is typed and stored by the WP specialist?

True/False
1. Dictation equipment cannot be used for recording conferences.
2. Thermocouplers are excellent forms of discrete media.
3. Occasionally the tape in an endless loop system will have to be changed by a WP specialist.
4. To dictate effectively, an originator should use an environment without interruptions.
5. Lockout is a feature that enables WP specialists to prohibit originators from dictating.

Exercises

Exercise 4.1. Give some examples of specific applications of machine dictation by the following people in their professions:
1. Doctor,
2. Salesperson,
3. Student, and
4. Teacher.

Exercise 4.2. Mr. Larson, an up-and-coming young executive, chooses to use machine dictation for his method of input to the WP center. His boss, Mr. Hughes, however, has dictated for years to his secretary, who takes his dictation in shorthand. A number of other originators in the organization, not the least of whom is Ms. Lorentzen, write their correspondence and reports on yellow tablets. Mr. Hughes has recently instituted a staff development program to help the executives in his company learn to do a better job. He has asked all of them to prepare a short presentation on techniques they use to be more effective. Mr. Larson feels very strongly that his method of transmitting his correspondence and other documents is an excellent one. However, he needs help in putting the presentation together. Prepare a short presentation which details the important points he should emphasize.

Exercise 4.3. Visit an office where dictation equipment is used. Discuss the frequency of use, the type of equipment chosen and why, the percentage of input by machine dictation, and the savings as a result of the use of machine dictation. Which media did this office choose? Why? What do the users feel the advantages of these media are for their organization? Why? What is the likelihood of their changing to another form of equipment and/or media? Why?

Case Problem

Horton, Limited, is expending considerable time and research on the choice of an input system. There are a number of factors they are reviewing, such as:
1. Capabilities for dictation.
2. Even distribution of transcription between WP specialists.
3. A need to permanently store some dictation.
4. A need for a cost-effective system since theirs is a large company.
5. A need to limit time lost because of equipment breakdown.

Based on Chapter 4, what category and type of dictation equipment would you recommend? Why?

Chapter 5

****

Output Equipment

Chapter Objectives

After reading Chapter 5 and completing the end-of-chapter activities, the student will be able to:

1. *Define output.*
2. *List the criteria for the selection of WP systems.*
3. *Describe the four major categories of WP systems.*
4. *List the types of output media.*
5. *Compare and contrast the categories of output equipment.*
6. *Compare and contrast output print devices.*

Output Defined

Output is the phase of WP in which a document is produced. The document is keyboarded, revised as necessary, printed for reproduction, telecommunicated, and stored on magnetic media by WP specialists on one of the many WP systems on the market. Generically, output equipment may be called WP systems, text editors, automated typewriters, word processors, and word/information processing systems. These terms may be used interchangeably.

There are five basic parts to a WP system—keyboard, display, logic unit, print device, and media unit. The documents are created from the typing done at the keyboard. This includes original typing and revision typing.

light-emitting diode (LED)

The display unit is a cathode ray tube (CRT), **light-emitting diode (LED)**, or gas plasma device that provides a television-like screen on which the document being keyboarded or revised may be seen. Older WP systems often do not have displays.

The logic unit which is often housed with the keyboard will range in size and capabilities. The logic unit may be called a central processing unit (CPU) or electronics module.

WP systems also have to have a way to print the document. This may be a print device, such as a print wheel housed in the keyboard unit, or a separate printer.

Lastly, the WP system must have a media device to house the software that provides system capabilities and to record what has been keyboarded. Some systems have internal storage; others have external or removable storage called media. Commonly used media today are diskettes, hard or rigid disks, and magnetic cards. These will be discussed more fully in later sections.

The advantages of these WP systems are:

1. Typing time for error-free copy is reduced.
2. Corrections become trivial.
3. Updates and revisions are easily handled.
4. Repetitive typing is a one-time job with easy replay.
5. Information can be sorted, selected, and produced in a variety of forms.

Depending on the kinds and amounts of documents, WP systems can significantly increase productivity. If revisions are common and repetitive work is frequent, productivity improvement may be as high as 40 to 50 percent. It appears that 90 percent of all offices would profit by the installation of some kind of WP system. In fact, WP systems as a market will continue to be high growth. Forecasts of a 30 to 50 percent growth rate through 1984 are common in the industry.

Output Equipment

There are many brands and types of output equipment, with diverse capabilities for keyboarding, revising, printing, telecommunicating, and storing documents. How does an organization know which to select?

There are considerable differences in the capabilities of equipment available in the marketplace for the production of documents. In fact, a newcomer to the industry may be overwhelmed by the amount of variety that exists. First of all, there are several levels or categories of equipment, depending on capabilities, which in turn often determine price. It is extremely important to acquire equipment with the capabilities that are needed to do the work of the organization without overbuying. A common mistake made by organizations acquiring equipment is that they are so awed by the bells and whistles of a system that they forget their own primary applications. Applications determine choice of equipment. After it is clear which systems being considered can be used easily to do the types of documents commonly produced in the organization, then decisions among equipment on the basis of price become important.

Generally speaking, the more capabilities the machine has, the more expensive the unit. When an organization is acquiring equipment, it should also consider service and support, two major factors. How long does it take for a service representative to arrive when the equipment is reported down? It does not take a lot of down time to affect productivity significantly. How many people are employed locally by the vendor to assist in teaching complex applications on the equipment? These individuals, called market support representatives (MSR), or service engineers (SE), teach the vendor's system to customers and assist in customer applications on equipment. Using a system to its optimum capability is important, and it is often helpful to have the assistance of the vendor's MSR or SE the first time through an especially difficult application.

Ease in learning to use the system is another important consideration; overlooking this could be costly. Not only does the time an organization spends in training WP specialists translate into many dollars, but users of the system must also be trained with respect to capabilities. Backup support when a WP specialist is out is also necessary. Are temporary services able to provide replacements, or does the organization have people trained as backup support?

Categories of WP Systems

firmware-driven
software-driven

A wide range of capabilities and prices of WP systems exists in the marketplace. There are several ways that this equipment can be categorized.

A common method of categorizing equipment is to distinguish **firmware-driven** or hardware-based equipment from **software-driven** equipment. If equipment is said to be firmware-driven, or hardware-based, it is equipped or updated with features and capabilities that are activated from within the equipment itself. Hardware is equipment. **Firmware** is the logic built into the hardware that makes it perform its functions. On the other hand, equipment that is software-driven has features and capabilities that are activated by software such as magnetic cards or diskettes. **Software** means programmed media. For example, some equipment can be instructed to right justify, design forms, number lines, read or record magnetic cards from a diskette, change pitch or vertical line spacing, and compute mathematical information with the insertion of a programmed card or diskette. These capabilities will continue to grow as vendors continue to add software options.

firmware

software

WP systems are also either standalone units or shared systems. They may be self-contained units that provide for all functions—keyboarding, playback, and storage. They may also be a group of devices that provides for keyboarding, logic, playback, and storage in an integrated or shared fashion. For example, several keyboard stations use or share the same logic device (central processing unit) or the same printer.

To work with the wide-ranging capabilities more easily, the industry has grouped WP systems into four major categories:

1. Electronic typewriters
2. Standalone units
3. Shared systems
   a. Shared logic
   b. Distributed logic
   c. Shared resource
4. Computer-related systems
   a. Time-share systems
   b. Mainframes, minicomputers, and microcomputers using WP software

Let us look at the equipment in each of these categories, as we focus upon where each fits best in various types of organizations, remembering that equipment in each category often blends into the next category.

Electronic Typewriters

electronic typewriter

Electronic typewriters (Figure 5.1), sometimes called intelligent typewriters, are upgraded versions of the electric typewriter. They are at the extreme low end of the WP market and are designed for use primarily at an individual secretary's desk. They are wholly contained in a single compact unit. Their market includes small businesses, one-person secretarial support staffs in departments of large companies, and those companies who are reluctant to convert to WP and want to ease into automation. Electronic typewriters require little special training to operate and look very much like an ordinary electric typewriter. They come equipped with varying levels of capabilities. Many have automatic functions, such as centering and underscoring, that are performed manually on electric typewriters. Other features are automatic error correction, format storage, electronic margins and tabulators, column alignment, right margin justification, automatic indent, phrase storage, and automatic carrier return. These machines often have limited memory and are not capable of performing extensive text-editing functions such as massive insertions, deletions, and rearrangement of text.

Electronic typewriters are available with both elements and daisy wheels as print devices (see p. 82). The speed of playback ranges from 15.5 characters per

Figure 5.1. IBM Electronic Typewriter, Model 60. The upper right picture illustrates that four sets of margins and tabs can be stored. The code key (lower left) used in conjunction with a dual function keybutton activates automatic operations. Instruction cards in the lower right may be pulled out for quick reference. Courtesy of IBM Corporation.

second to 45 characters per second. Telecommunications are also available on some electronic typewriters.

Ultimately, probably all manufacturers of electric typewriters will manufacture electronic typewriters. Some experts say that electronic typewriters will entirely replace electric typewriters. Electronic typewriters generally cost less than $3000.

Standalone Word Processors

standalone unit

This category of WP system is the most common type of unit used in offices in the nation today. It is often called the workhorse of WP. The **standalone unit** (Figure 5.2) is a single work station that is complete in itself; that is a WP specialist can keyboard, revise, store on media, and print or play out on it. The functions found on most electronic typewriters are found on most standalone units in addition to other features such as:

1. The ability to locate certain sections of a document (called accessing) in which revisions are necessary and make the correction, with the ability to delete or insert new text.
2. The ability to create repetitive letters, that is, the same letter sent to two or more persons.
3. The ability to store documents.
4. The ability to merge lists of names and addresses or other variables with text and to create repetitive letters or memos.
5. The ability to scan documents; that is, to look for necessary hyphenation decisions at the end of each line and the appropriate number of lines for each page.
6. The ability to print unattended. The limits of the playout usually are dependent on such factors as ribbon length on the playout portion of the unit and amount of text that can be loaded into the unit to play out at one time.
7. Telecommunications—the ability to talk to another standalone automated typewriter via telephone lines and connector devices.

Electronic typewriters and standalone units may be divided into two separate categories—display and blind or nondisplay.

video display terminal (VDT)
display unit
gas plasma tube
viewing window

Video Display Terminals. **Video display terminals (VDT)** are **display units** (Figure 5.3) with television-like screens. They are also called cathode ray tube (CRT) devices, **gas plasma tubes**, and **viewing windows**. A cathode ray tube (CRT) is a TV-tube-like device used to display text. Gas plasma is a video display screen employing a gas plasma or discharge technology, characterized by an exceptionally

Figure 5.2. A. B. Dick's standalone with a one-line display and 8000-character memory. Courtesy of A. B. Dick Company.

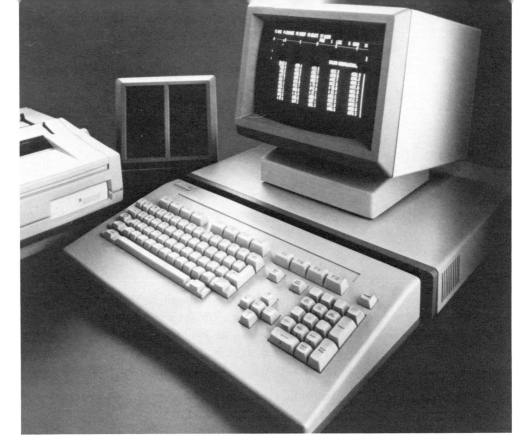

Figure 5.3. Exxon's 520 Information Processor—a display unit with full word processing capabilities including a 50,000-word dictionary, with a 10,000-word additional capacity that checks and corrects spelling. Courtesy of Exxon Office Systems Company, a Division of Exxon Corporation.

thin window

clear, flicker-free image. A viewing window or **thin window** is the term generally applied to a one-line or partial-line CRT or gas plasma display giving a window to see into the memory. The screens permit the WP specialist to see instantly what is being keyboarded or what is being added or deleted. These displays range from one line to partial page to two full pages (Figures 5.4 and 5.5). The greater the display, the greater the viewing area. It is helpful to be able to move or **scroll** the text up and down or left and right. Moving text up and down is called vertical scrolling; vertical scrolling permits the WP specialist to see previous parts of a page and previous and succeeding pages of a document. Moving text left to right is called horizontal scrolling; it allows the WP specialist to see keyboarded text that is wider than 8½ inches by 11 inches. There is often considerable discussion as to which is preferable and worth the money—the one line, the partial page, or the full page display.

scroll

The two page display system has some particular advantages for the WP specialist. If the WP specialist prefers, one large over-sized page may be used instead of two pages. This may be particularly helpful for applications such as accounting or statistical statements. Eye fatigue may be helped by the ability of the unit to show larger pitch type styles. When a document is being revised, it may be helpful for the WP specialist to be able to see both the original and the revised page. When a new document is being created from stored paragraphs or pages, it may be helpful to be able to see the stored text on one page and work with the insertion on the other page.

Opinions differ on eye fatigue and proofreading advantages of the various amounts of text displayed. Opinions also differ as to the best color of characters and background of the CRTs. A few that are used are green on black, red on black, black on white, and white on black. Several CRTs can be tilted for the best angle of vision.

5. Output Equipment

Figure 5.4. IBM's Displaywriter, a software-based text processing system features a large (66-line by 100-character) screen or the 25-line by 80-character display. Courtesy of IBM Corporation.

Figure 5.5. The Xerox 8010 Star information system offers a two-page display screen on which a wide range of text and graphics can be created. Courtesy of Xerox Corporation.

blind unit

Blind Units. **Blind units** (Figure 5.6) do not have a screen. A WP specialist can see only the printed text on hard copy as it is playing out, just as with an electric typewriter.

Shared Systems

shared system

Shared systems are several work station configurations which share one or more resources. The sharing of the resource contributes to a price reduction. The shared resource may be the logic, the media, or the printer. The types of WP systems with shared resources are:

1. Shared logic
2. Distributed logic
3. Shared printer/media

Shared Logic. Shared logic (Figure 5.7) is a multiunit system of work stations or terminals which share the memory and logic of a microprocessor, as well as the printer. The sharing of the electronic logic can give instant access to a large library of documents that are stored. Also, more than one WP specialist can perform various operations on a large volume of text simultaneously or several WP specialists may perform the same functions at the same time.

The number of keyboard work stations that may be used with a system varies with the vendor. Usually, the greater the number of work stations, the less the cost per work station. Some systems with a large number of capabilities might be prohibitive in cost as a standalone unit, but can be very attractive cost-wise when spread over a number of work stations. Thus, shared logic systems can provide greater control logic, greater editing capabilities, larger memory capacity, and larger media storage capacity.

A difficulty sometimes is encountered when the logic is out of service. All the work stations with shared logic may be inoperative.

Figure 5.6. Adler's Model 1030 Electronic Typewriter with 8000-character memory. Courtesy of Adler-Royal Business Machines, Inc.

distributed logic

Distributed Logic.   A **distributed logic** system is much like a shared logic system, except that each work station contains logic and processing power. This means that a malfunction of one station or of the central logic does not completely shut down the entire system.

At first look, the cost of shared or distributed logic might seem high. True cost, however, must be measured on a per-station basis and on the processing capability of each station.

Shared Printer/Media Systems.   Many users have systematized their stand-alone WP equipment in order to increase productivity and flexibility of formatting as well as reducing costs. The most common system that has been configured is to use one printer that will serve several keyboarding work stations (Figure 5.8). This sharing of printing power, because of the significantly faster print speed of the daisy wheel, ink jet, laser, or line printers (see pp. 81–87), has significantly increased productivity. Because the WP specialist can print out unattended at faster rates of speed while doing something else, labor costs are reduced. In addition, these printers can often format documents easier and faster and with more capabilities than a standalone unit. For example, they may automatically print letters and envelopes

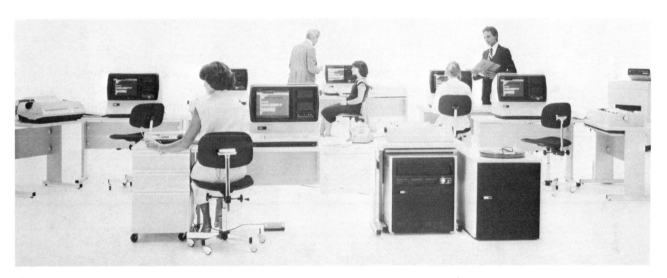

Figure 5.7.   The Lanier Shared Logic System, which can range from a single unit to multistation typing systems sharing a central memory/processing unit, magnetic storage, and printers. Courtesy of Lanier Business Products, Inc.

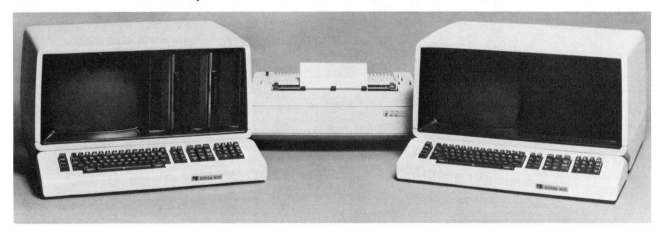

Figure 5.8.   These two NBI System 3000 work stations share a printer. Courtesy of NBI, Inc.

unattended, justify right margins, and so forth. Sometimes these shared printers are referred to as distributed media. You can see how the name is derived; the media are taken from one unit and distributed to another unit, the printer.

Computer-Related WP Systems

time-shared computer system

The computer with all its capabilities can be utilized to perform WP tasks from a DP terminal and also can be used in association with a WP system or terminal to tap into its database, capabilities, and storage (Figure 5.9). Many firms subscribe to **time-shared computer systems** with a commercial computer service bureau if there is not sufficient justification for an in-house computer for WP and DP activities. Since the cost of the computer is shared on a pro rata time basis among a number of users, this system provides an excellent access to the power at a reasonable price.

on-line

Customers of time-shared services access or call a computer from WP systems or terminals modified to be able to telecommunicate using ordinary telephone lines. Charges for each customer are based on the time **on-line** to the computer (time actually linked to the computer), the amount of computer capability utilized, and the backup services supplied by the vendor. Backup services may include the development of new programs, storage, training, and consulting. For example, if an organiza-

computerized WP system

tion needs to develop a new application to be processed on the **computerized WP system**, a new program may be required. This program can be written by the organization's personnel, or the company who owns the computer will develop the program for a price. In addition, the more text that is stored the more it costs. Some organizations want their text stored twice in case it is lost or scrambled. Time-shared computer vendors market DP as well as WP services. Advantages of using such a service include minimum financial outlay, massive storage, and often a higher level of storage capabilities than a typical WP system offers.

Figure 5.9. The Bowne Connection provides a unique way through which standalone word processing equipment such as the Lanier, Vydec, and Lexitron machines shown here can link into the capabilities of a computer (center) for special applications. Courtesy of Bowne Information Systems.

A second approach to WP time-shared computer systems is for organizations with in-house computers to dedicate a portion of the computer's capacity to WP functions. WP software for an organization's in-house computer in many cases costs only a fraction of what it would cost to install an additional WP system.

Use of WP software on mainframes, minicomputers, and microcomputers illustrates why many refer to WP as word/information processing. Increasing numbers of WP users are becoming interested in the integration of DP with their WP systems. They perform a variety of functions from WP and accounting to database access and inventory control. Some organizations with databases stored on their computer would like to tap into them and revise the information without rekeyboarding them. The computer can be programmed to permit this. In addition, it can perform many WP tasks, such as sending one letter to a list of people, revising and manipulating text that is permanently stored, and sorting information, such as selecting from a nationwide list only customers who live in certain areas and printing their names and selected information. All the databases of the computer can be accessible to the WP specialist.

Not only does the computer offer massive storage capabilities, but also, depending on the programming of the software, many other capabilities may be available. For example, a user can ask the computer not only to print and store a document, but also to phototypeset or microfilm the document.

Because of the capability of the computer, its availability, and the continuing trend toward reduction in cost, the future of WP lies in great part with the computer. This is particularly true with the large numbers of personal computers being purchased.

Personal computers range in price, memory capacity, and capabilities. Software programs determine capabilities and, therefore, applications. Most personal computers can be instructed to convert themselves into remote terminals capable of communicating with mainframes or minicomputers over a standard telephone. Very useful databases such as current business news, stock prices, legal and medical indexes, and legislative actions are accessible with the use of personal computers. Many personal computers are being used for WP. While their capabilities are not as extensive as word processors specifically designed for this purpose, basic capabilities such as error correction, insertion, deletion, and repetitive letters are very helpful for personal use.

Output Print Devices

type bar
element
print wheel
ink jet printer
laser printer
dot-matrix printer
line printer
impact printer

In the selection of a printer, the most important criterion is the quality. The second is the print speed. Next comes the reliability of the print device. Price, of course, is a very important consideration that must be balanced with the other factors.

To print the documents, one of the several types of devices may be used. These are the **type bar, element, print wheel, ink jet printer, laser printer, dot-matrix printer,** and **line printer.** An important distinguishing feature among some of the print devices is whether or not they are **impact printers**; that is, whether or not the print device impacts or strikes the paper as it prints. The type bar, element, print wheel, dot-matrix, and line printer are impact printers. The ink jet and laser printers are not. An important and necessary use of impact printers is the creation of carbon pack forms. Since the decision to acquire a printer may involve some tradeoffs, let us take a look at each type of output print device.

Type Bar Devices

Type bar devices (Figure 5.10) were used in some early electronic typing systems and many electric typewriters. The type bars sit in a well in the typewriter below the platen; each type bar is individually struck to print a character. Type bar devices did not have the type style flexibility many users want. The type style and pitch the user chooses when acquiring the typewriter is installed on the keys and cannot be changed. However, users have a variety of type styles, including foreign language symbols, from which to choose to equip the typewriter initially.

Because the print speed is dependent on the speed at which the individual strikes the keys, there is no standard print speed on electric typewriters. The print speed for WP systems with type bars as the print device when playing back is approximately 15 characters per second, which is equivalent to 180 words per minute. (This is calculated as follows: 15 cps times 60 seconds in a minute divided by 5 characters or strokes per average word.) This speed is, of course, much faster than the average typist's rate of typing; however, it is slow when compared to today's WP print standards.

Element Devices

Most electric typewriters as well as several WP systems use a single element (Figure 5.11) for their printing device. IBM patented the element in 1963 and it is being used by many typewriter manufacturers today. The element allows secretarial support staff to change type styles and pitch on documents easily. It is available in both pica and elite type as well as proportional spacing. Many styles of type, as well as OCR, foreign languages, Greek, and technical symbols, are available.

WP systems that use an element have a print speed when playing back of approximately 15.5 characters per second, which is equivalent to 186 words per minute. Because of this relatively slow print speed as well as formatting capabilities, many organizations are choosing to use WP systems with elements primarily for keyboarding and to use separate print wheel, ink jet, laser, dot-matrix, or line printers for the printing of a document.

Print Wheels

A print device common to many WP systems as well as separate printers (Figure 5.12) is the print wheel, which may also be called a daisy wheel or qume print wheel. The print wheel (Figure 5.13) looks like a wheel, with each letter, number, or symbol on

Figure 5.10. The Adler Model 131D Electric Typewriter which uses the type bar print device. Courtesy of Adler-Royal Business Machines, Inc.

Figure 5.11. The element print device has a rated speed of 15.5 characters per second and is used in electric typewriters, word processing work stations, and separate printers. Courtesy of IBM Corporation.

Figure 5.12. The IBM 5257 Printer used for the 5520 Administrative System is a qume printer with a daisy print wheel. Courtesy of IBM Corporation.

Figure 5.13. Daisy wheels, also called print wheels or qume printers, print in many type styles at a variety of speeds. Courtesy of Xerox Corporation.

the end of a spoke. The name of daisy wheel was given because it looks like a daisy in a flat one-dimensional circle with the characters on the end of each petal. The wheel is rotated to strike the paper as the keys on the typewriter are depressed. This print device was originally developed by Diablo Company, but is used today by many other manufacturers of WP systems. The print speed of the print wheel ranges from 25 to 60 characters per second, which is equivalent to 300 to 720 words per minute playback speed. Many manufacturers who use print wheels in their units have designed and engineered the print wheels to print bidirectionally; that is, the print wheel plays back from left to right on one line, then prints the next line from right to left.

Many type styles are available in print wheels. In fact, many of the common type style characters available on elements are also available on print wheels.

Another dimension of the print wheel is the twin track or twin head design (Figure 5.14). When two type styles are needed for a document, a twin track or twin head is particularly advantageous. It permits the use of two print wheels simultaneously for ease in combining different typefaces in one document and eliminating the necessity of changing wheels during document production.

A form of printer which uses a thimble-shaped element with more symbols than an element or conventional daisy wheel is the Spinwriter (Figure 5.15). This is an impact printer which prints at the rate of 55 characters per second.

Ink Jet Printer

In 1976, IBM introduced the ink jet printer, which electronically sprays a stream of tiny, electrostatically charged ink droplets on the paper through an electronic font in the shape of the character (Figure 5.16). Finished documents are printed by the ink jet printer at speeds of up to 184 characters per second (2208 words per minute). Besides the fast rate of print speed, the ink jet printer allows for a variety of formats, type styles, and type sizes. For example, if a document has been keyboarded in one type style, the printer can be instructed to play out in a different type style. The printer creates documents on command from stored paragraphs or segments, or

Figure 5.14. This Wang Twin Head Printer uses two daisy print wheels simultaneously for easy type style mixing within one document, at a rate of 40 characters per second. Courtesy of Wang Laboratories, Inc.

Figure 5.15. The print thimble used in the NEC Spinwriter. Courtesy of NEC Information Systems, Inc.

merges text with names and addresses. It is the only printer which prints both letters and envelopes in sequence. It prints up to seven type styles in ten or twelve pitch or proportional spacing and switches from one to another, automatically printing various combinations. It will accommodate a wide variety of paper sizes as well as envelopes. The ink jet printer can read, format, and print text from magnetic cards.

There are two models of the 6640 ink jet printer, the regular and the dual-speed model. The dual speed model can print in regular high quality at 92 characters per second and in draft quality at 184 characters per second. It also can combine the two by printing the first copy at high quality and subsequent copies at draft quality.

One disadvantage of the ink jet printer is that it cannot print on multipart carbon packs. It has to print additional identical copies to serve as carbons. Many companies, such as insurance companies, however, have a need for output using carboned forms.

Laser Printers

laser

Laser printing is a new technology taking the office automation industry by storm. There are currently more than seventy companies working on laser imaging and printing projects. **Laser** technically translates to *l*ight *a*mplification by *s*imulated *e*mission of *r*adiation. It is a technology which transmits an extremely narrow beam of electromagnetic energy in electrophotographic printing.

A laser device which allows high quality, high volume, and high speed printing and processing is the IBM 6670 Information Distributor. Using a low-powered helium neon laser beam and mirrors, it forms the characters on the photoconductor for transfer to the paper. It also performs other functions, such as:

1. Telecommunicates to automated typewriters and other printers as well as to the computer.
2. Creates documents by processing with a variety of formatting capabilities.
3. Collates.
4. Duplexes (prints on both sides of the paper).
5. Serves as a convenience copier.

A very important capability is that of printing computer output. It can reduce 11 inch by 17 inch computer printouts to a very legible, high quality, 8½ inch by 11 inch document. These laser printers work in a system with word/information processing

Figure 5.16. The IBM Ink Jet Printer prints 92 to 184 characters per second in a variety of formats. Courtesy of IBM Corporation.

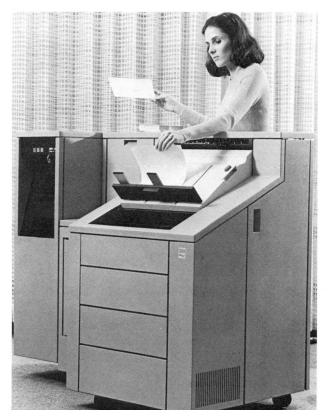

systems, DP systems, and other separate printers. The speed allows up to 36 pages per minute.

The Xerox 5700 is a high speed printer that combines computer, laser, and xerographic technologies to print data, textual material, and forms up to 43 pages a minute. It also has powerful telecommunications capabilities.

The Wang Laser Printing System (Figure 5.17) using laser-based xerographic technology prints in 10, 12, and 15 pitch or proportional spacing. It operates at an average speed of 12 pages per minute.

Line Printers

A line printer prints a line at a time. There are several types of line printers. The dot-matrix printer is an impact printer that prints a whole line at a time. Each character is formed by a grid or matrix pattern of dots. Several WP and DP equipment manufacturers have designed and engineered a draft quality line printer for the organizations who have applications that do not require high quality. High quality text and graphics printing is also available for those users who require these capabilities. The DP or WP center printing an internal document or one that will require revisions can benefit from this unit.

Figure 5.17. The Wang Laser Printing System, which uses laser-based xerographic technology, operates at an average speed of twelve pages per minute and interfaces with Wang OIS, Alliance, and VS systems. Courtesy of Wang Laboratories, Inc.

Figure 5.18. Wang's High Speed Line Printer, which prints at a speed of 425 lines per minute, can be used with Wang Word Processing Systems. Courtesy of Wang Laboratories, Inc.

The fastest impact printer being marketed is the high speed line printer (Figure 5.18). This is a device that prints an entire line of characters as one unit. As the industry evolves, these printers may focus more and more on the WP market.

Output Media

Output media are the removable magnetic materials on which digital information or recorded and stored text can be accessed by the system. Depending on the equipment, magnetic tape, cards, diskettes, hard disks, or computer media may be used. Some WP systems have internal storage rather than external or removable media (Figure 5.19).

The term *magnetic* as it is applied to media means that the media can be used again and again, just as a standard cassette may be used repeatedly in a tape recorder. Frequently, output media are *not* interchangeable between brands and types of output equipment. The ability to file and retrieve documents stored on media quickly and easily is essential. This is one of the primary benefits of WP (Figure 5.20). This filing and retrieval process is discussed in Chapter 6.

Tape

In older WP systems magnetic tape was a standard cassette tape or any of a variety of tape cartridges with different sizes, lengths, capacities, and costs. In fact, these factors were important considerations for tape systems in WP's early days. Most magnetic tapes hold 25 to 60 pages of text, up to approximately 300,000 characters.

Magnetic Card

A magnetic card (Figure 5.21) is an oxide coated mylar film cut to the size of the 3¼ inch by 7⅜ inch punched paper card used in keypunch applications. Many users prefer a card-to-page relationship; that is, each card represents a page of text. Magnetic card capacities range from 50 to 100 lines, holding 5,000 to 10,000 characters.

Figure 5.19. IBM Memory 100 Typewriter with internal storage for 100 pages. Courtesy of IBM Corporation.

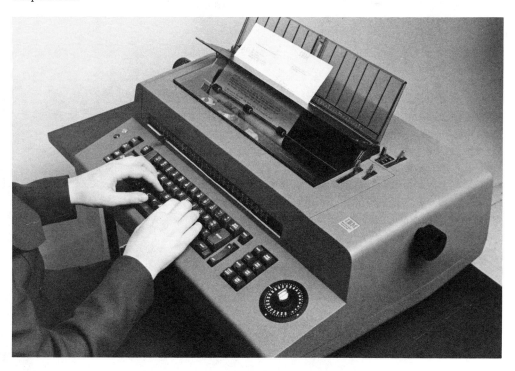

Figure 5.20. Magnetic cassette tape stored in a cassette album for easy access. Courtesy of American World Processing Company.

Figure 5.21. The magnetic cards being recorded in the IBM Mag Card II will be printed on the IBM 6670 Information Distributor (laser printer) in the background. Courtesy of IBM Corporation.

Double-sided cards with magnetic coating on both card surfaces double storage capacity and are available for all equipment that uses magnetic cards. Magnetic cards commonly have a writable area in the corner for identifier or index marks. Writable cards provide the user with space to annotate the information necessary for quick and easy filing and retrieval. An infrequently used card is the magnetic strip card, which holds about a paragraph of text.

Diskettes, Disks, Discs

A magnetic diskette or disc (floppy disc) is a thin, circular piece of flexible mylar that is coated with iron oxide to give it its magnetic recording properties. It resembles a 45 rpm record and may be called disk, disc, diskette, or floppy, depending on the vendor. There are minidisks (5.25 inches in diameter), standard discs (7.8 inches in diameter encased in an 8-inch envelope), and microdiskettes (3.5 inches in diameter).

Standard diskettes have quite a range in recording capacity since some are single sided and others are double sided. Double-sided diskettes may also be dual or double density, which means they hold much more data. Standard floppy discs (Figure 5.22) have concentric tracks upon which information may be recorded. These tracks are divided into pie-shaped wedges called sectors. The sector on each track provides a data block for information. For example, the IBM OS6 diskettes have 8 sectors with 77 tracks, for 616 data blocks of information and a system for locating documents. Diskettes are permanently contained in envelopes that protect them from dust and handling and, they provide more storage capacity than do tapes or cards; specifically, they permit storage of 70,000 to 30 million characters and from 60 to 500 pages of text. They provide random access memory (RAM) which makes instant access possible. In many cases, software for the WP system is also stored on the diskettes.

Information can be stored on or through WP equipment for computer media— tapes, diskettes, or hard or rigid (fixed) discs.

Figure 5.22. Diskettes are the most common medium in the word processing marketplace. Courtesy of American Word Processing Company.

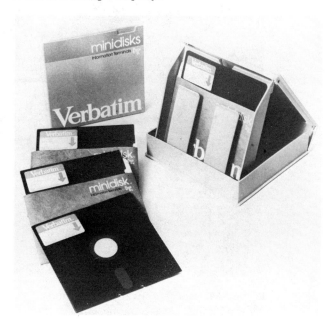

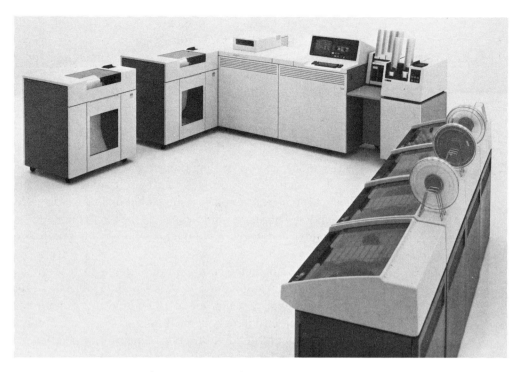

Figure 5.23. IBM System/38 computer with magnetic tapes. Courtesy of IBM Corporation.

Figure 5.24. Sperry Univac 1100/60 computer with disc packs. Courtesy of Sperry Univac, a division of Sperry Corporation.

5. Output Equipment

A disc is a rigid, random access, high capacity magnetic storage medium. Discs may be removable (cartridges) or nonremovable. Capacities range from 250 to more than 750,000 pages of text. WP systems are able to telecommunicate with computers to dump or transfer documents for storage. More and more organizations are choosing this method of electronic storage to reduce the amount of paper stored in file cabinets and the amount of WP media handled.

Some WP vendors have begun to offer 8 and 14 inch Winchester rigid disc drives for text storage. These fixed or nonremovable disc drives offer all the advantages of rigid computer discs and are capable of holding approximately 325 to 150,000 pages, depending on the size of the disc. They are sealed in a filtered enclosure so that the cleanliness of the disc is assured.

Future Trends

As WP and DP evolve toward combined information processing, more and more capabilities will be interchanged on hardware. DP equipment will have increased WP functions, and WP hardware will have more DP capabilities.

Media will trend toward greater amounts of storage. New technologies such as the video disc, which stores both text and pictures with random access capabilities, will find a marketplace; their manufacture will become commercially feasible. Much of the potential of this technology lies in education and training.

Printer capabilities will be faster and shared to provide higher price performance per work station. As costs are reduced, the use of high-speed printers will become more common.

Summary

Output is the phase of WP in which the document is keyboarded, stored on magnetic media, revised as necessary, and printed. WP specialists use WP systems to yield significantly higher production for documents. These electronic typing systems provide for keyboarding at rough draft speeds, easy corrections, and revisions; they have automatic features that permit electronic performance of such tasks as centering and underscoring.

The factors that most significantly affect the decision-making process when selecting equipment are applications and price. As the equipment increases in capabilities, the cost generally increases.

WP systems are commonly categorized as follows:

1. Electronic typewriters.
2. Standalone units.
3. Shared systems.
4. Computer-related systems.

The printer device for the system may use the type bar, element, or print wheel. For increased productivity, however, many organizations use high speed, high volume printers such as ink jet, laser, line, and dot-matrix printers.

Output media are the magnetic materials on which information is recorded and stored for access and revision. Today's WP equipment utilizes magnetic cards, cassettes, diskettes, hard or fixed discs, and computer media for storage.

The future promises greater integration of functions between DP and WP hardware. More common use of greater printing power and media storage are anticipated.

Key Terms

Blind unit	Distributed logic	Element
Computerized WP system	Dot-matrix printer	Firmware
Display unit	Electronic typewriter	Firmware-driven

Gas plasma tube	On-line	Thin window
Impact printer	Print wheel	Time-shared computer
Ink jet printer	Scroll	system
Laser	Shared system	Type bar
Laser printer	Software	Video display terminal
Light emitting diode (LED)	Software-driven	(VDT)
Line printer	Standalone unit	Viewing window

Self-Check Questions

Completion

1. _____ is the phase of WP in which the document is produced; that is, keyboarded, revised, and printed.
2. An individual trained to teach a WP system to a customer and assist in customer applications of equipment is called a _____.
3. _____, sometimes called intelligent typewriters, are an upgraded version of standard electric typewriters.
4. Standalone units are divided into two separate categories—_____ and _____.
5. _____ are several work stations that share one or more resources.
6. WP hardware uses _____, _____, _____, and _____ _____ for storage.
7. If the printing device actually hits or strikes the paper, it is called a _____ printer.
8. A print device which resembles a daisy is called a _____ and the printer it is used on has a print speed of _____ to _____ cps.
9. The IBM 6670 Information Distributor, which uses a helium laser beam and mirrors, is called a _____ printer.
10. A _____ printer prints a whole line at a time.

Matching

Write the letter of the definition to the left of the number of the term.

Terms

_____ 1. Winchester disc

_____ 2. Firmware

_____ 3. Software

_____ 4. Standalone unit

_____ 5. Distributed logic

_____ 6. CPU

_____ 7. MSR

_____ 8. Blind units

_____ 9. Print Wheel

Definitions

a. Operation of a WP or DP terminal directly connected to the CPU of a computer.

b. Rigid, nonremovable, magnetic, oxide coated, random access disc sealed in a filtered enclosure with the read/write heads and head actuator.

c. Interchangeable print font used on many WP electronic typing systems; it produces faster print speeds than an element print device.

d. Specific logic capabilities permanently placed in control memory in DP and WP equipment.

e. Nondisplay WP system in which keyboarded data are printed on paper in the unit.

f. Individual employed by the vendor to train customers to use equipment and to apply it to their environment.

g. Stored set of instructions or programmed media for the operation of DP or WP hardware.

h. WP system that has more than one work station, all of which share one or more resources, such as logic, media, and printer.

i. Single station, self-contained WP unit that provides keyboarding, logic, playback, and storage of data.

j. Unit which controls the storage, logic, and manipulation of the data on a computer and shared logic WP system.

5. Output Equipment

k. Multiterminal system which shares peripherals and sometimes storage and logic but with intelligence (logic) and processing power also in each terminal.

_____ 10. On-line

Exercises

Exercise 5.1. As an individual or as a class, visit two vendors of WP output equipment. Choose an application such as repetitive correspondence or statistical work. Ask the marketing support representative or service engineer of each company to demonstrate the application. Compare the ease with which it is completed both times. Compare time, quality of document, access to the document, and ease of operation. Which equipment was the most effective? Which media were the most effective? Write a short report reacting to each equipment demonstration.

Exercise 5.2. Compare the production time of a 32-page document by element, print wheel, and ink jet printer. Assume that each page has 25 double-spaced lines typed in elite type with a 6-inch line length. Show your calculations.

Case Problem

Dr. Reiswig and her two WP specialists, Ms. Addington and Ms. Harris, have just attended the annual International Information/Word Processing Syntopican. They spent many hours visiting the exhibitors' demonstrations as well as listening to the leading practitioners explain new techniques and equipment applications in the seminar sessions. They know their present equipment does not have all the capabilities of some of the new equipment at the show. What criteria should they use to decide to change or upgrade equipment? All the documents used up to now are stored on the media of the present equipment. What difficulties are faced with a media change? Ms. Addington and Ms. Harris are very well trained on the present equipment. How long will it take them to be equally as competent on new equipment? In general, what is involved in a decision such as this one?

Chapter 6

****

Document Production

Chapter Objectives

After reading Chapter 6 and completing the end-of-chapter activities, the student will be able to:

1. *Differentiate between media-bound and memory-equipped WP systems.*
2. *List the steps required to revise a document.*
3. *Reference necessary sources for decision-making in printing a document.*
4. *Discuss the advantages of databases and magnetic media storage.*
5. *List and describe the basic categories of documents.*
6. *List and describe the major types of sources from which documents are created.*
7. *List and describe the ways a document may be produced.*
8. *Describe the benefits of transcribing from machine dictation.*
9. *List the forms of media used in transcription.*
10. *Employ good procedures for effective transcription.*
11. *Identify the components of transcription equipment.*

Keyboarding into Memory

You can produce documents much faster on a WP system than on an electric typewriter because you do not have to be concerned about the errors you make. This rough draft typing speed is, in itself, a boon to productivity.

Keyboarding on an electronic typing system can be a powerful feeling. At your fingertips are the controls for effective document formatting, production, and distribution. The feel of the alphabetical and numerical keys is similar to that of an electric typewriter. In addition, there are keys that permit you to do many different types of formatting functions, such as automatically centering, underscoring, and indenting paragraphs. Quality documents that aid in important business decisions may be your responsibility. The push of a button can send a document around the world.

memory

A major benefit of keyboarding on WP equipment is that what is typed is recorded either on media or in the memory of the equipment. **Memory** is the ability of the equipment to remember what has been keyboarded, revised, and stored. It is a significant addition to the equipment.

The early units, such as the MTST and the Mag Card I, both manufactured by IBM, had no memories. On these units, the keyboarded text was recorded directly on the media, that is, magnetic tapes and cards. These early units were media-bound.

If an insertion, deletion, or correction was required, the WP specialist had to access the point of revision and insert or delete the text. In the case of insertion, new text, if it was more than was deleted, was typed over good material; this text, then, had to be at least partially retyped. In the case of deletion, the gap between the original text and the deletion had to be closed up to provide continuous material. Small deletions were much easier than large ones. The right margin could be adjusted to close gaps caused by small deletions. **Pagination**, that is, making the text on the media equal to a page length of a chosen number of lines, was sometimes a problem. Even with these limitations, however, the abilities of these first units to insert, revise, and delete text were considerably better than those of conventional typewriters.

pagination

Revisions are significantly easier with a memory-equipped WP system. The impact of the memory logic on the industry has been dramatic. With memory there is never any retyping of good text when new material is inserted. Instead, the memory actually allows the old text to open up and move over for the new, much like throwing a rock into a pond—the water moves over and makes room for the rock. When deleting material, the specialist uses the delete instruction to remove and close the gap around the text to be deleted and the remaining material electronically. What is in memory can be stored easily on media and can be recalled just as easily. To **access** sections of the document in memory is easily accomplished. Memory is to WP systems what automatic transmissions are to automobiles—work savers and devices that permit higher performance. The amount of memory varies from model to model; a unit may have as little as one line of memory or as much as many pages.

access

Memory used to store text as keyboarded is called **random access memory** (RAM). Random access memory allows documents to be stored randomly and retrieved immediately by a system of document identification. RAM is said to be a **volatile memory** if it is lost when the power to the system is shut off. Word processing specialists quickly learn not to turn off the equipment until they have stored the text.

random access memory

volatile memory

A system can access the identified text directly; hence, information may be retrieved more speedily from random access memory than by serially searching through media such as the cassette or cartridge tape. A sequential search through the media of older WP systems is called **sequential access memory (SAM)**. To access page 45, pages 1-44 must be searched through.

sequential access memory (SAM)

Memory may also be **read only memory** (ROM) or **read only storage** (ROS). Read only memory or storage is frequently used for storing instructions for machine functions. Some vendors increase machine capabilities by increasing ROM.

read only memory

read only storage

Bubble memory represents the newest solid state memory technology. It provides for retention of an even greater amount of data in a very small storage area. Perhaps a billion bits of information can be stored in a device the size of a cigarette package and accessed very quickly. Bubble memory uses magnetic fields to create regions of magnetization. A pulsed field breaks the regions into isolated bubbles. Digital information is represented by the presence or absence of a bubble. External electromagnetic fields push the bubbles past the reading and recording sections of memory. Bubble devices are tiny and have **nonvolatile memories**, which means they retain the data when the power is turned off. Because of the compactness of the technology, if prices come down within competitive ranges, bubble memory may soon find its way into WP systems.

bubble memory

nonvolatile memory

Common Features of WP Systems

Although there are over one hundred models of WP equipment, many systems perform similar functions. The keys on the keyboard or the functions may be called by different names, but the results are similar. Keyboards commonly have, in addition to alphabetical and numerical keys, format, access, edit, and operation keys. These keys enable the WP specialist to create documents electronically and tell the system what to do. Perhaps grouping keys into functions and citing names given by different equipment manufacturers will help you relate the functions on several systems.

Format

format
Format is a contraction meaning *form of material.* It designates a predetermined arrangement of text and/or data for output. The format keys or functions determine what the page layout of a document will look like. Some examples of format keys (Figure 6.1) with their functions are:

1. Tab—indent or align.
2. Carrier return—end the line.
3. Automatic center—center text on the line or between designated points.
4. Automatic underscore—underscore characters, words, or segments of text without backspacing and underscoring on a character-by-character basis.
5. Decimal tab—align columns of figures around a decimal point, also called number alignment.
6. Automatic headers/footers—put header/footer text at the top or bottom of the page (also called header/footer or top/bottom margin text).
7. Margin set or adjust—change margins with one command.
8. Automatic page numbering—generate page numbers within a document at the top or bottom of a page.
9. Pagination—produce pages of a specified number of lines.
10. Justify—print text with flush left and right margins.
11. Stop code—stop during printout for such procedures as changing elements or inserting variable information.

Access

An access key locates a point in the memory at which you can enter new text or make revisions. On a display system a cursor (a lighted indicator) usually shows the position. Examples of access keys and their meanings are:

1. Recall—go to the next page of the document or to the next document.
2. Character, word, line, sentence, paragraph, page—go to the next character, word, line, sentence, paragraph, or page, respectively.

Figure 6.1. Wang keyboard illustrating types of functions. Courtesy of Wang Laboratories, Inc.

6. Document Production

3. Search—go to a point specified, i.e., a group of characters or a word, by searching through text matching groups of characters.
4. Find—go to a specific record or listing in a file/sort document.
5. Previous page—go back to the preceding page.
6. Scroll—go through a document, usually in forward, backward, and up and down directions.

Edit

Edit keys are used to revise the document. Examples with their functions are:

1. Insert—add new text.
2. Delete or erase—remove text.
3. Move, block and jump, or save and recall—change the location of text from one area of a page or document to another.
4. Copy or block and save—locate and reproduce specific text in another section of the page or document as well as leave it in its original location.
5. Column move/delete or field update—move characters vertically within a column and move, insert, or delete a column with a minimum number of instructions.
6. Column wrap—adjust text among columns to conform to a new or specified format.
7. Skip—pass over certain segments of text and edit beyond the skipped area.

Operation

Operation keys are those keys or functions that identify major tasks you may wish to perform. Examples of operation keys and their meanings are:

1. Text or new document—create a document.
2. Print—generate printout of the document.
3. Merge file/text—combine selected information from a file or listing with text or document; e.g., a list of names and addresses with a letter.
4. Cancel—stop performance of task and revoke instruction.
5. Communicate—put the machine into a mode of operation to transmit documents electronically.
6. Execute—perform the command instructed.
7. File—create a file or list of information that can be qualified or manipulated.
8. Index—create a list of stored information on the media.
9. Document build or assembly—create a new document interactively or automatically, using stored segments of text.

menu

Some systems use a **menu** (Figure 6.2), a list of possible actions, for performance of tasks.

mnemonic code

Many systems use **mnemonic codes** to give instructions. This means that a "code" or "command" key (Figure 6.3) is used in conjunction with alphabetical or numerical keys to give a direction. The direction may be a format, access, or edit function. An example of a mnemonic code is "Code + C" to center text automatically. Other examples are "Code + J" to justify text and "Code + M" to move text.

Revisions

Everyone makes mistakes! Revision is the process of changing the keyboarded data. The author, when creating a document, and the WP specialist, when producing the document, are both subject to error. The good news is that revisions and corrections are easily made on WP equipment. Corrections can be made immediately for those

Figure 6.2. The menu shown on the display of this Apple III computer equipped with Apple Writer III software indicates the choices available to the operator. Courtesy of Apple Computer, Inc.

Figure 6.3. The code key (upper left) on this IBM Electronic 75 Typewriter when used in conjunction with other keys gives them dual function capabilities. For example, Code plus "C" provides for automatic centering. Courtesy of IBM Corporation.

6. Document Production

errors that the specialist feels the instant they are made. Most systems have a simple backspace to eliminate the error so that the correct character or characters can be retyped. For the relatively small percentage of errors that the specialist makes but does not recognize until later, there are other correction techniques, which are also used for author revisions.

Let us take a look at how you might correct an error that you catch as you are proofreading the document:

1. Access or locate the place in the memory of the WP system or on the media where the error is.
2. Delete the error by using the delete function; most equipment deletes text by character, word, line, sentence, paragraph, or page, which means you delete only as much as necessary.
3. Insert any necessary new text by keyboarding it into the appropriate location in the material. It does not matter whether the insertion is one character or many paragraphs; the equipment will allow for the insertion.
4. Sometimes a revision does not require the deletion of any material; a simple addition after accessing the point of insertion is all that is required.
5. Sometimes a deletion is all that is required; it is accomplished by simply accessing the point of deletion and using the delete instruction.

A WP specialist frequently needs to rearrange text by changing the order of paragraphs, pulling a paragraph or paragraphs from one page and inserting them in a different place on the page or on a different page. This can be done in a variety of ways, depending on the media and the equipment. Display systems have prompts or messages to aid in revising text. Blind or nondisplay systems often use lights.

Text rearrangement is an important process in document revision. Some machines have a method of identifying text, pulling it out of memory, and saving it for insertion at a different place. Different vendors call it different names: "save and recall," "block and jump," "copy and move." A manual technique is to duplicate the text to be inserted in another location in the document onto blank media, then play out the document, deleting the text where it was originally located and inserting it manually from the newly duplicated media in the appropriate position.

Global search and replace is another helpful revision technique. If a document has been produced with, say, *U.S. Government* throughout the text and the author wishes it to be *United States Government* instead, all the WP specialist need do is to instruct the system appropriately, and the system will move quickly through the document, making the changes.

An important decision a WP specialist often makes is whether to revise or start again from scratch. If revisions are too numerous or complex, sometimes it is easier to rekeyboard the material. For example, a WP specialist may have the option of moving a few sentences to another page in the text or rekeyboarding them where needed and deleting them where not needed. For just a few sentences, it may be easier to rekeyboard. Longer amounts of text definitely merit the moving operation. Experience is a good teacher for these types of decisions.

Playback or Printing the Document

Automatic playback procedures are similar on many nondisplay WP systems or printers. You can play back characters, words, lines, sentences, paragraphs, or pages at a time. You can play back by increments to access certain areas of the document for revision and to verify your position in the document before you start revising. You can also instruct the equipment to play back continuously or stop, as you wish, instantly. The equipment will do precisely as you instruct it—no more, no less.

Line-ending or hyphenation decisions are very important in playback. Even though the equipment may have a dictionary built into it to help with the decision, ultimately the WP specialist is responsible for making the decision. These decisions must be made, of course, not only in accordance with appropriate machine procedures, but also with correct word division usage rules. A dictionary and a reference manual are important publications for a WP specialist to have within arm's reach.

Page-ending decisions are also important in document formatting. Organizations usually adopt a standard format for letters, memos, reports, and other documents. The WP specialist must format accordingly. This includes playing back or printing the correct amount of text on a page, a function called pagination. Many systems will help the WP specialist count the lines to be printed. This avoids having the document print too high or too low on the page. Again, however, the WP specialist ultimately controls and is responsible for the formatting decisions. Here again, a reference manual is important for making sure grammar is correct.

parallel operation
background printing
trail printing

Newer WP systems have the feature of **parallel operation** or **background printing** so that printing may go on while another document is being keyboarded or revised.

Another feature in the newer WP systems is that of **trail printing**: the printing of one page of a document while the next is being keyboarded or revised.

Storage and Filing of Magnetic Media
archiving

After a document is keyboarded, revised, and printed, it is important to be able to store it for future use or reference. **Archiving** is the term used to refer to the transfer of text from memory or on-line storage to off-line storage media. This is needed because most systems have volatile memories; that is, if the power of the machine is turned off, the information is not retained. This storage of data, called file or data management, consists of:

1. Input—putting data into the system.
2. Identification—classifying, categorizing, labeling, numbering, or naming data.
3. Storage—recording data on a magnetic medium.
4. Retrieval—recalling and reviewing stored data.

As stated in Chapter 5, text may be stored internally within some equipment or it may be stored on external media in other equipment.

Many organizations are creating databases on their media for the production of documents. Just as the name implies, a database is a storehouse or library of recorded documents. Databases are helpful to authors, because frequently documents are created from text material that has been used in previous documents. Examples of these documents are proposals and specifications for engineering and technical organizations and legal research for law firms. An engineer may author one document as a proposal and find it possible to use this document or portions of it repeatedly. This not only saves the rewriting time, but also the WP specialist's rekeyboarding time. The text is simply retrieved and assembled as required. Some organizations are finding that their more advanced WP specialists are working more in creative document assembly rather than initially keyboarding.

key word

Databases that index and store information for many fields are being created and sold. For example, attorneys can research a case using a databased legal library much more quickly than using many books. The databases are **key word** searchable. This means a user can find information on a given subject in the data repository by asking for a main word used in the text. If an attorney researches the data base for all cases on dog bites, the key word *dog bites* is used. All cases on dog bites and their resolution for a requested region and time frame will be provided, in minutes. Easy access and retrieval are the benefits.

document coding system

It is important to have an orderly, safe, and economical system of storing and retrieving the media. Documents and media are usually identified by name or number. A **document coding system** is used for easy retrieval of the document. Organizations use many systems of identification—author, subject matter, client code, department, date. Sections 4.28–29 of the WP Specialist's Procedures Manual illustrate examples of coding or identifying documents. Media may be numbered or color coded. After this identification of the media for easy reference, they may be stored in a variety of ways. Trays, binders, boxes, and stands are a few of the devices used to house media (Figures 6.4 and 6.5).

Basic Categories of Documents Keyboarded

Regardless of the method of output, type of equipment, print device, or media, there seem to be seven basic categories of documents used by most organizations. These are:

1. Correspondence.
2. Repetitive correspondence.
3. Text.
4. Forms.
5. Statistical documents.
6. Document assembly.
7. File/sort information or records processing.

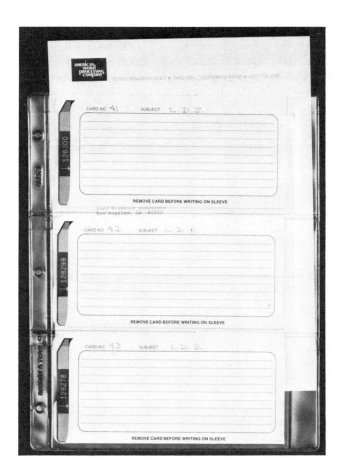

Figure 6.4. For easy storage and retrieval, magnetic cards are stored in these plastic sheets in three-ring binders. Courtesy of American Word Processing Company.

Figure 6.5. This tray housing diskettes both protects them and displays them for easy access. Courtesy of American Word Processing Company.

The three major sources from which these documents can be created are:

1. Original material, submitted in longhand, by machine dictation, by OCR, or dictated to a stenographer taking shorthand.
2. Revisions of previously recorded documents.
3. Prerecorded or **boiler plate** material and/or formats—repetitive-use text that is databased for reuse in another document and prerecorded formats that once set up can be used again.

boiler plate

Now that you know the sources of documents from which the WP specialist works, let us consider each type of document.

Correspondence

correspondence

Correspondence, a written message to a recipient, includes documents such as letters and memos. Since documents of this nature represent the vital link in communications, this category represents a large portion of business documents. They range from one page or less to many pages. Letters, in particular, represent the organization, and top quality is required. Memos are documents used within the organization and represent approximately 65 to 75 percent of all correspondence.

Repetitive Correspondence

repetitive correspondence

variable information
constant information

Most organizations have a number of applications that are frequently used, such as letters or memos that have the same or nearly the same content with minimum differences, such as names and addresses. This is called **repetitive correspondence**. The personalized touch given by WP equipment rather than a blank to be filled in on a mimeographed form is appealing. To produce repetitive letters, many WP systems have a capability of merging the **variable information**, which is different for each letter or memo, with the **constant information**, which is the same. Some equipment can produce these documents unattended; that is, the letters or memos can be set up to print without the WP specialist's being there. Many WP specialists increase production significantly by keyboarding the data for the documents, storing it on media, and setting up the equipment to print the documents while they are away from the office. When they return from lunch or arrive at the office in the morning, a supply of documents has been produced and is waiting for distribution.

Text

text

Text, a term used to refer to documents such as reports, manuals, and manuscripts, is generally narrative information. Frequently, WP specialists lump everything that does not fit into the other six categories into this general category.

A text application often difficult for conventional typewriters is scientific report typing. WP equipment manufacturers offer foreign language, Greek alphabet, mathematical symbol elements and print wheels to assist in the production of technical documents. Easier methods of typing superscripts and subscripts than is provided for on conventional typewriters are features of WP equipment.

Forms

form

Forms are high use, standard, information-supplying documents. Printed form typing is often difficult on conventional typewriters because forms are not designed for typewriter spacing. The variable line spacing of many WP systems can change the height of the writing line and, therefore, fit more printed forms. In addition, some WP systems permit the specialist to create a format or replica of a form that is on the display screen of the WP system. The form itself can be drawn in bold so that the form can easily be completed, stored, and duplicated.

Forms on oversized paper are also easier to work with on WP systems.

Statistical Documents

statistical document

Statistical documents require the keyboarding of statistics, that is, numbers arranged in multicolumnar form. Statistical applications become an easier assignment with WP equipment. For example, the columnar alignment feature found on most equipment aligns the columns automatically around the decimal point—no more spacing over to align digits. Also, WP systems set up tabs for the columns automatically.

Some systems have the ability to move, insert, or delete partial or whole columns. Often an author decides to expand or contract a statistical table, that is, to add or delete columns; with WP equipment, the whole table will not have to be retyped.

Document Assembly

document assembly

Document assembly is the combining of stored or databased text with new material to create a new document. Use of the stored or databased text saves having to write and keyboard the entire document. These new documents may be created automatically and unattended if the WP specialist enters an instruction for a combination of paragraphs or pages along with the keyboarding of the new text.

For ease in creating a document, the originator is provided with a file or binder containing typed copies of the stored text. All that is necessary is for the originator to select the stored material desired and note the changes pertaining to the new document being prepared. In the case of correspondence, the originator must specify the new recipient. The WP specialist, using a similar file or binder and the media on which the text is stored, produces the document complete with the pertinent changes. This type of document preparation is beneficial both to the originator and the WP specialist. Time savings for both the rewriting and rekeyboarding are considerable.

File/Sort

file/sort
qualify

Because of the massive amount of list information that needs to be processed and made available in the business world of today, manufacturers have equipped their WP equipment with **file/sort** capabilities, a method that can electronically create, revise, process, add, delete, merge, search, and **qualify** (select) the volume of records kept and maintained. This process may also be called records management, records processing, files management, and list management. Lists or records maintained by organizations may range from a roster of employees to a city telephone directory. Before WP, and even now in many organizations, this information is created and maintained manually—a very costly effort. Card files, ledgers, and lateral and vertical files are full of such information. These files take up valuable space. Expensive personnel are used to maintain them. Many represent duplication of effort by different departments in the organization. Lists may not be current; they are available only in the form in which they were written.

WP equipment has changed this situation. A list that is keyboarded and updated by one WP specialist can be available throughout the organization, which prevents duplication of effort. Information can be keyboarded in one form and rearranged in many different forms without being rekeyboarded. Information needed for one particular application can be selected. For example, an organization may list all of its employees' names, addresses, home telephone numbers, birth dates, department assignments, office room numbers, and office telephone numbers. A personnel manager may then ask the WP specialist to output a list of only the employees in the marketing department born after 1950 with their home addresses. In just a very few minutes another list with different information can be selected or qualified from the same database and printed out, with no additional keyboarding. For example, the building manager of the same company may ask for a list of only the employees in the "100" building and their office telephone numbers. This printed list would be available very quickly. The significant point is that the information was keyboarded only once, but parts of that information were selected and drawn upon in various formats. Imagine the time required to separate the information needed in these examples manually, not to mention the time needed to keyboard them again and again.

Methods of Production

There are several ways a document may be produced. These include:

1. The document may be keyboarded on a WP system and printed or played out on the same machine (Figure 6.6).
2. The document may be keyboarded on a WP system, terminal, or work station and printed or played out on a separate printer (Figure 6.7).
3. The document may be keyboarded on a single-element typewriter and read or scanned through an optical character reader (OCR) and into a WP system for revisions and printed (Figure 6.8).

Let us look at each one of these methods of output.

Figure 6.6. This IBM Mag Card A Typewriter is a machine on which a document may be keyboarded and printed. Courtesy of IBM Corporation.

Figure 6.7. Each work station of the Honeywell Administrative System 4 may be used for keyboarding a document to be printed on the separate printer. Courtesy of Honeywell.

Figure 6.8. The AlphaWord III OCR may take its input from standard office typewriters or word and data processing printer/copiers as well as from high quality facsimile. Courtesy of CompuScan, Inc.

Keyboarding and Playing Out on the Same Machine

This is usually the method thought of when considering output. The WP specialist is given a document via machine dictation, shorthand, or handwriting and is asked to produce it. He or she then sits down at the WP system and keyboards it, using all the power of the machine and its many functions. After keyboarding and revising the document, and making corrections as necessary after it has been edited, the WP specialist inserts the paper and prints or plays out the document in final form, being sure to format appropriately.

Keyboarding on a WP System and Playing Out on a Separate Printer

In order to reduce the expense of WP equipment, many users are configuring systems rather than using individual units. A system can consist of one or more work stations and one separate printer serving several work stations. Printers can frequently be printing one document while the WP specialist is keyboarding or revising another. This is called parallel operation, background, or trail printing. Printers are equipped with devices such as the print wheel, ink jet, laser printer, or line printer. Thanks to the rapid print speed of this equipment, productivity is significantly increased. It is easy to see the cost savings that result when an organization has to purchase only one printer to serve several work stations. Because the printer outputs so rapidly, there is less backlogging of documents. The separate printers have a variety of document formatting capabilities that are not always available on the automated typewriter.

Output Using Optical Character Recognition

Managers who want all secretarial support staff to have the capabilities of WP but do not wish to acquire a WP system for each individual secretary frequently implement the OCR system discussed in Chapter 4. The system consists of using single-element typewriters with an OCR recognizable element. As the secretary types, the OCR element prints the characters on the paper or hard copy so that they will be recognized by the OCR reader/scanner. As the hard copy is read into the reader/scanner, after the originator has edited it, the text is transferred to the memory of the media or the WP system. The WP specialist can then quickly make the revisions shown on the edited original and output the final document.

Transcription for Output

magnetic media

Transcription from machine dictation is the process of listening to and keyboarding the documents recorded on **magnetic media**, reusable devices used for recording or storage of text and software in WP and DP systems. Although machine dictation is only one source of input for daily production, as originators become more knowledgeable about the advantages of machine dictation, the WP specialist will have an increasing amount of transcription. The WP specialist is the other half of the document preparation team, in partnership with the originator. It is the WP specialist who must be able to understand the originator's instructions for the production of the document and the dictation of the text. The use of transcribers with WP systems significantly improves productivity and makes the task easier because of the correction and revision capabilities.

Even though dictation is almost always transcribed and revised, first in rough draft and then in final form after the author's changes, the rate of transcription is significantly faster from machine dictation than from transcribing shorthand or typing from longhand. The rate of 20 to 25 words per minute is typical from machine dictation, while 10 words per minute is average when typing from longhand and 15 words per minute is average when transcribing shorthand. A primary reason for this increased rate is that the WP specialist does not have to look up from the typewriter to read longhand or shorthand notes. This may also improve accuracy.

Transcription Equipment

As discussed in Chapter 4, there are two types of media: discrete and endless loop.

Transcription equipment using discrete media is similar to dictation equipment. In fact, many vendors use the same basic unit for both dictation and transcription. With the same basic unit, a footpedal and an earphone (Figure 6.9) are used by the transcriber instead of the microphone which is used by the dictator.

Figure 6.9. The Dictaphone Micro Master desk-top transcriber includes an electronic information display that eliminates indexing slips. Courtesy of Dictaphone Corporation.

Transcription equipment for endless loop media usually consists of a footpedal, earphones, and an electronic device with hand controls for volume, speed, and tone. Both kinds of transcription equipment have several common features.

Earphones

There are several types of earphones—a lightweight ear clip which covers one ear, a lightweight headset which hangs under the chin from the ears, and a heavier over-the-head headset. The lightweight headset provides sound to both ears. The heavier type is helpful when there is background noise at the work station.

Footpedals

The footpedal, when depressed, activates the sound. It also permits review capabilities. Usually one side of the footpedal is used to advance the text for transcription; the other side is to back up the media to the specific transcribed text to ensure that what was dictated was indeed transcribed.

Scanning Devices

scanning devices

Scanning devices can be manual or electronic. Some manual transcription equipment uses index slips. These are paper strips that show the end of each document and the location of special instructions from the originator. Other newer transcription equipment has electronic scanners to show the same information. This information is important to the WP specialist for producing first-time final transcription.

Other Features

Volume, speed, and tone control are important for producing normal, natural dictation. Some transcription equipment also has conference playback features so that the sound can be heard by all within range of the unit.

Transcription Media

Although the most common discrete magnetic media for transcription equipment are cassette tapes—standard, micro, and mini sizes—discs and belts are also being used. In fact, dual media transcription equipment is presently being marketed (Figure 6.10).

Discrete Media

Whether the WP specialist is working in a centralized, decentralized, or combination environment, dictated text on discrete media from a portable, desk-top, or centralized unit can be transcribed from a desk-top transcription unit. Because the media are handled physically, the cassettes, discs, or belts can be shared with several WP specialists for transcription. Another advantage of discrete media systems is that the recorded media may be stored.

Endless Loop Media

Unlike media that can be physically handled, the endless loop medium is a long magnetic tape housed in an electronic tank-like device which has variable recording, reviewing, and erasing capabilities.

An advantage of the endless loop system is that the WP specialist can transcribe just seconds after the originator starts the dictation; the entire document does not have to be completely dictated before transcription can begin. As the WP specialist

Figure 6.10. The IBM portable dictation unit, the Executive Recorder, records minicassettes that can be inserted into this dual media transcriber unit, also used for IBM 6:5 magnetic discs which are placed in a cartridge that can contain up to 25 magnetic discs, with each disc holding up to six minutes of dictation. Courtesy of IBM Corporation.

transcribes the dictation, the tape recycles for use again by an originator. Another advantage is that monitoring the system to replace used cassettes, tapes, or belts is not required.

A disadvantage of endless loop media is that most endless loop systems can assign one tank of dictation to only one WP work station at a time.

Transcription Procedures

Successful transcription is the result of good procedures followed by both the originator and the transcriber. Some key procedures that WP specialists might use for effective transcription are shown in the following:

General Procedures

1. Clear your work station so that you will be able to concentrate more effectively on the project.
2. Determine the priorities of the documents you are to transcribe. This priority may be explained at the beginning of the dictation or may be marked physically on the index slip or electronically according to the type of scanning device.
3. Keep reference manuals, procedure manuals, and dictionary within arm's reach.
4. Be sure supplies are readily available.

Equipment Preparation

1. Set up the transcription equipment and scan the media for special instructions and priorities.
2. Set up the WP system with correct formatting, the appropriate stationery, and number of copies.

During Transcription

1. Use effective listening techniques. Tune out the noise around you and concentrate on the project. Occasionally, it may be necessary to fill in a word or words from the context because of poor or inaudible dictation.
2. Strive for a continuous flow of keyboarding as you listen to the dictated text. Increasing the amount of material retained in an earful as you continuously keyboard is an important goal in raising transcription productivity.
3. Reduce the number of words you set for playback when backing up and reviewing what has been dictated. The range of review capabilities on most transcription equipment is from zero to as many as six words.
4. Remember your language arts skills and use them properly:

   a. Sound-alike and troublesome words.
   b. Paragraphing.
   c. Punctuation.
   d. Spelling.
   e. Numbers.
   f. Capitalization.
   g. Word division.
   h. Abbreviations.

After Transcription

1. Proofread carefully, using one or more of the methods discussed in Chapter 7.
2. Note the productivity measurement information for the document, discussed in Chapter 7.
3. Evaluate the dictation for the author's benefit and improvement, if your organization uses this procedure.
4. Store the media, both input and output, if required.
5. Submit the document to the editor or originator for approval.

Summary

Output equipment has been significantly improved with the addition of a memory feature. The amount of memory varies from machine to machine. Memory contributes significantly to the production of documents.

Revisions are the process of changing the recorded document. They are easily made using WP equipment. They range from the immediate correction of a key-boarded error to the massive rearrangement of text from one part of the document to the other.

The WP specialist is responsible for important final print decisions such as line endings and page endings. Knowledge of language arts skills provides the specialist with the appropriate background for making these decisions.

Many organizations are creating databases from a library of stored documents from which new documents may be created. Significant amounts of time may be saved in rewriting by the author and in rekeyboarding by the WP specialist if the databases are used appropriately.

Seven basic categories of documents are used frequently by organizations. These are: correspondence, repetitive correspondence, text, forms, statistical documents, document assembly, and file/sort. These documents are largely created from three sources: original material, revisions, and prerecorded material.

A document may be produced in at least three ways: keyboarding and printing on the same machine, keyboarding on a WP system and producing on a separate printer, and keyboarding on a single-element electric typewriter and using an OCR reader/scanner to transmit it to a WP system for storage, revision, and final print.

Transcription is the process of listening to and keyboarding the recorded document stored on the magnetic media of the dictation equipment. Transcription is significantly faster from machine dictated text than from longhand or shorthand notes.

Transcription equipment for discrete media uses the same basic unit as the dictation unit. Instead of a microphone used by the dictator, earphones and a footpedal are used by the transcriptionist. Transcription equipment for endless loop is simply earphones, footpedal, and an electronic control device for volume, speed, and tone.

Key Terms

Access	Format	Random access memory (RAM)
Archiving	Form	Read only memory (ROM)
Background printing	Key word	Read only storage (ROS)
Boiler plate	Magnetic media	Repetitive correspondence
Bubble memory	Memory	Scanning device
Constant information	Menu	Sequential access memory (SAM)
Correspondence	Mnemonic code	Statistical document
Document assembly	Nonvolatile memory	Text
Document coding system	Pagination	Trail printing
File/sort	Parallel operation	Variable information
	Qualify	Volatile memory

Self-Check Questions

Completion

1. _____ is the process of keyboarding the recorded message that is stored on media from dictation.
2. The rate of _____ to _____ words per minute is common when typing from machine dictation, while _____ words per minute is average when typing from shorthand.
3. A manual scanning device which is inserted in the dictation equipment for marking documents is called a _____.
4. Other dictation equipment has _____, which mark documents for transcription, but are operated electronically.
5. Handling of the media is not possible with the _____ system.
6. Transcription of discrete media is done using a _____ transcription unit.

7. Locating the place in memory or on media where revision is to be made is called _____.

8. The _____ has the responsibility for making line-ending, hyphenation, and page-ending decisions.

9. A _____ is used to create a new proposal from an old one.

Short Answer
1. Name the seven basic categories of documents.
2. Describe the three methods of document production.
3. Briefly describe media conversion that uses OCR.
4. Define and describe database.
5. What is the purpose of numbering, categorizing, color-coding, or otherwise identifying the media.

True/False
1. Mnemonic codes are function keys on WP hardware used to give format instructions.
2. Bubble memory provides large amounts of storage in a very small area.
3. Line-ending decisions are the primary responsibility of the WP equipment.
4. OCR can make a significant contribution to the production process.
5. File/sort capabilities are seldom needed on today's WP equipment.
6. Volatile memories retain information when the power is turned off.
7. RAM suggests that accessing is best accomplished by searching through each document, page-by-page, to find the section you need.

Exercises

Exercise 6.1. As a class or individually, visit an organization that has WP. Discuss the types of documents the organization produces and the volume per week or month of each type. What types of document production are used in the organization? What responsibilities for formatting are retained by the WP specialist?

Exercise 6.2. Read an article on memory technology, its uses, its potential, and its capacity. Write a short report summarizing your findings.

Case Problem

Although transcription is increasing the productivity for Stewart Savings and Loan, Ms. Addington, supervisor of the WP department, knows they are not achieving the 20 to 25 words per minute in output rate. A new endless loop centralized dictation and transcription system has been recently installed. It works well mechanically. What can be the problem? What should be done?

Chapter 7

****

Output Procedures

Chapter Objectives

After reading this chapter and completing the end-of-chapter activities, the student will be able to:

1. *Define procedures and identify their uses.*
2. *Locate and apply the information in a procedures manual to a document to be produced.*
3. *Process a document through the work flow procedure.*
4. *Apply the techniques of effective proofreading to documents produced.*
5. *Measure output productivity.*

What Are Word Processing Procedures?

WP procedures are guidelines used by WP personnel to create and produce documents. Effective procedures are a necessity for proper use of equipment and maximum utilization of time. Efforts spent in developing, writing, and following procedures are repaid many times over in increased time savings and efficiency in the processing of paperwork.

These procedures must satisfy many objectives. They must:

1. Define WP functions within the organization.
2. Define the users' responsibilities.
3. Provide general information about the organization.
4. Provide specific information about document production.
5. Determine media handling, storage, and retention including purging of information that is no longer needed.
6. Establish work flow from input of original (or revision), through delivery of finals.
7. Define the responsibilities of each member of the WP staff.
8. Provide training for the users and WP staff.
9. Identify methods to use statistics needed for productivity measurement.
10. Identify information available from stored media.
11. Provide for modification of procedures applying to specific situations.

Word Processing Procedures Manual

standardized procedures

A procedures manual is a must for any organization operating a cost-effective and smooth-flowing management support system using standardized procedures. This guide is the key to good communications, ease of production, and effective use of equipment and personnel.

Standardized procedures mean that everyone keyboards, revises, and prints exactly the same way, according to company procedures. They are essential so that if one person keyboards a document, another can revise or print it. Standardized procedures also allow for:

1. Increased efficiency of personnel.
2. Cost-effective use of equipment.
3. Ease of training for new or temporary employees.
4. Consistency in style and format.
5. Sharing of work among WP personnel.
6. Ease of revision.

The manual should be distributed to WP and AS staff. Originators should have that portion of the manual that relates to the origination, copying, and telecommunication of documents. A procedures manual is an excellent method of acquainting new staff with the management support system. The new support staff will learn to be effective more easily and faster with the manual. New originators will also be able to use the system quickly.

A User's Procedures Manual and Word Processing Specialist's Procedures Manual have been included as Parts IV and V to familiarize you with general procedures used in a WP environment. Please study them as a practical application of the theory you read in this text.

Work Flow

Document requests from users in most organizations have a specified work flow. Let us look at likely paths the document may take.

Centralized or Production Center

logging

editor

The users dictate a document or give the document to the WP supervisor, who logs it in. **Logging** is recording incoming and outgoing work to monitor work flow. The document log in the WP Specialist's Procedures Manual shows an example of a form used for logging. If the user requests, an individual with good language and writing skills, called an **editor**, will take a look at the document for clarity, correctness, and completeness. The document is then keyboarded, proofread, and printed by the WP specialist. The proofreader will give it a final check for accuracy and pass it on to the supervisor, who will log it out, charge it to the appropriate user or project, and arrange for its return to the user. Of course, users may return the document if they decide to change the content.

Decentralized or Custom Work Station

Because the decentralized work arrangement is similar to the mode of the traditional secretary who has been given WP equipment for greater effectiveness, the work flow of the document is somewhat traditional. The user gives the document to the secretary/WP specialist, who keyboards, proofreads, and prints the document. It is then returned to the user for content editing, checking, and signing. If there are changes, the document will be returned to the secretary/WP specialist for revisions.

Proofreading

Proofreading is the process of verifying that a completed document is identical in all respects with the original text. It is done to determine whether a document is error-free or whether revisions are necessary. Proofreading is a major step in the production of a document. Since the image of the organization is often projected by the written document, it is important that proofreading be done carefully.

A letter meant to solicit business probably will not be successful if the reader notices misspellings and typographical errors. Where will the reader focus attention first, on the fine intent of the letter or on the misspelled word? Although all errors have damaging effects, some are more serious than others. For example, if you read the statement, "I hardly share your concern," which should have been transcribed as, "I heartily share your concern," what would be your reaction?

Proofreading initially starts with the author, after he or she writes or dictates the document, by rereading or listening. An editor-proofreader can make a significant contribution by proofreading the document before it is prepared or typed. The WP specialist also shares the responsibility for proofreading the document for errors. However, the author has the ultimate responsibility for the document. If an originator misspelled a name while dictating, only he or she would be likely to catch it. Some content errors are the WP specialist's responsibility; he or she must watch for obvious nonsensical content, repeated information, and information that is incorrect according to organizational policy or data given earlier in the document. Figure 7.1 shows the steps in the proofreading cycle.

Several vendors have equipped their WP systems with dictionaries to aid in proofreading and spelling verification of English and foreign language words (Figure 7.2). The number of words in the dictionaries of the various units varies from vendor to vendor. Some units permit WP specialists to add technical terms or terms unique to an organization or industry to the dictionary. This dictionary provides an aid to proofreading and significantly reduces revisions due to spelling and typographical errors.

A good proofreader recognizes the importance of producing error-free documents and takes time to do a thorough job. To be a good proofreader, he or she must know the basics of capitalization, punctuation, and spelling and must pay attention to small details. If the proofreader is error-conscious and aware of where mistakes are most commonly made, the chances of proofreading well are significantly increased. Some things to look for include: misspellings; missing words, lines, sentences, paragraphs, and pages; misplaced words; excess words; typographical errors; wrong dates; time

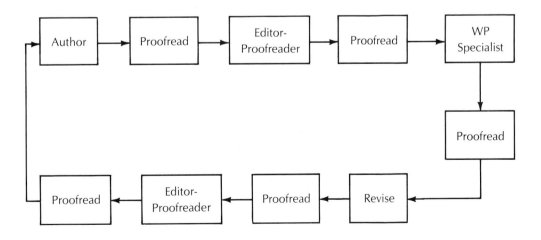

Figure 7.1. Proofreading cycle.

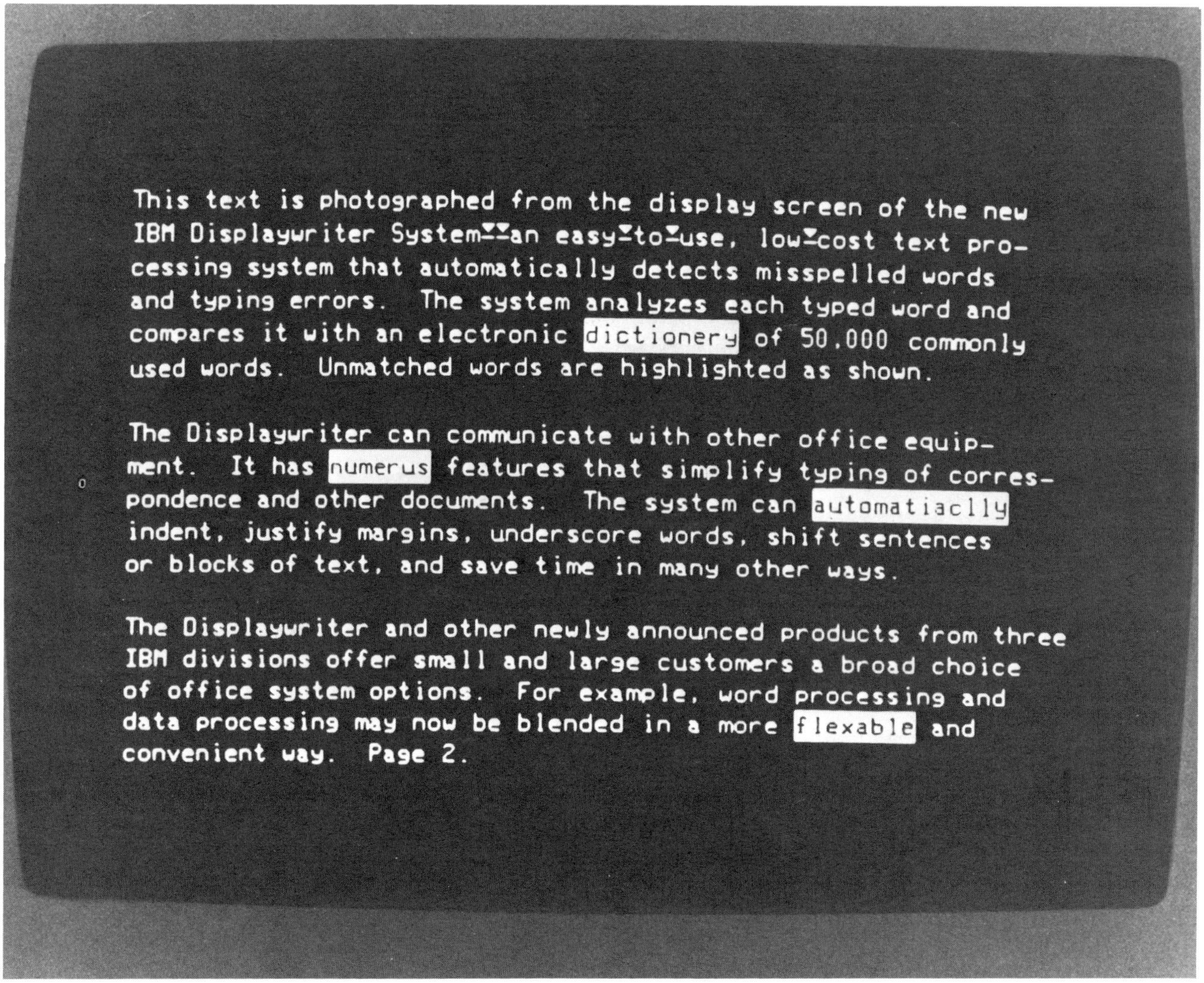

Figure 7.2. The IBM Displaywriter uses an electronic dictionary that checks the spelling of about 50,000 words and offers up to seven choices to replace a misspelled word. Courtesy of IBM Corporation.

sensitive data; improper format; abbreviations; clarity and proper meaning; and punctuation.

A research study by Staples[1] showed that the ten typewriting errors most frequently undetected are found:

1. In headings and subheadings.
2. Near the beginning and ending of lines.
3. Near the bottoms of pages.
4. In long, frequently appearing words.
5. In omissions involving simple, frequently appearing words.
6. In transpositions of letters or characters.
7. In captions and footnotes.
8. In proper nouns.

[1] John Dixon Staples, "An Experimental Study to Identify the Basic Abilities Needed to Detect Typescript Errors with Implications for the Improvement in Typewriting," University of North Dakota Ed.D. dissertation, 1965.

9. In vertical enumerations.
10. In number combinations.

Knowing where the most common proofreading errors are made may help the proofreader to pay close attention to these areas and to be more accurate.

As you proofread the document you have produced, watch for:

1. Clarity.
2. Typographical errors, incorrect grammar, and punctuation.
3. Omissions or repetition.
4. Consistency.
5. Dollar amounts, figures, numbers.

Some proofreading methods you might try include:

1. Scan the document before starting detailed proofreading. This is particularly useful in detecting format errors.
2. If you have an impact printer—the paper bail method—before removing the paper from the typewriter, roll the paper down so that just the first line shows above the paper bail. Roll the paper through the machine one line at a time, reading as you roll.
3. Read silently left to right, top to bottom.
4. Read the typewritten copy aloud, while someone else reads the original draft.
5. Read backwards from bottom to top.
6. Read aloud to yourself.
7. Ask someone else to read for clarity, content, sense, and errors.
8. Read while reviewing the dictation.
9. Put the document aside after completion and do another task before proofreading.
10. Use a guide such as a ruler, line advance mechanism, or finger to help improve your powers of concentration. Sometimes a mask of cardboard with holes cut in the cardboard to show only the data being proofread, such as one line or a partial line, may be helpful.
11. Read first for content; then a second time for spelling, abbreviations, punctuation, word division, capitalization, footnotes, and number use.
12. Check figures and unfamiliar terms character by character.
13. Retotal columns of figures to ensure correctness. If your system has a math feature, this is an excellent way to use it.
14. When you find an error, watch for another nearby; errors often come in multiples.
15. Look at the pages upside down and sideways to catch spacing and format errors.

Uniform use of standard proofreaders' marks by all members of the organization will speed up the revision process. Section 1.10 of the User's Procedures Manual contains a chart of standard proofreaders' marks. Use them consistently for marking copy.

Measuring Productivity

The business world is concerned with its cost of operating, its productivity, and its responsiveness to its clients. Many organizations, therefore, measure the productivity of their WP systems. To measure productivity, the numbers of documents, pages, lines, or characters produced by each WP specialist as well as by the group as a whole are counted and monitored. This count is analyzed against time for cost of production. Information derived from this measurement serves several purposes:

1. WP equipment and personnel are justified to management.
2. Future equipment, personnel, and procedural decisions can be made on a documented basis.
3. Turnaround time can be determined.
4. Employee performance can be measured.
5. Chargeback costs can be determined.

Let us look at each of these purposes.

1. WP equipment costs thousands of dollars. Even more expensive than the equipment are the personnel who use it. In addition, dollars are spent in designing and implementing the system as well as in educating the users and training the support staff. All business decisions should be checked and rechecked to be sure the decision (in this case, to use WP equipment) was and continues to be a sound one and that the business is operating on a profitable basis.

2. The WP industry is a rapidly changing one. It has been said that there is enough technology sitting on the shelves of vendors to make an equipment introduction every three months for the next ten years. New procedures are constantly being developed. An organization must be sensitive to new equipment developments as well as to procedural innovations in order to keep the system most cost-effective. Perhaps no other industry must be so alerted to change.

3. The turnaround time of documents in an organization can be critical. Money can be made or lost if a document is not complete when needed. For example, a bid or proposal that is late probably will not be accepted. A successful WP system needs to be sensitive to the shortest turnaround time possible.

4. People are the most expensive but most important commodity of any business. Their performance can often make or break a business. If employees need help, often they cannot bring themselves to ask for it. The work performance may show the need for help from the supervisor.

5. A very important reason for measuring productivity is to determine to what extent the WP system is being used for certain projects or specific departments. In order to allocate the costs of a project, the costs of the WP system must be included.

chargeback system

A **chargeback system** identifies the production times and costs for that project or department and charges the budget for that amount. This is most frequently used in large companies.

standard

Over time, a WP supervisor develops a **standard**, the level of achievement of an average WP specialist. This standard takes into consideration factors such as the following:

1. Types of documents. Some documents, such as statistical ones, are more time-consuming than others.
2. Employee considerations. Occasionally employees have difficult personal problems that may affect work performance.
3. Equipment downtime. Productivity can be reduced considerably if the equipment is not working properly.

To measure productivity, each document is counted as it is printed. It may be counted in terms of lines, full pages, partial pages, keystrokes, and so forth. In fact, over 45 different methods of counting documents have been devised. However, most WP supervisors seem to prefer to count the number of lines or full pages each WP

production log

specialist outputs each day. A **production log** (in the WP Specialist's Procedures

Manual) is the form on which the WP specialist lists each document and the information about it.

Most production logs contain the following information:

1. The name of the WP specialist and the date for which the form is being completed.
2. The information required for each document completed:
   a. The originator's name and department.
   b. The source of the text (original, revision, prerecorded).
   c. The form in which the material was received (handwritten, machine dictation, copy type).
   d. The date and time the document was received.
   e. The date and time the document was returned to the originator.
   f. The production count of the document.
   g. The turnaround time of the document.
   h. Administrative time required to produce the document (the time spent talking to the originator or supervisor about the document and its production).
3. Administrative time spent by the WP specialist not related to a specific document (meetings, training, and so forth).

Each WP specialist combines daily production logs for a week to create a weekly and then a monthly log. All of the monthly production logs are combined to demonstrate productivity for the WP center for the month.

To show cost savings, WP supervisors often compare the amount of document production in the time period being studied to the amount of time it would take a secretarial support staff to generate the same number of documents using conventional methods. There are many sources supervisors may use to show the time it takes to produce a given number of documents using conventional methods. Supervisors also compare departments' and specialists' productivity of that month, quarter, or year to other time periods.

You may wonder how to determine the production count for each document. Counting documents by full or partial pages is no problem; they are counted sequentially. Most organizations that count by characters or keystrokes have equipment that counts for them.

line count

A **line count** may be manually calculated. A transparent overlay (a clear plastic sheet) is marked with numbers that correspond to the lines on the typewritten page. Figure 3 in the WP Specialist's Procedures Manual illustrates one. There is a scale for single-spaced, space and one-half, double-spaced, and triple-spaced documents. Using the appropriate vertical line-spacing scale, overlay the plastic sheet, align the top line with the first printed line, and note the number of the last printed line. Filling in the production log the first few times may take a few minutes. After you have done it several times, however, the time spent is negligible.

Production Procedures

For a WP specialist, knowledge of and ability to follow organizational procedures is equally as important as operating the equipment. The Word Processing Specialist's Procedures Manual for Arnco, Inc., which provides AS and WP services, shows how to produce documents according to Arnco's design.

A description of the organization and its employees helps the WP specialist to see how he or she fits into the organization. How to handle such things as supplies and equipment repairs is important. The work flow, that is, how a user requests a document using a job request form and the path the document takes to completion, is essential information. The WP specialist also needs to know how the priorities, overtime, and confidential documents are handled. The user can submit a document in several ways: longhand, machine dictation, or OCR. The manual addresses all of these.

Keyboarding procedures are crucial. WP specialists in an organization must follow the same procedures so that all can revise each other's work or finish a document started by someone else. The WP specialist must proofread documents even though there is a proofreader. Occasionally, a WP specialist may be asked to help another specialist proofread an especially technical document. Editing and proofreading marks are provided for the WP specialist's use; these same marks have been given to the users. A language arts section has been provided for reference. Knowledge of the language is a must for WP specialists. If in doubt, look it up!

All of the documents produced must be counted. Section 7 of the manual provides procedures for this. Every document that is produced must be stored, even if it is only temporarily. The manual provides instructions for temporary, short-term, and permanent magnetic media filing.

When WP organizations have a number of clients, each may have its own style guide. When producing a document, the WP specialist must follow these steps:

1. Check the style guide for the client to see if a similar document is shown.

2. If no document is shown that is similar, refer to the general style guide. If a similar document is shown there, follow it.

3. If there is no similar document to use as a guide, use your best judgment. Often the WP specialist is called upon to create a new format.

Future Trends

As personnel in organizations learn more about using systems to the optimum, procedures manuals will be used more routinely.

Increased emphasis on improving productivity will necessitate productivity measurement. Equipment will routinely provide productivity measurement statistics.

Equipment will have increasingly sophisticated proofreading or spelling verification capabilities in all languages. These features will become more accommodating.

Summary

Procedures are guidelines for both users and WP personnel in the creation and the production of documents. Good procedures are critical for optimum use of equipment and maximum productivity.

A procedures manual for both the user and WP personnel is a guide to good communications, ease of production, and optimum use of equipment and personnel.

Work flow in an organization should be well-designed for the production of the document in the shortest period of time. Appropriate proofreading and revisions will contribute to the overall effectiveness in the document cycle.

Proofreading is the verification of the accuracy of the document. Checking for correct capitalization, punctuation, and spelling are important skills in proofreading.

Productivity measurement is counting and monitoring the output produced by each WP specialist and the group as a whole. Most commonly, documents, pages, and lines are measured.

Key Terms

Chargeback system	Logging	Standardized
Editor	Production log	procedures
Line count	Standard	

Completion

1. Procedures are guidelines for the _____ and the _____.
2. A _____ is a must for all WP personnel when standardized procedures are needed.
3. An individual with good language and writing skills, often employed to check a document for correctness, clarity, and content, is called a(n) _____.
4. The total time that passes between the originator's giving the document to the WP specialist and the time it is returned is called _____.

Short Answer

1. Standardized procedures promote several important benefits. List three of them.
2. Discuss the necessity for quality proofreading.
3. Name two examples of when an originator is solely responsible for proofreading.
4. List three locations for the most commonly undetected errors.
5. List three reasons for measuring productivity.
6. What is the purpose of a line count?

Matching

Write the letter of the definition that matches the term in the space to the left of the number of the term.

Terms

_____ 1. Proofreaders' marks

_____ 2. Procedures

_____ 3. Work measurement

_____ 4. Line count

_____ 5. Administrative time

_____ 6. Production log

_____ 7. Chargeback system

_____ 8. Standards

_____ 9. Turnaround time

Definitions

a. Time that elapses between the submission of a document for completion and its return to the originator.

b. Symbols used to mark corrections required in the production of a document.

c. Level of average production of WP specialists.

d. Guidelines for the performance of tasks, documents produced, and equipment operated.

e. Method of charging projects, individuals, or departments for WP or DP production time and costs.

f. Count of productivity in terms of document volume, time, and cost.

g. Form on which documents are listed with pertinent information about them for the purpose of calculating productivity.

h. Number of typewritten lines per page or per document.

i. Time spent talking to the originator or WP supervisor about the formatting and production of the document.

j. To locate documents or sections of documents within the memory or media.

Exercises

Exercise 7.1. Proofread the resume on page 122. Circle all errors. Compare your proofreading with the corrected copy that follows yours.

Exercise 7.2. Proofread the letter on page 123 and circle the errors. Did you find all 33 of them? A corrected copy follows yours for comparison.

➤ Patricia de Lina, 1300 Adams 17N, Costa Mesa, Ca 92626 ◄

CAREEER OBJECTIVES: To combine mine experience and creative abilities in related to people in the areas of managment, merchandizing, training, public relation's or sales with a progressive firm providing chalenging work

POSITION DESIRED: Retail training-merchandizing coordinator, sales representive.

EXPERENCE: Presented Sales Representative Thousand Flowers Jewelry Inc, San Fransisco, CA. Responsible for servicing outhern California area and five-state territory, writing orders; prospecting new accounts, promoting maximum exposure-setting up gift shows in major markets, from designing and construting booths to displaying merchandise.

1976–1979 Bullocks Department Stores, Westwood, CA (Max Factor, Mens Frangrances). Counter Manager-Cosmetic Sales Consultant - full charge of all counter activity, including supervising salespersons. Responsible for for product display, merchandising; ordering and sales reports.

1974–1976 Bullocks Department Stores, Sherman Oaks; CA (Shiseido) Cosmetic Sales Consultant. Taught customers the corect method of skin care and cosmetic application, created displays, merchandized products for maximum sales potential.

1972–1974 May Co. Department Stores, North Hollywood, CA (Charles of the Ritz). Counter Sales Consultant-developed proper technique for for evaluating customer skins care needs. Given the added responsibility of aiding assistant cosmetic manager with sales and production records, purchase register, and sales planing.

SUMMERY OF QUALIFICATIONS: Creative-people oriented-work well under presure-preceptive-desire challenge,

EDUCATIONS: University of San Diego College for Woman,

1966–1968 San Diego, CA. Sociology and Political Science Major.

1968–1971 University of California at Los Angeles
B.A. Degree-Political Sience

➤ Patricia de Lina, 1300 Adams 17N, Costa Mesa, Ca 92626 ◄

CAREEER OBJECTIVES: To combine mine experience and creative abilities in related to people in the areas of managment, merchandizing, training, public relation's or sales with a progressive firm providing chalenging work

POSITION DESIRED: Retail training merchandizing coordinator, sales representive.

EXPERENCE: Presented Sales Representative, Thousand Flowers Jewelry Inc, San Fransisco, CA. Responsible for servicing Southern California area and five-state territory, writing orders prospecting new accounts, promoting maximum exposure setting up gift shows in major markets, from designing and construting booths to displaying merchandise.

1976–1979 Bullocks Department Stores, Westwood, CA (Max Factor, Mens Frangrances). Counter Manager Cosmetic Sales Consultant full charge of all counter activity, including supervising salespersons. Responsible for for product display, merchandising ordering and sales reports.

1974–1976 Bullocks Department Stores, Sherman Oaks CA (Shiseido) Cosmetic Sales Consultant. Taught customers the corect method of skin care and cosmetic application, created displays, merchandized products for maximum sales potential.

1972–1974 May Co. Department Stores, North Hollywood, CA (Charles of the Ritz). Counter Sales Consultant developed proper technique for for evaluating customer skins care needs. Given the added responsibility of aiding assistant cosmetic manager with sales and production records, purchase register, and sales planing.

SUMMERY OF QUALIFICATIONS: Creative people oriented work well under presure perceptive desire challenge

EDUCATIONS: University of San Diego College for Woman,

1966–1968 San Diego, CA. Sociology and Political Science Major.

1968–1971 University of California at Los Angeles
B.A. Degree Political Sience

April 6 1980

Ms. Donna deLuna
Accounts Manger
Markham Stores
7899 Front Streeet
Springfield, Il 62701

Dear Mrs. De Luna;

This is to confirm our telephone conversatoin of April 7 concerning you're participation in a panel discussion on "Getting the Most From Your Dollar at the convention of the Bankers' Assoc.

The meeting will be held in the Noel Room of the Hyatt Hotel in in Springfield, Illinois, from 10 a. m. to Noon. You should allow fifteen minutes for your presentation and an editional 30 minutes for discusion, questions, and anwers,

The meeting will be followed by a lunchon from 12:30 P.M. to 2 P.m. You are of course, invited to be our guest for lunch.

We are look forward to you're participation in teh program on April 17.

Sincerely Yours

Harold Nelson,
Director

ds:

April 6, 1980

Ms. Donna deLuna
Accounts Manger
Markham Stores
7899 Front Streeet
Springfield, Il 62701

Dear Mrs. De Luna

This is to confirm our telephone conversation of April 7 concerning you're participation in a panel discussion on "Getting the Most From Your Dollar at the convention of the Bankers' Association

The meeting will be held in the Noel Room of the Hyatt Hotel in in Springfield, Illinois, from 10 a. m. to Noon. You should allow 15 minutes for your presentation and an additional 30 minutes for discusion, questions, and answers.

The meeting will be followed by a luncheon from 12:30 P.M. to 2 P.m. You are of course, invited to be our guest for lunch.

We are looking forward to you're participation in teh program on April 17.

Sincerely Yours,

Harold Nelson,
Director

ds:

Case Problem

Goldberg Electronics, a small engineering firm, recently purchased three WP machines and some dictation/transcription equipment. Mr. Stamper, the owner, then asked his secretary, Ms. Brown, to take the responsibility for overseeing the implementation of a WP system. There are five administrative secretaries working on a one-to-one basis, three clerk-typists who share the clerical support responsibilities of the ten draftspersons, and one mail-file clerk.

Ms. Brown assigned the three clerk-typists to the WP department.

Several months later, Mr. Stamper encountered the following situation:

1. The draftspersons were complaining that work was sometimes lost in the system, and many documents were returned with grammatical as well as typographical errors.
2. The secretaries enjoyed the luxury of having their lengthy documents processed in the WP department because this gave them more time to organize their desks, and they now required little or no overtime. Their only complaint was the formatting of the documents. Because the WP staff divided the lengthy projects, the format was frequently inconsistent.
3. Mr. Stamper felt that the expense of the equipment was not justified because of the various complaints, but he really had no facts upon which to base a decision. In fact, the dictation/transcription equipment was so seldom used it had been moved to a storage room to save desk space.
4. Deadlines were missed because the WP department was backlogged. The WP specialists were having difficulty keeping up because their efficiency was hampered by excessive overtime, deadline pressures, and constant telephone interruptions.

How should Mr. Stamper or Ms. Brown handle this situation?

Part III
****

THE REPROGRAPHICS AND DISTRIBUTION PHASES OF WORD PROCESSING

Chapter 8

****

Reprographics and Reprographics Systems

Chapter Objectives

After reading this chapter and completing the end-of-chapter activities, the student will be able to:

1. Describe each of the five reprographic processes.

2. List the advantages and disadvantages of each process.

3. Select the correct process for duplicating a document.

4. List the organizational designs for duplicating functions.

5. Describe the advantages and disadvantages of each type of organizational design.

6. List the advantages of phototypesetting.

7. Describe the methods used to phototypeset documents.

Factors To Be Considered

reprographics
image processing
duplicating
copy processing

It has been said that the business world is a paper mill. Charles E. Wilson, past president of General Motors, once told a congressional committee, "No physical activity goes on in our modern age without a piece of paper going along to guide it."[1] Almost every document must be reproduced with a copy for everybody. The reproduction of a document may be called **reprographics, image processing, duplicating,** or **copy processing.** In the time cycle of a document, it is the third phase. The use of WP systems has created an enormous flood of information. The job then becomes to reproduce the documents effectively and economically.

This phase includes copying, duplicating, or printing, as well as assembling, collating, and binding the document.

There is a variety of ways in which two or more copies of a document may be made. Common methods of duplicating a document are printing on a WP or DP printer, carbon copies, spirit duplicating, stencil duplicating, offset duplicating, and photocopying. The key question is, Which method is appropriate for which document? Since copies are sent to people both inside and outside the company, the methods of reproduction are largely dependent on what the purpose of the document is and who is going to receive it. The factors usually considered in choosing a reproduction process include:

[1]"Pieces of Paper," *Better Letters*, vol. a, no. 2, (Fairfield, N.J.: Economics Press, Inc.).

1. Quality of the document (appearance).
2. Cost of duplicating the document.
3. Time required to duplicate the document.
4. Quantity needed of the document.

These factors vary considerably among the processes. They are the same factors that an organization considers when looking at a WP support system for its executives. Cost, efficiency, quality, and volume of documents are uppermost in the minds of management as they consider how to make the written communications of the organization run smoothly and economically.

Carbon Copies

Carbon copying is the most economical copying process for six or seven copies since no special duplicating equipment is required. It is also very easy with WP systems with impact print devices. The WP specialist who is outputting the document simply puts carbon paper and second sheets (onionskin or mylar) behind the paper on which the original is being produced and prints the document. It is possible to buy the carbon and second sheets already assembled; these are called carbon sets. It is also possible to buy a specially treated paper which can reproduce copies with no carbon paper. This is called NCR (no carbon required) paper. There is no time involved in producing carbon copies since they are produced simultaneously with the original. In addition, no time is required to correct carbon copies since the text is perfected in the memory of the WP system before the document is printed error-free.

Costs of carbon copies are minimal; they involve the paper and carbon paper only. A restricting factor is that of quantity. Depending on the quality of the carbon paper and the thickness of the stationery, only five or six readable copies can be made.

Photocopying

photocopying

Photocopying is the process of photographing a document. It is probably the most common method of reproduction in use today. Billions of dollars are spent annually photocopying documents. There are several reasons for this:

1. The process is fast and easy.
2. The process produces a very high-quality document.
3. As many copies as are wished may be made in a relatively short period of time.

A major drawback to the photocopy process, and it is an important one, is cost. Cost per copy ranges from approximately three to ten cents.

Two processes of photocopying are used today, direct and indirect. The older process is the direct process, which uses a copier that requires a specially coated paper. This specially coated paper has contributed to the gradual demise of the direct process because it is more costly and heavier than plain paper. The indirect process, which uses plain or bond paper, is the more popular. People, in general, prefer the copies produced on the bond copier.

The reprographics industry divides photocopiers/duplicators into two categories

convenience copier
intelligent copier/printer

—**convenience copiers** and **intelligent copiers/printers**. Convenience copiers (Figure 8.1) are the smaller copiers which are used for one to ten copies. Intelligent copiers/printers (Figures 8.2 and 8.3) are used for high-volume production. Both categories produce a high-quality document. The intelligent copiers can produce a large quantity faster and less expensively.

A key advantage to the photocopying process is that no master is required. The copier or duplicator can photograph a drawing, typewritten document, or printed document.

8. Reprographics and Reprographics Systems

Figure 8.1. The Xerox 2830, a convenience copier, can make multiple oversize copies from single originals. Courtesy of Xerox Corporation.

Figure 8.2. The IBM Copier/Duplicator, Series III, produces high quality copies at a speed of 4500 copies per hour. Courtesy of IBM Corporation.

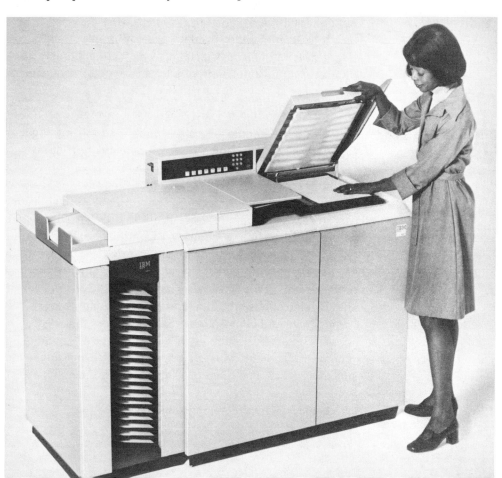

Figure 8.3. The Kodak 150AF produces high quality copies and duplexes, counts, collates, and staples them. Courtesy of Eastman Kodak Company.

The misuse of copiers is a common problem in the management of a duplicating facility. Staff may use the copier for personal documents. Overcopying or generating more copies than required is common. If these costly problems occur it may be necessary to implement stringent controls. These controls may include closer supervision, an autotron which counts copies as well as activates the machine, and a chargeback system (a method of allocating costs to each individual or department). It is important for the staff to be educated on the costs of copies. Time expended going to and from the copier and extra file space required for filing the extra copies are often unidentified but associated copying costs.

duplex   Intelligent copiers/printers are multifunction units with logic systems built into them which photocopy documents as well as **duplex** (copy both sides), reduce, collate, and staple. Interruptions can occur and the system can restart in the appropriate place.

Printing on a WP or DP Printer

WP and DP vendors are also manufacturing intelligent copiers/printers. Several vendors have high-speed, high-volume ink jet or laser printers, which make the printing of several copies of a document easy, fast, and economical. Quality varies with the model and type. When activating from a WP or DP system, little additional effort is needed to produce two or more copies. The print speed is high. No labor is involved; the equipment does it all. If a WP or DP specialist no longer has to walk a document to be reproduced, a significant savings is realized. The quality is also excellent because all the copies are originals.

The ability to telecommunicate documents to and from an intelligent copier or WP system is a very useful feature in the integration of office communications. Intelligent copiers/printers represent the ultimate merger thus far between document production and reproduction. Their high-speed, high-quality print characteristics, graphics capabilities, and type style choices offer many of the services of a commercial print shop. The intelligent copier is another example of modern technology which mechanizes routine functions such as collating and stapling and makes it possible to

Figure 8.4. The IBM 6670 links word and data processing, printing computer-based information in typewriter-like quality with customized formats at a rate of up to 36 copies a minute. Courtesy of IBM Corporation.

Figure 8.5. The Xerox 5700 electronic printing system responds to the operator's touch on the control screen. The system combines word processor printing, remote computer printing, direct copying, and telecommunications to another 5700 in a different location in three seconds. Courtesy of Xerox Corporation.

do more routine work with fewer people. As well as speeding up the task, this frees people to do more challenging tasks.

Some intelligent copiers utilize the technologies of fiber optics and laser beams. Fiber optics technology uses lasers transmitted over hair-sized glass fibers and converts a digital signal to charged dots on the zinc oxide sheet master of the copier. The image is then transferred to paper.

Laser technology transmits an extremely narrow beam of electromagnetic energy in electrophotographic printing. The IBM 6670 Information Distributor (Figure 8.4), introduced in 1979, employs a laser beam to print documents at a speed of up to 36 pages per minute. It also communicates with mainframe computers, other 6670s and communicating WP systems. The 6670 also serves as a convenience copier.

The Xerox 5700 (Figure 8.5) combines computer, laser, and xerographic technologies to print data, textual material, and forms at a speed of up to 43 pages per minute. The 5700 user can choose from 200 standard font styles. It has extensive communications capabilities for both priority and standard mail.

Minolta manufactures an intelligent copier that can be linked to facsimile machines, WP systems, and computers. Several other manufacturers join Minolta in the bid for the small business community's need for laser printing and are continuing to introduce other laser copier/printers.

Offset Duplication

offset duplicating

The **offset duplicating** process is an ink and water process based on the fact that oil and water do not mix and that impressions may be offset from a plate or master to an intermediate and then to a page. This process is used for high-volume production. Offset duplicators range in size from small table-top to large printing units (Figure 8.6).

Users of this process prefer it because it is:

1. High in quality.
2. Capable of reproducing a large volume of material.
3. Inexpensive on a per copy basis.

The equipment requires an experienced operator. The process takes time and is not as fast as the carbon and photocopy processes. The cost per copy is dependent on the number of copies to be made and ranges from one to five cents.

Unlike the photocopy process, a master is required for the offset process. There are three types of masters: metal plate, paper plate, and electrostatic.

The least expensive master should always be used for a job. Two considerations that determine the type of master to be used are the total number of copies needed and whether or not the master is to be stored for later use.

A metal plate or master is used for the highest volume—1,000 to 50,000 copies. Metal plates can also be stored for use again at a later date. A developing process much like that with the development of film is used to prepare a metal plate for running off on the offset.

Paper masters are used for short runs to 500 copies. Because the paper master is less expensive than others, it is advantageous to use for small numbers of copies.

An electrostatic master is the master prepared from an original such as an already typed document, a picture, or a pasteup—something that already exists that you would like to reproduce onto a master and then, in turn, make a number of copies of it. This is done using a converter unit, a photographic process which reproduces the image of the original onto the master. Electrostatic masters can produce up to 5,000 copies, but they cannot be stored for later use.

Offset duplicators come in three sizes or configurations. The table-top model is

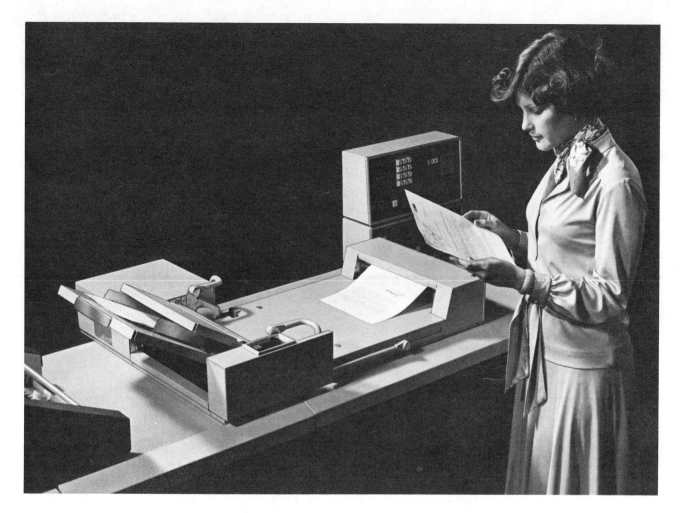

Figure 8.6. A. B. Dick's 1700 CDS Computerized Duplicating System produces 9000 copies per hour. Courtesy of A. B. Dick Company.

the type most often found in an office environment. It is a simple to operate office duplicator. A second type is the floor-type offset, usually found in large reprographic centers or commercial print shops. The third type is the automatic duplicating system with an automatic plate maker. The criterion for selection of configuration is often volume of production.

Spirit Duplication

spirit duplicating

The **spirit duplicating** process uses masters with aniline dye and a fast drying alcohol fluid to transfer the image to paper. It is also called fluid or liquid duplicating. Spirit duplicating is used primarily by schools, churches, and government offices. The process is inexpensive, versatile, and good for up to approximately 300 copies.

The equipment is easy to operate. The per copy cost ranges from slightly less than one cent to two cents per copy, depending on the number of copies made. Masters are easy to prepare. Because masters are available in red, green, black, blue, as well as the usual purple, it is possible to be versatile in reproduction. The masters may be written, typed, or drawn.

Typewritten spirit masters are particularly simple to create using a WP system with an impact print device. The text is keyboarded and perfected in the memory of the electronic typing system; the master is then inserted and the document is printed on the master and then run.

By a heat process, thermal spirit masters can be used to transfer a facsimile of an original copy to a duplicating master.

The primary drawback of spirit duplicating is quality. It is satisfactory for use for in-house documents where superior quality is not required. It is generally not used where documents are going to outside customers and high quality is desired.

Stencil Duplication

stencil duplicating

Stencil duplicating is a process that reproduces using an inking machine and a master called a stencil. The process is also known as mimeographing.

The stencil can be written, drawn, or typed. By a heat process, thermal stencils can be used to transfer a facsimile of an original to a stencil. This process also is used primarily by churches, schools, and government offices because of its versatility and economy.

The versatility is illustrated by the different sizes and weights of paper that may be used, ranging from 3 inch by 5 inch cards to 8½ inch by 14 inch paper. Ink is also available in a variety of colors—red, blue, yellow, and black. Special effects can be achieved by using a colored paper with a complimentary color of ink. It is also possible to use more than one color of ink on copies.

The cost ranges from slightly under one cent per copy to two cents per copy, depending on the number of copies made. Stencils that can reproduce up to 3,000 copies are available.

Some training is required to create stencils and to operate the mimeograph. WP equipment is ideal for creating stencils since the text can be keyboarded and perfected in the memory of the WP system. The stencil is inserted, the ribbon turned to the stencil setting, and the document is played back through the use of an impact printer onto the stencil which is then run.

This process is satisfactory for in-house documents because of its level of quality. It would generally not be acceptable for use for documents going to customers or the public.

Organizational Design for Reprographics

An organization's philosophy on duplicating can cost or save an organization many dollars. Part of this savings depends on the accessibility of the duplicating facilities. Organizations need to look at the kinds of reproductions which will be required for their operations. The decisions they need to make include the following:

1. What is the quality of reproduction that is necessary? Will documents be produced for customer presentations? For in-house use? For both?

dedicated operator

2. How much mechanization is desirable? Some systems require more operation, in fact, a **dedicated operator** (an individual whose primary responsibility is to operate the reproduction equipment). Some systems perform tasks, such as stapling, that are not cost-effective when done manually.

3. What amount of money is the company able to budget for equipment and what will be the cost per copy?

4. How much collating, stapling, binding, and so forth will need to be done?

5. Are there sufficient applications for phototypesetting to justify equipment and personnel? Will a phototypesetting service do if media or OCR recognizable hard copy are provided?

6. Are graphics used to any extent?

7. How many conveniences, such as reduction, are needed?

There are many ways an organization may approach the design of reprographic facilities. However, three basic designs are generally applicable to location: centralized, decentralized, and a combination or specialized production. Centralization locates the duplicating equipment and staff in one advantageous location. Usually this type of system permits the organization to have a variety of reproduction processes along with sophisticated assembling or binding techniques, phototypesetting, and graphic artwork. This design often requires a chargeback or accounting system to individuals or departments. Unfortunately, travel time to and from the facility is labor intensive and costly. Some users may not like the inconvenience when just a copy or two is needed. The larger the organization, the more difficulties encountered if all reprographic equipment is in one location. For small organizations, generally no other design is appropriate.

A decentralized system provides basic duplicating services in locations convenient to the users. Often, the photocopy process is used for everything in this type of system; any other reprographic needs that occur within a company are sent out to commercial printers for completion. For large organizations, decentralization locates equipment in a number of departments. This spreads usage over several machines and saves travel time. Controls are often less stringent with this design.

The combination or specialized production design is used for companies that need a center for large and special duplicating orders, but also wish to have small duplicating facilities such as a quick copy center. Labor costs for the user can be kept down if areas are established so that minimum time is devoted to making just a copy or two. This design requires more equipment, but the savings in travel, cost, and convenience may offset the initial outlay.

Phototypesetting for Reprographics

Many written and graphic communications are creatively phototypeset (in different sizes and styles of type via an electronic system) onto photographic paper or film. It is an output process that is used to reproduce a document attractively and economically. Some documents that are commonly phototypeset are manuals reproduced in large quantities and promotional literature. Today's typesetters require two kinds of information: (1) the actual letters, numbers, or symbols in the text to be set, and (2) the commands or instructions concerning how the copy will be set. Commands include typeface, point size, line length, vertical line spacing, indents, et cetera.

phototypesetting

Phototypesetting is also called photocomposition, although photocomposition usually refers to creating an entire page at a time rather than a partial page with little or no pasteup required. Phototypesetting is modern technology's answer to yesterday's manual typesetting where a printer would arrange metal typefaces for printing of the document—a slow, cumbersome, and costly process by today's standards. Using a photographic process, a phototypesetter snaps images of type characters at high speed and assembles them in the size and style of type desired and instructed. These images are photographed on a specially treated paper which is developed to create the phototypeset document.

There are several methods of producing a phototypeset document:

1. The document is keyboarded on a phototypesetter (Figure 8.7) which has been directed to use the correct size and style of type with the appropriate layout (positioning on the page). The illustrations are then inserted manually (also called pasted up although paste is not used) and the typeset image is ready for photographing for the final product.

camera ready

2. The document is keyboarded on a direct impression unit—a WP system which produces proportionally spaced characters in a variety of type styles and sizes on the paper. This is called direct impression because the hard copy is created **camera ready** for printing direct from the typewriter unit. An illustration can be pasted up in the space that is designed for it with the words around it.

Figure 8.7. This Comp/Edit with terminal phototypesetter is used to set type. It interfaces with the AM Jacquard word processing systems. Courtesy of AM Varityper, a Division of AM International.

interface

3. The document can be keyboarded and stored on WP media with space left for illustrations. An **interface**, a device which allows two dissimilar machines to work together to create the finished product, is used to transmit the words stored on the media of the WP system to the phototypesetter. The text stored on the media of the WP system is converted and recorded on media that can be read by the phototypesetter. The conversion strips out the unnecessary WP instruction codes and replaces them with appropriate typesetting commands such as type size, type faces, and document positioning to create the typeset image. This conversion eliminates rekeyboarding for typesetting, reduces the need for proofreading, and speeds production.

4. A document can be keyboarded on a WP system equipped with a telecommunications option. The document can then be electronically communicated to a typesetting system.

5. A computer that has been appropriately programmed can produce phototypeset documents. The document would be keyboarded on a WP system and communicated to the computer, or keyboarded on a computer terminal. When the text is resident in the computer's memory, the software can enable the document to be printed in the desired typeset form.

6. Typewritten text produced on a single-element typewriter using an OCR recognizable font can be read into the typesetting machine through an OCR reader/scanner. Not only can programmable OCR units scan typewritten copy, but they can insert the desired typesetting commands to indicate changes in typeface sizes and styles and copy position.

Why do we need to be concerned with all this? Why not just produce the document on a WP system and be done with it? Some of the reasons include cost, appearance, ease of reading, higher comprehension rate, and greater formatting capability.

As we have discovered throughout this book, cost is usually a major reason for adopting a procedure. Phototypesetting is no exception. Because phototypeset pages hold 40 percent more than a typewritten page, a 100-page manual becomes a 60-page manual. This permits a bulk reduction in the paper, ink, printing, collating, stapling, storage, and postage/distribution.

A document which has been typeset looks better and is easier to read than a typewritten one. The allowance of just the right amount of space for a character is pleasing to the eye. Research shows that phototypesetting permits higher comprehension of the material; more is retained. The important facts in the text—key words or headings, which may be highlighted with a special type size or style, are emphasized for the reader. Because of the many different type styles and sizes, as well as the layout capabilities of the equipment, far greater formatting possibilities exist.

Almost any type of document can be phototypeset—forms, manuals, booklets, brochures, reports, contracts, policies, proposals, certificates, ads, directories, and on and on. It is probably safe to say that phototypesetting is destined to grow to massive proportions for document production.

Procedures for Reprographics

One or two copies of a document are seldom enough for an operating business. Reprographics then becomes very important. Since copies can represent a significant expenditure, it is important to choose the best process for the job. Effective, well-communicated procedures aid in this effort. Section 1.15 of the User's Procedures Manual contains reprographics procedures.

Choosing the appropriate process considering the available methods, cost, time, quantity, and quality is an important decision. Who will make that decision is also important; otherwise, there may be problems. Procedures should clearly state this.

Arnco provides photocomposition services to its clients. Selecting a type face and size is necessary; the manual shows the range of choices available. Reports often need to be bound; the options for this decision are presented. Enough lead time for the ordering of supplies is important. Most users are concerned about the cost factor and how charges are handled. The manual details for each process the cost based on the number of copies and services needed to complete the job. Once the job has been reproduced, there is still paperwork. The production log offers an analysis of the work performed by the reprographics or duplicating specialist. Communicating the chargeback costs for billing completes the process.

Future Trends

Color photocopies will be more commonly used as a reprographic process. Because the use of color is effective, particularly with graphics, and costs should decrease, users should make good use of this tool.

The photocopy process is expected to be integrated with the facsimile or long-distance copying process for greater power in both areas.

Phototypesetting will become more commonly used as a production process for documents in the office as office systems equipment integrates more easily and effectively.

Graphics will be frequently integrated with text in the production of documents to make a more complete presentation. As equipment integrates graphics with text, production of documents will be activated from the same work station.

A systems approach to the total office environment which includes reprographics will become commonly used. This should reduce the costs of the production and reproduction of paperwork.

Summary

The reproduction of a document may be called reprographics, image processing, duplicating, and copy processing. This third phase in the cycle of a document includes duplicating, assembling, collating, and binding the document. Common methods of duplicating a document are carbon copies, spirit duplicating, stencil duplicating, offset duplicating, printing on a WP or DP printer, and photocopying.

The popularity of carbon copies is being revived with WP equipment. The photocopy industry has been taken by storm by the intelligent copier/printer, a high-speed, high-volume printer using laser technology. The offset duplicator continues to provide high-volume printing at an inexpensive per copy rate. Spirit and stencil duplicating have been made easier with the WP system.

The four factors upon which the choice of duplicating process depends are: cost of duplicating the document, time required to duplicate the document, quality, and quantity needed.

How the organization designs its reprographic facility may be costly or cost effective. The three designs most generally used are centralized, decentralized, and a combination of the two.

Phototypesetting is an economical process for creating manuals, brochures, and promotional and sales literature. It sets different sizes and styles of type via electronic systems onto photographic paper or film.

There is a variety of methods of producing a phototypeset document: keyboarding the document on a phototypesetter or on a direct impression unit, keyboarding on WP equipment and converting it to phototypesetting through an interface device or telecommunications, keyboarding on a computer terminal for production instructed by computer software, and typing text on a single-element typewriter and reading it into the phototypesetter using OCR.

Phototypeset documents are easier to read, provide a higher comprehension rate, and give a more attractive appearance at less cost. The phototypesetting system has greater formatting capabilities.

Key Terms

Camera ready	Duplicating	Photocopying
Convenience copier	Image processing	Phototypesetting
Copy processing	Intelligent copier/printer	Reprographics
Dedicated operator	Interface	Spirit duplicating
Duplex	Offset duplicating	Stencil duplicating

Self-Check Questions

Short Answer

1. Define reprographics.
2. List the five reprographic processes and give the advantages and disadvantages of each.
3. Give two examples of how a WP system can be used in reprographics.
4. Name four important factors to consider when choosing a reproduction process.
5. List some advantages of the offset duplicating process.
6. List and briefly describe the methods of producing a phototypeset document.
7. Name five reasons for using phototypesetting.
8. Give one reason phototypesetting has been shown to increase reader comprehension.
9. Name three types of documents that lend themselves to phototypesetting.
10. Name two reasons phototypesetting a document is cost effective.

Completion

1. The most commonly used method of reproducing a document is the _____ process.
2. _____ copiers are small units designed to make one to ten copies for each original.
3. A multifunction, high-speed, high-volume copier with a logic system is a(n) _____ copier.

4. The IBM 6670 Information Distributor uses _____ technology to print and telecommunicate.
5. The Xerox 5700 prints at a speed of up to _____.
6. _____ is an output process of producing a document with different type sizes and type styles via an electronic optical system onto photographic paper or film.
7. A phototypeset page holds _____ percent more than a typewritten page.

Exercise

Exercise 8.1. Individually or as a class visit an organization that uses a variety of reprographic methods. Write a brief summary containing the following information:
1. What reprographic methods are used?
2. What types of documents are phototypeset?
3. Is a chargeback system used?
4. Does the organization continue to increase the amount of material phototypeset?
5. What is the cost per copy on each form of reproduction?
6. What savings has the organization experienced that can be attributed to the phototypesetting process?
7. Which method is used for phototypesetting?
8. Is there any misuse of copying?

Ask to see documents reproduced by different processes and in the various stages of the phototypeset process. Compare a finished phototypeset document with a typewritten one.

Case Problem

The Knowles Insurance Company recently opened and as yet has only a small, table-top bond copier. Knowles has a need for a great many forms, which they presently send out to a print shop to reproduce. The typists use carbon paper to produce the necessary three copies of some of these forms.

In addition, Knowles Insurance distributes a weekly one-page newsletter to 12,000 clients. The newsletter is produced by a local print shop. Increased costs have forced Ms. Simmons, the manager, to consider dropping the service.

From your knowledge of reprographics, suggest some reproduction processes which the Knowles Insurance Company might use to increase productivity while controlling unnecessary costs.

Chapter 9

****

Physical and Electronic Distribution Processes

Chapter Objectives

After reading this chapter and completing the end-of-chapter activities, the student will be able to:

1. *Define distribution.*
2. *Define the major categories of distribution.*
3. *List and describe the categories of physical distribution.*
4. *List and define the types of electronic distribution.*
5. *Determine the best method of telecommunications for a given application.*
6. *List the advantages and disadvantages of each type of electronic distribution.*
7. *List and define examples of telecommunications networks.*
8. *Define micrographics.*
9. *List and describe the various microforms.*

Distribution Defined

Let us take a look at the fourth phase of WP, that of distribution. The Exxon study[1] showed that 74 percent of the time cycle of a document is devoted to distribution. Nineteen percent of the document cycle cost is in distribution.[2] To demonstrate the monetary importance of this phase, consider the amount of money that has has been spent on typewriters since 1868 when Christopher Sholes first invented it. Imagine the tremendous amount of money spent on WP systems since 1964, when IBM began marketing the MTST. The research and development costs as well as the purchase or lease costs of typewriters and WP systems over the past century must be astronomical. Yet the output phase accounts for only 3 percent of the time cycle of a document. Since the distribution phase accounts for 74 percent of the time cycle, it may well be the most important phase of WP. It merits major consideration as to dollar expenditures.

distribution

What is **distribution**? It is the mailing, delivering, transmitting, and filing of a document. It is the reason for everything we have discussed up to this point, because unless the documents produced are easily accessible and are delivered to the people

---

[1]"The Exxon Corporation Study," *Communication News*, June 1975.
[2]"Electronic Mail," the Butler Cox Foundation, Report Series No. 17, February 1980.

physical distribution

electronic
  distribution
electronic mail

electronic filing

who need the information, we have performed a useless exercise. The two major categories of distribution are physical and electronic. **Physical distribution** is the delivering or mailing and filing of a document by manual or physical means. It includes mail, internal carriers, courier service, and manual files. **Electronic distribution** is the electronic mailing or delivery of a document via telephone or satellite transmission. **Electronic mail** is another name for telecommunicating a document electronically over telephone lines or satellites. Also included in electronic distribution is the **electronic filing** of a document, a part of which is the science of micrographics.

Physical Distribution

Mail

Mail is the most commonly used physical distribution method. It has two major problems—time and cost. It is estimated that three-fourths of all U.S. mail takes three or more days to be delivered. Internal mail is not much better. Surprisingly, 65 to 75 percent of all mail going through a mail room never leaves the site; it is going to another office on the same site. It takes 71% of the mail an average of 3 days to move from one office to another internally.[3] Consider the implications of this. A great deal of money is spent on systems design, personnel, and equipment to originate, produce, and copy a document in the fastest and most efficient way possible, only to mail it and lose complete control of it. Perhaps we have sacrificed our efficiency totally when we mail the document. The effects of delay can be costly to a company in terms of its own operation as well as opportunities for potential business. The increasing costs of the U.S. Postal Service verify that mail service is becoming more and more expensive.

private carrier

As an alternative to the U.S. mail, some companies have begun to use **private carriers**, businesses who deliver packages. These include such carriers as United Parcel Service, Federal Express, and some commercial airlines and railroads which offer a variety of mail services such as overnight delivery or freight. The cost for these services is higher than that for mail, and they do not service all cities in the nation, but they do provide a useful service.

Internal Carriers

internal carrier

Internal carriers, as the name implies, are responsible for the internal delivery of mail within an organization. The mail room of any organization has never been an inexpensive operation because of the number of personnel involved. Any time that a function involves primarily labor, it is called labor intensive and is expensive. Many organizations are looking for equipment and systems which can reduce the number of personnel required and, therefore, costs. In fact, there is an automated machine which can be programmed to travel a floor of a large organization with the mail. The staff at each office simply removes its mail and sends the robot merrily on its way down the hall for other deliveries. Through the use of sophisticated systems design, large organizations using such devices as conveyor belts and special elevators for automated mail delivery have reduced significantly the number of personnel required. For example, one organization spent approximately one million dollars to design and install a system of conveyor belts and elevators for the delivery of mail. After only one year of operation, a significant portion of that million dollars has been recaptured as a result of lower personnel costs.

You may begin to think that people will soon be replaced entirely by machines.

[3]"Report on Facsimile," the Yankee Group, Cambridge, Mass., December 1976.

This has not turned out to be the case. In the 1950s, when computers began to impact business heavily, there was considerable concern that they would take away many jobs. In reality, they have created more jobs than may have been eliminated. Fortunately, machines require people to set them up and work with them. In addition, functions that take extra steps frequently must be performed by people. It probably is true to say that people are going to need a higher level of skills and that the jobs they perform will be of a more complex nature. A benefit of mechanization is called **value added**. This means that many things that could not be done before because of work force capabilities can now be done.

value added

Courier Service

courier service

Courier service is the procedure of having a document hand-delivered by commercial carrier. It is frequently used when meeting a deadline. For example, a subcontractor submitting a quotation for bid may send an employee by jet to the contractor to deliver it. An attorney service may pick up a document from a lawyer's office and hand carry it to the courthouse to file it. No doubt this is an expensive way to deliver documents. If it is not possible to mail it and guarantee delivery in time to meet the deadline, however, without question the document must be hand-delivered.

Manual Filing of Documents

manual filing

The **manual filing** of documents involves the classifying, indexing, filing, and preserving of documents. The need for filing is unquestioned for operating a business, providing legal documentation, recording historical data, and complying with some hundreds of regulations issued by nearly sixty bureaus and offices of the federal government, not to mention the state and local governments. A manual system of filing hard copy is people operated and labor intensive and, therefore, costly. Of course, the storage of hard copy in file cabinets is also space consuming and expensive.

Another major problem with manual filing is that of retrieval. Documents may be misfiled, mislaid, or lost. What business person has not experienced difficulty locating a document? Frequently, the problem of retrieval occurs when a document is needed most quickly and urgently. In addition, misfiling a record is costly.

There may always be a need for some manual filing of documents because of the need to have hard copies of documents for a working file when a project is in progress. Limiting the amount of manual filing and working files may be one key to a good system.

Document retention is a study in itself. Which documents need to be retained and for how long? What is the best way to catalog or index? What is the best way to purge hard copy files and when? At the price of square footage for office space and the amount of space consumed by file cabinets, these are important questions.

Electronic Distribution

Electronic distribution is the electronic transmission of documents via telephone lines, microwaves, hardwired cables, or satellites. Just as physical distribution includes manual filing of documents, electronic distribution includes micrographics, the science of recording permanent files on film in miniature form.

electronic data transfer
electronic document distribution
integration

Electronic distribution or telecommunications, which is also called electronic mail, data transmission, **electronic data transfer** or dissemination, and **electronic document distribution**, is the key to the integration of systems in WP, DP, voice mail, photocomposition, and micrographics. The ability to move information in usable form from one device to another is called **integration**. For example, an AS secretary

9. Physical and Electronic Distribution Processes

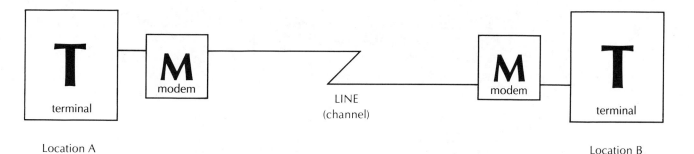

Figure 9.1. Telecommunications.

types a document using an OCR element. After the author marks necessary revisions, the document is scanned by the OCR reader/scanner and telecommunicated to the WP system, where it is transferred to magnetic media and the revisions made. The document is then telecommunicated to the intelligent copier for thirty copies and stored. It can also be telecommunicated to the computer for storage. The computer can also be instructed to put the document on one of the forms of micrographics. All four of these devices have the capacity to communicate within the same building and within or between cities, states, or countries.

Many organizations are using telecommunications effectively to communicate with branch locations since document delivery time is reduced by approximately 75 percent. For example, a pharmaceutical manufacturer in California telecommunicates daily with its Georgia and Puerto Rico offices. An engineering firm telecommunicates with its international and other domestic offices. One campus of a college system telecommunicates with its other campuses. Courts using electronic mail have reduced document delivery time significantly. Examples of telecommunications abound in industry. What kinds of documents do companies telecommunicate? A wide range of monthly reports, internal memos and letters, and documents with multiperson distribution for review are all telecommunicated. There are two major benefits gained from telecommunications—speed and accuracy. In the case of the pharmaceutical manufacturer, since pharmaceuticals are manufactured at all three locations, if there is a change in the formula, instant notification is necessary. It takes less than a minute to telecommunicate a page. Further, telecommunications is absolutely accurate. Nothing can be changed or mistaken in the process.

An important factor for many organizations doing classified work is security. Branches or other organizations can be locked in or out of telecommunications by use of such techniques as passwords and keylocks. Only those whom an organization wishes to access its information can do so, provided appropriate security procedures are used.

When designing a telecommunications system, it is important for an organization to identify the types of telecommunications applications it will have, in order to ensure the optimum equipment for the least money. It is also important to determine with whom the organization will communicate, in order to acquire compatible equipment.

It is possible to use several different types of equipment to send and receive information electronically. The specific applications of an organization determine the method of telecommunications to be used. The four major methods of telecommunications we will be exploring are:

1. TWX/Telex, for brief messages.
2. Facsimile, for sending charts, graphs, and so forth.

3. Terminal-to-terminal, or **point-to-point**, for telecommunications among WP systems, OCR, and intelligent copiers.
4. Terminal-to-computer for telecommunications between a WP system, OCR, or an intelligent copier and a computer.

TWX/Telex

TWX/Telex

One of the oldest and most common forms of telecommunications is **TWX/Telex** (Figure 9.2). These are teletypewriter networks of Western Union, originally developed by American Telephone and Telegraph. The TWX/Telex network is the largest public electronic mail network, with 120,000 terminals in the United States. They have different speeds, they can both send to and receive from their own units and to and from each other. Although a delay in message relay occurs when communicating TWX to Telex, there is no delay communicating TWX to TWX or Telex to Telex. The TWX/Telex process is relatively slow, but inexpensive if messages are brief. Because of the relatively slow speed of transmission, long distance charges would be too great for lengthy documents. For a short message, the cost of TWX/Telex is less than one-half the cost of a three-minute long distance telephone call. If the call is placed after hours it is even more cost-effective. Setting the machine up to be able to receive unattended is a good technique for cost-effective transmission after hours. In addition to the cost, appearance or quality of the document is another reason the TWX/Telex is not used for long documents such as letters, memos, and reports. TWX and Telex messages are printed on special paper stock with all capital letters. They cannot compare with a typewritten document.

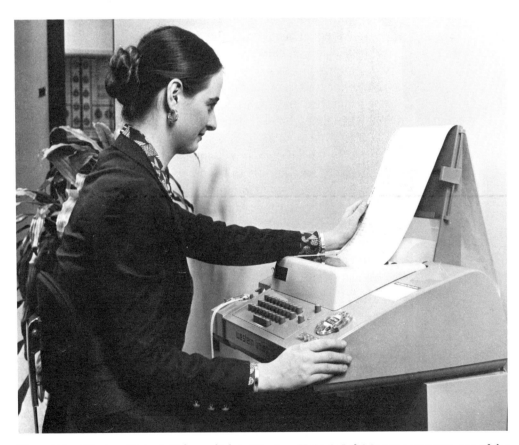

Figure 9.2. Western Union's Telex, a link to Western Union's InfoMaster computer, one of the most advanced message-switching computer centers serving the communications industry. Courtesy of Western Union Corporation.

The established network is an important advantage of TWX/Telex telecommunications. A directory of organizations across the world is published with the name of the company and the number to dial to reach the TWX/Telex office of the organization. This makes it possible for every user to communicate with every other user in the TWX/Telex network. TWX/Telex systems do have the disadvantage of requiring the documents to be typed onto the teletypewriter. This is, of course, labor intensive and costly. Also, the difficulty of not being able to store as much on the same amount of paper tape from a TWX/Telex machine as can be stored on magnetic cards, tapes, or discs is a disadvantage. Of course, revisions on paper tape from TWX/Telex are not possible as compared to a communicating WP system which not only transmits messages, but also has editing capabilities.

Facsimile

facsimile

Facsimile, sometimes abbreviated to *fax*, is the transmission and reproduction of charts, graphs, drawings, and pictures as well as signed documents and other images over a distance by electronic means. Some people think of this equipment in terms of long distance copying. A facsimile device (Figure 9.3) can be thought of as a copier which electronically sends an original document to a remote location where it is reproduced as a copy or facsimile of the original.

It is an old process, first tried in 1842 when Alexander Bain, a young Scot, transmitted a document over a short distance. It has been used by some industries for a number of years. Publishers and news services use this method to transmit photographs for reproducing in newspapers. Another use is signature verification by financial institutions. Transmission of military maps displaying reconnaissance information is a third use.

Facsimile is the least expensive way to transmit pictures. It offers the flexibility of maintaining the original format of the message with no possibility of transposition or omission errors.

There are many brands of facsimile units, and they have varying transmission speeds. To send a document via facsimile, it is helpful to have compatible units. If you have one brand of facsimile and your branch office has another, you may not be able to communicate. Manufacturers strive to create a standard of compatibility.

Figure 9.3. The QWIP 1200 facsimile with the telephone device for the handset of an ordinary telephone is all that is needed for telecommunications. Courtesy of QWIP Systems, a Division of Exxon Corporation.

Figure 9.4. Rapicom, Inc.'s 6350T/6300R Transmitter/Receiver transmits a wide variety of document sizes and graphic forms, including typewritten and handwritten letters, charts, diagrams, and drawings, in speeds of less than one minute. Courtesy of Rapicom, Inc.

Compatibility is more common with the large manufacturers in the industry and is an important factor to consider when acquiring units.

With compatible units, all that the sender need do is attach the original appropriately, set the machine for length of sending time, length of document, and so forth, call the receiving party, place the telephone handset into the acoustic coupler (the device that connects the units via telephone wires), and the process will be started. The receiver of the document, upon receipt of the telephone call alerting him that a document is being sent, puts the appropriate size paper on the machine, sets it up as necessary, places the telephone into the coupler, and the process can begin. In the sending unit, electronic impulses are responsible for the long distance transfer of information. In the receiving unit, the image is actually etched on the paper as a series of dots, thus creating the shape of the chart or graph being sent.

It is important to note that any telephone can be used; nothing special is required. The facsimile unit itself has a built-in data communications device called an **acoustic** *acoustic coupler* **coupler** which permits the machine to transmit the message over the telephone lines (Figure 9.5). There are other technical hookups that can be made with special telephone company equipment in combination with the facsimile units. A facsimile machine may be located anywhere power and a telephone are available. Different units take longer or shorter times to transmit, depending on the brand of the unit, the darkness of the original, and the length of the document. The range of transmission time varies from 30 seconds per page to 12 minutes per page. Many units transmit an 8½ inch by 11 inch page in 4 to 6 minutes, depending upon the clarity of the original.

A distinct advantage of facsimile is that anything on paper can be transmitted. No typing or retyping is required. Transmitting after hours is cost-effective because

Figure 9.5. A. B. Dick's Magna I Communication Option, with acoustic coupler and telephone, provides asynchronous telecommunications. Courtesy of A. B. Dick Company.

of lower long distance rates. Setting the machine up to receive unattended is also an advantageous procedure. Facsimile cuts the largest and most important hidden business cost—time and money lost in waiting for information.

Facsimile does have limitations. One disadvantage is that when a document has been received, it can only be read; it cannot be revised without retyping the entire document. The second disadvantage of facsimile systems is poor quality of output document.

Terminal-to-Terminal Telecommunications

terminal-to-terminal

Terminal-to-terminal, also called point-to-point, telecommunications is one WP system, printer, intelligent copier, or OCR terminal sending to or receiving from another WP system, printer, intelligent copier, or OCR terminal (Figure 9.6). Many organizations are discovering the benefits of this instant and accurate form of electronic mail. It produces high-quality documents, correctly formatted, providing information in a timely and security-conscious manner. For example, a Houston-based engineering firm telecommunicates with its Chicago, North Carolina, and London offices.

In order for the equipment to talk it must be compatible. Compatibility involves the speed of transmission and the protocol. The difficulties of incompatibility have been partially solved with interface devices, sometimes called black boxes, that make it possible for equipment with different protocols or speeds of transmission to talk. These black boxes convert the codes or protocol of one unit to that of the other. The equipment can then communicate. All brands of WP equipment cannot at this

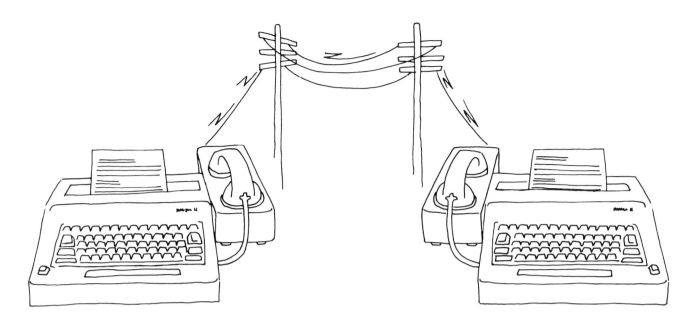

Figure 9.6. Terminal-to-terminal telecommunications.

time have all codes and protocols converted. However, equipment of major vendors currently can communicate with that of other major vendors through such interface devices. The computer, with the appropriate programs or software, also has the capability of meshing incompatible equipment to make communications possible.

The communications process has two methods for most WP systems—dial-up and hardwired. Using dial-up telecommunications, the message is keyboarded and recorded on the magnetic media used by the WP system. The media are then inserted appropriately in the WP system as it is set up to send. The telephone number assigned to the recipient's equipment is dialed. The recipient is asked to set up the receiving equipment with the correct amount of media to record the document. The proper procedure for sending and receiving is then followed. The message goes from the sender's equipment through a **modem** (an internal or external device that changes the recorded data into the necessary form to travel the telephone wires) to the recipient's equipment.

modem

Three elements are necessary for terminal-to-terminal telecommunications (Figure 9.1). They are terminal, modem, and channel or line. The terminal serves as the unit that inputs data to be sent, outputs received data, and houses the communications control functions. The modem changes the letters and numbers of the text to sound waves to allow them to travel over the line. The line is the channel or path between the two terminals.

To explain further, typewriters have letters and symbols that represent the language. Communicating typewriters talk in electronic patterns called digital codes. You may have seen the ones and zeros of the binary language of a computer; this is the electronic pattern of digital coding. Since communication is carried in sound waves over telephone lines, the typewritten message must be changed from letters and symbols to the digital coding of ones and zeros to sound waves (Figure 9.7). This sound wave form of communication is called analog coding. It is the modem that changes the electronic pattern of digital coding of the WP system to the analog coding of sound waves, so that it can be transmitted over telephone lines. At the receiving end, another modem changes the analog coding back into digital coding so it can be played out on the WP system as letters and symbols. The term *modem* comes from the contraction of *mod*ulate and *dem*odulate.

Modems may also be called acoustic couplers when they are in the form of external box-like devices into which the telephone receiver is placed with the two rubber cups for the earpiece and mouthpiece. Modems may be called data sets when they are built to resemble telephones with extra buttons. In addition to modems, data sets, and acoustic couplers, which are technical equipment necessary to make the telecommunications process work, the telephone company often requires a **Data Access Arrangement (DAA)**, which is an interface attachment that connects a data communications device such as a modem to a telephone line to protect the public telephone network from a sudden surge of power or interference.

With all these required devices, it is nice to know business people still use a handshake. In telecommunications, a handshake is a preliminary exchange of predetermined signals performed by modems and/or terminals to verify that communication has been established and can proceed.

A second method of telecommunicating between WP systems, intelligent copiers,

Data Access Arrangement (DAA)

Figure 9.7. Modem.

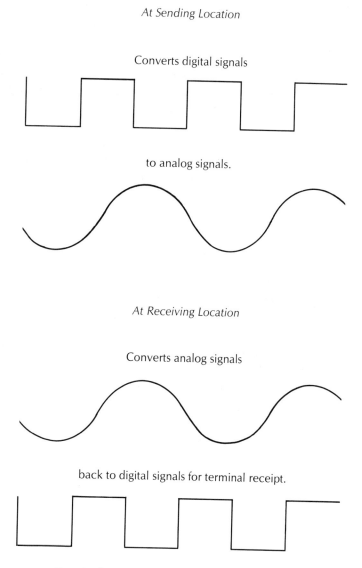

At Sending Location

Converts digital signals

to analog signals.

At Receiving Location

Converts analog signals

back to digital signals for terminal receipt.

terminals, printers, or OCR is hardwired or cable-connected. This means that units are wired directly together and no dial-up is required in the operation. One machine is simply instructed by the pushing of a button on another machine to perform an operation. For example, an OCR hardwired to a WP system will transfer text from a piece of paper read by the OCR reader/scanner to the media of the WP system with the push of a button.

The transmission devices primarily used for telecommunications today are telephone wires, because of their accessibility and the relatively low cost. There are over 2,500 telephone companies in the world today, the largest of which is American Telephone and Telegraph. Greater use of the other methods is being made. These include coaxial cables (a cable that has one conductor within and insulated from another conductor of larger diameter) connecting two hardwired terminals, and microwave and satellite systems. Satellites will result in even faster and less expensive communications and will also permit telecommunications to places difficult to access at present because of lack of telephone availability.

It is important to note a technical difference about point-to-point telecommunications. Although the term is widely applied, it technically limits communications to two points at a time. For example, an organization's branch office in New York telecommunicates to another in Houston, which then calls Boston with a second document. A **multidrop line**, also called a **multipoint line**, is one that serves multiple terminals on one dedicated line in a polling mode, that is, going from one telecommunications address to another checking for messages.

multidrop line
multipoint line

Terminal-to-Computer Telecommunications

terminal-to-computer

Terminal-to-computer, also called point-to-computer, telecommunications is the process of electronically transmitting information from a WP system, intelligent copier, or terminal to a computer.

The same two processes of telecommunications are used with terminal-to-computer as with terminal-to-terminal, that is, dial-up and hardwired telecommunications. For terminal-to-computer, telephones and modems are used much as they are for terminal-to-terminal telecommunications. The procedure is essentially the same. The document is keyboarded and recorded on magnetic media, the computer system's telephone number is dialed and answered, and the message is transmitted using the appropriate procedures of the terminal, WP system, or intelligent copier and the computer system. The same process of modulation and demodulation is used, with the modem converting the message from digital coding to analog coding and then back to digital coding for printing in letters and symbols. A similar procedure for hardwired telecommunications is used. The push of a button on one machine activates an operation on another.

There are a number of advantages to terminal-to-computer telecommunications. The computer provides access to documents without retyping. A WP system can also serve as a DP terminal, which results in a cost savings of one machine. A WP system or intelligent copier makes computer printouts, which are often difficult to understand, easy to read because it is possible to extract just that amount of information necessary from the computer printout. Certainly the appearance of a document printed out on a WP system or intelligent copier is superior to that of a computer printout.

Computers are able to store vast amounts of data; therefore, many organizations choose to store their permanent documents in the computer rather than on magnetic media. This eliminates extensive handling of media. An example of this application is found in legal and medical libraries, where the attorney or physician simply calls up the topic in the computer, which searches for the information.

Figure 9.8. Anderson Jacobson terminal and acoustic coupler with a telephone communicating to a host computer. Courtesy of Anderson Jacobson, Inc.

Computers can manipulate large amounts of data easily and quickly. For example, an insurance agent wishing to sell a life insurance policy may send a letter which is already stored in the computer that can be personalized with the prospective client's name. In addition, an actuary chart using that client's date of birth can be computed to be included with the letter. Organizations are becoming convinced of the value of having a large computer with centralized data files and terminals at all locations in the organization. This system is being adopted because of the efficiency of the large databased/data communication systems.

teleprocessing

Another development is that of **teleprocessing**, which is simply the processing of documents during telecommunications transmission. For example, names and addresses can be merged with a letter and telecommunicated to the named persons almost simultaneously. Since the computer telecommunicates the finished product to a WP system or printer, the quality of the document is excellent. The range of speeds at which WP systems communicate to computers is similar to that of point-to-point telecommunications. The printout speed may be much faster. A high-speed printer driven by the computer can generate several thousand lines per minute.

Some organizations cannot afford to have a computer of their own. An alternative may be to use a time-shared computer service. This service is provided by an organization which has one or more large computers and contracts with many organizations to do their work. Customers are charged only for the time it takes the computer to perform their functions and for storage space required for their amount of text. Since the computer operates at a very high rate of speed, it can do one function for one company, then switch over to perform another company's tasks, and then switch back again, as each is inputting, messaging, and outputting data.

A common example of terminal-to-computer telecommunications is Western Union's Mailgram. You may telecommunicate with Western Union's large computer using a TWX/Telex, a WP system, or you may telephone the local Western Union office and dictate the message to the operator, who types it on a terminal. The message is sent to the computer in West Virginia and then is sent on to the terminal at the post office nearest the recipient's zip code. Delivery is always guaranteed by 9:00 A.M. the following day. Recently, one organization found a good use for mailgrams. It found that its telephone number was to be changed. There was no way to delay the telephone number change to allow for notification of the organization's clients. Since this organization was a pharmaceutical house, it was possible that it could be a matter of life or death for a client to know the telephone number to check pharmaceutical information. The organization chose to send mailgrams to all of its clients, all of whom received notification by 9:00 A.M. the next day.

Protocol

compatibility of equipment
protocol

In each of the categories of telecommunications, TWX/Telex, facsimile, terminal-to-terminal and terminal-to-computer equipment, **compatibility of equipment** is important and includes several factors of protocol. **Protocol** is a set of conventions that include modes, speed, character length, and code. These conventions govern the format and relative timing of the data exchange. The most common protocols are IBM-compatible (2741, 2780, 3780 are numbers assigned to them for identification) and TTY-ASCII (American Standard Code for Information Interchange)-compatible.

Baudot
Correspondence code
EBCDIC
SNA

There are also other protocols or transmission codes: **Baudot, Correspondence code, EBCDIC (Extended Binary Coded Decimal Internal Code),** and **SNA (Systems Network Architecture).** All equipment must use the same protocol. Let us look at some of the factors of protocol.

synchronization technique

Mode. The equipment must have a similar **synchronization technique** or method of transmission. The methods are: bisynchronous (also called synchronous), asynchronous, and Synchronous Data Link Control (SDLC). The first method of transmission is used when some equipment can call another unit and batch or transfer information to it in **blocks of characters.** The common block sizes are 128, 256, and 512 characters. The data can be revised and then **batched** back. This type of transmission is called **bisynchronous** (Figure 9.9) by its inventor, IBM, and **synchronous** by other vendors. Synchronous protocol does not require a start and stop bit or instruction at the beginning and the end of each character. The second method of transmission is **asynchronous.** This means that one unit can send information one character at a time with a start instruction before each character and a stop instruction after each character. This is a relatively slow process.

blocks of characters
batched
bisynchronous
synchronous

asynchronous

The range of transmission speeds for the asychronous mode is 50 to 2400 bits per

Asynchronous = one character at a time

Bisynchronous = block of characters at a time

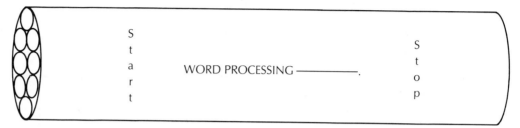

Figure 9.9. Asynchronous and bisynchronous word flows.

second. The bisynchronous or synchronous mode ranges from 600 to 9600 bits per second, or 75 to 1200 characters per second.

Synchronous Data Link Control (SDLC) is a line protocol by IBM. It is a subset of Systems Network Architecture (SNA) developed by IBM to improve telecommunications. SDLC, like bisynchronous communications, sends blocks of information, but it can send up to seven blocks of information before a response by the receiving equipment has to acknowledge receipt; this results in greater line utilization. SDLC also makes it possible to reduce communications costs because devices or equipment can share leased telephone lines rather than being required to have one line for each type of equipment. SDLC also provides for terminal sharing from a host computer. Rather than having one or more terminals for each type of application from a host computer, an operator can log on or off the terminal and use it for different applications.

baud
bit

byte

Let us look at characters, bits, bytes, and baud for a moment. **Baud** rate is the unit of transmission speed and generally equates to the bits per second rate. A **bit** is an abbreviation for a binary digit and is the smallest unit of information in a binary system. A **byte** is a sequence of bits and is equivalent to a character. Depending on the protocol or transmission code, there are different numbers of bits in a byte. For example, in the Baudot code used in some Teletype machines, there are five bits to a byte or character; in the correspondence code used by the IBM Mag Card I, there are six bits in a byte; in the ASCII mode there are seven bits in a byte; in the EBCDIC mode, there are eight bits in a byte. Since binary digits or bits are expressed in 0's and 1's, a unique combination of 0's and 1's in a byte represents each character of the alphabet. For example, an upper case "A" is represented by 11000001 in EBCDIC (note the eight bits); whereas an upper case "A" is represented by 1000001 in ASCII with seven bits.

The EBCDIC mode is synchronous transmission. For example, suppose the transmission speed is 2400 bps (bits per second) synchronous transmission. This translates to a transmission speed of 300 characters per second (2400, the baud rate in bits per second, divided by eight, the number of bits in an EBCDIC byte or character).

Most communicating units must also check for accuracy of transmission; this is called **parity check**.

Character Set. It is important to have all the characters needed to transmit data in all forms. All alphabetical characters, both upper and lower case, numbers, symbols, and word processing codes are important for transmission. The greater the number of bits in a byte, the greater the number of characters available for the character set. Let us take a look at this. Since bits and bytes are usually thought of

Figure 9.10. Derivation of transmission codes.

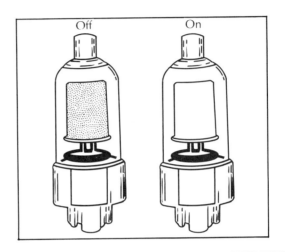

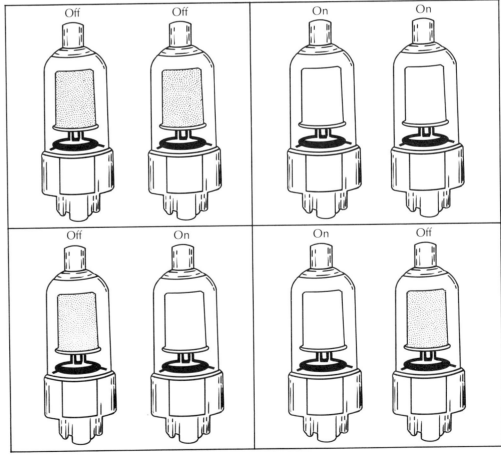

9.   Physical and Electronic Distribution Processes

in terms of data processing, we may use a data processing illustration to explain the derivation of character sets. The computer initially used vacuum tubes, so let us use vacuum tubes for the example. Think of one vacuum tube as one bit. See Figure 9.10. Notice that in the first square there is a vacuum tube shown as off and on. Because one vacuum tube has two states—off and on—it can represent two possible pieces of information, say a two-character alphabet. Now, think of two vacuum tubes or bits with two states—off and on—and the four conditions that can be derived—both off, both on, one off and one on, and the reverse of the one off and one on. These different configurations represent four possible pieces of information or a four-character alphabet. The number of pieces of information or characters in the alphabet will geometrically progress each time. If the example were extended to three vacuum tubes or bits with the possible configurations, an eight-character alphabet could be derived; with four vacuum tubes or bits, 16 characters; with five, 32 characters; with six vacuum tubes or bits, 64 characters; with seven vacuum tubes or bits, 128 characters; with eight vacuum tubes or bits, 256 characters; and so on. Therefore, the greater the number of bits the greater the amount of information that can be transmitted.

Speed of Transmission. The equipment must send and receive at the same speed for the transmission of characters to be accurate. For example, a communicating WP system that sends at 10 characters per second cannot work accurately with one which sends at 150 characters per second.

Direction Flow. Direction flow refers to the direction of transmission (Figure 9.11). **Simplex** means communications flow in only one direction. **Half-duplex** means that data transmission can occur in only one direction at any given time (send or receive). *Full-duplex* allows transmission to occur in both directions simultaneously (send and receive).

simplex
half-duplex

Noncompatible Equipment

Talk among machines using different protocols, speeds, and codes is something like two persons speaking in different languages. Communication is nonexistent or at least garbled.

Facsimile vendors have standardized transmission speeds which enables some previously incompatible units to talk.

TWX/Telex, both products of Western Union, also have no difficulty.

There are easily over 100 models of WP equipment. The functions, the way a machine operates, the media, and the codes used to key these functions differ from one system to another. Each vendor has designed a system he/she feels will best serve customers' needs. Many users, however, are demanding compatibility so that they can send documents from different WP systems, edit and revise them, and send them back. Unfortunately, this is an extremely complex issue because to interface

Figure 9.11. Direction flow.

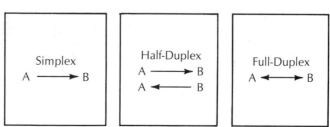

two WP systems, the manufacturer must analyze every feature and code of each model. Multiply that by over 100 models with many different options, and the economics of the problem seem unworkable. An international committee is working on the resolution of this problem.

There are some present alternatives available to users of WP equipment. Each has its limitations. Let us consider the various possibilities.

1. Computer software can be written and implemented for connecting WP systems with different codes and protocols.

2. A protocol translator or black box (Figure 9.12) can be acquired for the major manufacturers. This translates the coding structure of the sending machine into the code used by the receiving device.

3. A service bureau's software interface provides a way to input from one WP device and output to another through telecommunications links with a computer.

4. OCR is used to scan a printed document into another WP system.

Experts seem to agree that there is no existing approach that ensures 100 percent data transfer accuracy with incompatible equipment. Editing must be done at the receiving end to clean up the document or at least its format. However, a number of industry standard groups are working on the problem and are optimistic that there will be easier solutions in the future.

Cost and Other Factors

Also of primary consideration in the design of a telecommunications system is the cost of the transmission and the equipment features necessary to accomplish the organization's telecommunications goals. The cost of transmission is frequently dependent upon the speed of transmission, since long distance rates account for much of the cost. Other factors of cost are equipment and facilities. Organizations are appointing and training key personnel in telecommunications systems design and

Figure 9.12. Racal-Telesystems 303 Protocol Translator, an interface device that provides for telecommunications between data and word processing equipment having different protocols and formats. Courtesy of Racal-Telesystems, Inc.

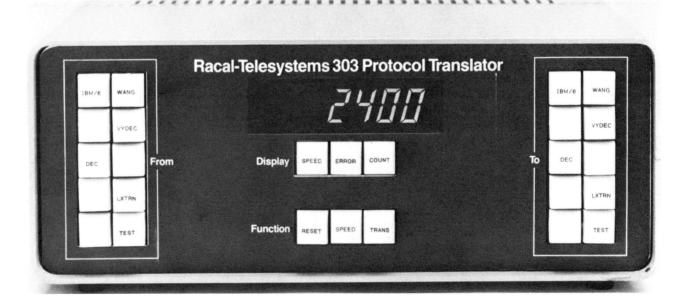

operation. Knowing and using the appropriate method for the specific applications is not only cost effective, but also beneficial to the operations of the organization.

Carriers

There are three kinds of carriers of telecommunications: common, specialized, and satellite. American Telephone and Telegraph and Western Union are common carriers, since they are government regulated telephone and telegraph companies. International Telephone and Telegraph and RCA are specialized carriers. Satellite carriers include Western Union, among others.

Telephone. The telephone line is the product of our common carriers. Most information today is still transmitted over telephone lines, although increasing amounts of microwave, fiber optics, and laser technologies are being employed by the common carriers to increase the service in a cost effective manner. Far more conversations can be transmitted over a laser beam than over pairs of copper cable. Because of the small diameter of fiber optics, copper cable is being pulled and replaced by fiber optics.

Bandwidth is the difference between high and low frequencies of a transmission band, described in cycles per second (Hertz). For example, the bandwidth used to transmit voice over telephone lines is 300 to 2700 or 3000 hertz; 300 is about the lowest a human ear can hear, and 3000 picks up a satisfactory level in the higher ranges.

TWX/Telex, facsimile, terminal-to-terminal, and terminal-to-computer all transmit documents electronically via telephone lines. Narrow bandwidth is used for teletypewriters (TWX/Telex) and facsimile. Voice grade is used for human conversation and data. Wide band is used for teleconferencing and other image transmission such as Picture Phones. Wide band is the most expensive. These bandwidths use digital information converted to analog since teletypewriters, facsimile, voice, data, and images are in digital form and have to be changed to analog to be able to traverse the telephone lines. Some organizations are beginning to use Dataphone Digital Service, which has recently become available. This service provides a means of transmitting digital information without converting it to analog.

There are two types of lines or networks provided by the telephone company. They are switched or dial-up networks and private networks or leased lines. As the name implies, a dial-up network is just that, pick up the telephone and dial anywhere. A private network is used when an organization wishes to be permanently connected to a branch office on a leased line. The only communication possible on this leased line is between the two offices of the organization.

satellite

Satellite. Telephone lines in some foreign countries are antiquated and working with them is difficult. In some geographic regions, there are insufficient numbers of telephone lines. Organizations which telecommunicate frequently are interested in lowering the costs of transmission. The answers to these difficulties may be **satellites**. For WP applications, satellite communications have the following impact:

1. Low cost, distance-insensitive electronic mail.
2. Faster, higher quality facsimile transmission.
3. Inexpensive data base inquiry via relatively low-cost WP or DP terminals.

There are several satellites orbiting. In 1974 Western Union launched two WESTARS (Figure 9.13). The Westar satellites link to five major earth stations, twenty designated satellite access cities, and five television operation centers within an 8,000-mile transcontinental network.

Figure 9.13. Western Union's Westar IV, a second-generation satellite designed to relay voice, data, video, and facsimile communications to the continental United States, Hawaii, Alaska, Puerto Rico, and the Virgin Islands. Courtesy of Western Union Corporation.

Satellite Business Systems (SBS)

Satellite Business Systems (SBS), which is made up of IBM, Aetna Insurance Company, and Communications Satellite Corporation (COMSAT), is also involved with satellites, as is RCA. SBS launched its first communications satellite, SBS-1, on November 15, 1980, and is offering a variety of advanced communications services which feature telephone communications, computer-to-computer communications, high-speed electronic document communications, and videoteleconferencing. Satellite technology promises to integrate various technologies that are currently incompatible. In addition, satellites will provide significant transmission quality advantages over terrestrial networks; these advantages may be significant with the use of facsimile.

Network Systems Design

network

Some organizations have begun to establish telecommunications **networks**, which are like electronic roadmaps connecting branch locations, the home office, major vendors, regulatory agencies, bidders, and so forth. These networks will be extended as telecommunications continues to grow. There probably are no two alike; however, several types of networks that have been designed and implemented will serve as examples.

Intraorganization

intraorganizational network

Intraorganizational networks are used for telecommunications among branch locations within the organization. An example of this would be an oil company headquartered in Houston, Texas, communicating terminal-to-terminal with its other locations in Emeryville, California; Shreveport, Louisiana; and Gulfport, Mississippi.

Interorganization

interorganizational network

Interorganizational networks are used for terminal-to-terminal or terminal-to-computer telecommunications between two organizations. An example of these applications would be a contractor telecommunicating with subcontractors during a bidding process.

Structured Network

structured network

The **structured network** is used in organizations where executive policies and directives are disseminated regularly and must be communicated quickly. A main office can communicate directly with each of the branch offices. Terminal-to-terminal telecommunications may be established for this purpose, but terminal-to-computer telecommunications probably has a more direct application. A main office can input into the computer the policy or directive for each of the branch offices for which it is intended and then activate the message signal on each branch office's electronic mailbox, the computer terminal. Each branch office can then simply call up the computer to receive the message and implement the directive.

Message Switching

message switching

Message switching or store-and-forward is being used more and more to provide timely data. A computer is at the heart of the network. Using a terminal or WP system, a message is keyboarded with instructions to whom it is to go. The computer alerts the recipient's mail file that a message is on hold. When a network user wants to "read the mail," he signs on to the computer and requests messages. Several commercial networks exist that provide this service.

Practical electronic transfer systems can replace a great deal of our paper society. Inventories or orders for goods can be sent through computer networks as purchases are made and registered on computer terminals.

Another form of message switching is that of computer teleconferencing, a system of ongoing information exchange, problem solving, and discussion via computer. A system for computerized conferencing has three basic elements: the computer, the terminals, and the network among terminals. An individual wishing to conference types the message into a terminal, edits it, and sends it to the receiver over the telephone.

An important consideration in networks design is that of 24-hour availability across time zones. It is important that many U.S. organizations be able to send and receive communications to and from Europe even though the time difference exists. Most telecommunications equipment can be set up to receive after hours unattended for this purpose. The feature by which an electronics typing system may receive text

automatic answer

unattended is **automatic answer** (Figure 9.14).

The problem is clear: business must stop moving paper and begin moving information. Telecommunications has significantly broadened the concept of an international economy and narrowed the distance around the world. In this decade much record handling will be electronic.

Tele-communications Procedures

Like all phases of the industry, telecommunications is as dependent, if not more dependent, on procedures as on hardware for success with electronic mail. Section 1.16 of the User's Procedures Manual demonstrates some of the important points to be considered in telecommunicating.

Many organizations designate specific personnel as telecommunications specialists and set up their equipment with all the necessary features. These individuals

Figure 9.14. This IBM Office System 6 is set up to receive unattended outside normal working hours when telephone rates are lower. Bisynchronous data can be transmitted and received at speeds of up to 2400 bits per second, depending upon the modem selected. Courtesy of IBM Corporation.

have a significant amount of responsibility. They, as well as the users, need specific procedures. Their manual should include a form such as the Resident Telecommunications Equipment form shown in the User's Procedures Manual, Section 1.16.9. This form gives all necessary information about the receiving party. The request from the user should be in writing on a job request form such as the one shown in Section 1.16. There should be no question about the authorization of the communication nor the time communication is requested. Priorities of transmission should take into account the timeliness requirement of the document, the lowest telephone rates, and after hours equipment availability. A telecommunications calendar, shown in Section 1.16.9 of the procedures manual, is an aid to remembering scheduled periodic communications. Verification of all messages sent or received is noted on the telecommunications log.

Time and cost savings are very important to most users and examples of both are shown in the manual. Format information in Section 1.16.11 enables the receiving WP specialist to print the document for its recipient just as the author approved it. Security becomes increasingly important, and a procedure for security (Section 1.16.10) is essential.

Records Management Through Micrographics

There are three images in today's office. These are:

Image	Form
Videoimage	CRT—media
Paper	Hard copy
Microforms	Microfilm, microfiche, and aperture card

Although paper today is very much a part of the working environment, many managers are asking for at least less paper if not the paperless office. While a project is in the working stage, some people still like to work with its documentation on paper. However, when the project is beyond the working stage and documentation is not used so frequently, an alternative may be preferable. Figure 9.15 shows the options. Considering the cost of manual filing, floor space, and file cabinets, there can be only occasional justification for retaining on a permanent basis the hard copy of a document. If the goal is to be as cost effective as possible, hard copies will not be used; instead, magnetic media and micrographics will provide an excellent records management program. Certainly any document keyboarded and stored can be accessed through the CRT for reference or printed on hard copy.

What about incoming documents? What about outgoing documents that need to show a signature? For these documents micrographics is a viable alternative.

Micrographics

micrographics

Micrographics is the process of recording and storing permanent records on film in miniaturized form. Since it is considered legal documentation, micrographics is being used more and more by industry, especially for incoming documents. The largest portion of micrographics users is financial institutions.

The ways in which micrographic records are stored are called microforms (Figure 9.16). The three types are microfilm, microfiche, and aperture cards.

Micrographics has become popular for many reasons. Storage space is reduced considerably; records on microfilm take as little as 2 percent of the space needed for the same records on paper. Film is more permanent than paper. Because of the

computer-assisted retrieval (CAR)

computer's indexing system used with micrographics **(computer-assisted retrieval, CAR)** retrieval is easier and faster. Microforms are less expensive to send through

Figure 9.15. Images and their forms in today's office.

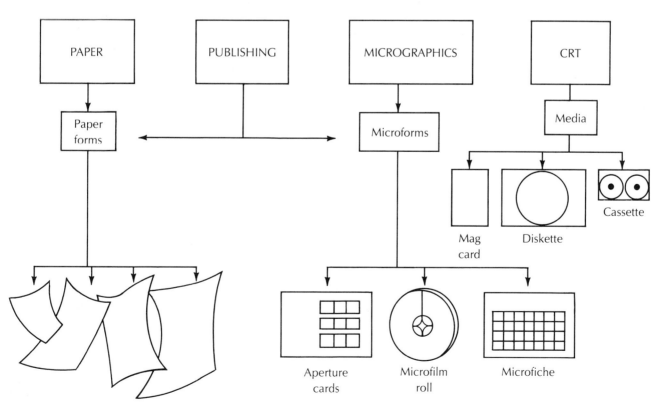

Figure 9.16. Microforms—microfilm, microfiche, and aperture cards. Courtesy of 3M Micrographic Products Division.

the mail in quantity then hard copy. Both paper and film copies are easy to duplicate. Documents are not misfiled, mislaid, or lost, because of fixed sequential filming. The security of documents is easier to maintain with micrographics than with hard copy. Improved customer service is possible thanks to easily accessible records. Information can be captured in just a fraction of a second by a flash of light.

There are also some disadvantages to micrographics. Optical magnifying devices or readers must be used to read the filmed document. Preparation costs are initially more expensive than hard copy files. Unless microfilm jackets or aperture cards are used, records that are in need of frequent updating often require complete refilming.

Microfilm is used for sequentially filmed miniaturized documents and comes in roll, cartridge, film strips, or jacket form. The form used depends on the type of information, how it is to be used, frequency of updates, need for rapid and easy retrieval, and overall cost. Roll film on spools is used primarily for records not requiring frequent reference. Roll film loaded into cartridges or magazines is used for automatic retrieval programs.

Because of the miniaturization, paper storage can be reduced by up to 98 percent; however, an optical magnifying device is required for reading microfilm. It is the most economical of all of the microforms, but documents filmed on roll or cartridge are also the most difficult to access. Microfilm can be 16, 35, or 105 millimeters wide and 100 to 215 feet long. Newspaper libraries use microfilm for easy access and retrieval in conjunction with computers. Each article has a number which is used to locate the story on microfilm. The advantage of having the story on microfilm is that users can see accompanying photographs. In this case, as in most cases, microfilm is black and white. However, some organizations, such as greeting card companies, film in the more expensive color.

A disadvantage of microfilm, except for microfilm jackets, is that if a document needs to be updated or added in sequence, the film will have to be spliced or refilmed.

The film is cut and loaded into jackets. Patient records in hospitals, student records in schools, and police records are examples of uses of jackets duplicated into microfiche for distribution.

A microfiche is a 105 millimeter by 148 millimeter (approximately 4 inch by 6 inch) sheet of film which contains multiple images in a predetermined grid pattern or format and can hold up to 450 data pages. The ability of fiche to accommodate multiple pages of data on a common subject, in one unitized format, makes it well suited to many business applications. Microfiche is easy to duplicate and distribute. Information is easily indexed and retrieved. Updating or adding and deleting information requires splicing the film or refilming. Frequently, the old fiche is discarded and replaced with a new one. Fiche can be interfiled without difficulty. Microfiche viewing devices are the most inexpensive available. An interesting comparison by Dr. William Mitchell, University of Wisconsin, Eau Claire, of a diskette and a microfiche shows that the cost of the diskette is in the $10 range and the cost of a microfiche is 10 cents, although they contain about the same amount of information. Microfiche are often color-coded for ease in identification of units of information.

aperture cards

Aperture cards are cards which have only one or just a few filmed images mounted on them. The process of updating with film is easy since so few images are used per card; a new card can be added or can replace an outdated one. Aperture cards are easier to handle than hard copy. The cards are much smaller than hard copy, particularly if the hard copy is an oversized document such as an engineering drawing. The aperture card is easier to mail than a drawing. Storage space is less. Aperture cards can also be written on, which can be helpful.

Ultrafiche (or ultramicrofiche) was developed by National Cash Register Company using a process called PCMI Microform System. This process permits tremendous reduction rates. For example, over 1,200 printed pages of the Bible are reproduced on about 2 square inches of film.

High-speed, high-quality, easy-to-operate cameras are available to film source documents. The two major types are planetary cameras and rotary cameras. These cameras can film one side of a document at a time or both sides simultaneously. Very little training is required to be able to operate these cameras. Film processors are available to those organizations which wish to develop their own film. Readers and reader/printers are available for viewing and/or printing the microforms.

Computer/Word Processing Output Microfilm

Computer Output Microfilm (COM) (Figure 9.17) is a process that permits information stored in a computer to be converted to roll microfilm or microfiche without first being printed out as hard copy. It also permits immediate retrieval from microfilm. WPOM combines WP systems, computers, and micrographics to produce microforms that are generated directly from the document produced on a WP system and interfaced through the computer using telecommunications to microfilm or microfiche. It eliminates the need to store one or more copies on paper. The manual process of filing the paper is also eliminated. The speed and economy of generating a microform by COM/WPOM surpass the benefits of paper. COM/WPOM also permits the effective and rapid retrieval of information stored in the computer indices. The speed or line rate of the COM/WPOM recorder is approximately 32,000 lines per minute, faster than most equipment used in today's office systems.

Many practices integrating various technologies are being explored. The future of the office information storage and retrieval system suggests an effective network using WP, computers, and micrographics. The benefits appear almost limitless.

Computer Assisted Retrieval

An important concept in the WP/DP-micrographics interface is computer-assisted retrieval (CAR) (Figure 9.18). The computer generates an index of all documents for ease in retrieval. CAR systems can be classified as (1) online index with manual retrieval of full text on microforms and (2) an online index integrated with automatic retrieval of microforms. CAR may be used to retrieve COM-generated microforms as well as source documents filmed, indexed, and added to the microimage library (all those documents stored on micrographics).

Documents manually filmed are assigned an image address by the computer just as are those images generated by COM. The computer then generates an index. This document control minimizes the number of printouts required. It reduces the proliferation of computer paper forms. Information can also be searched by the computer. For example, by keying in physical characteristics of a police suspect, the police can limit the number of suspects with the exact description.

Computer input microfilm (CIM) is a new method of duplicating existing microimages as the source document back into the computer. This has been done on an experimental or custom basis. There is some question as to the marketing potential of reading microfilm data into the computer; because of the historical nature of microfilmed documents, they may not need to be revised frequently.

Figure 9.17. 3M's 720 Series COM system, which provides offline, online, or switchable offline/online communications with a data processing system. Courtesy of 3M Micrographic Products Division.

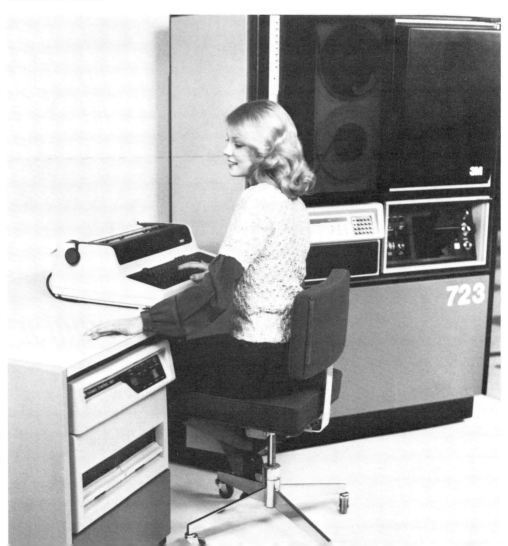

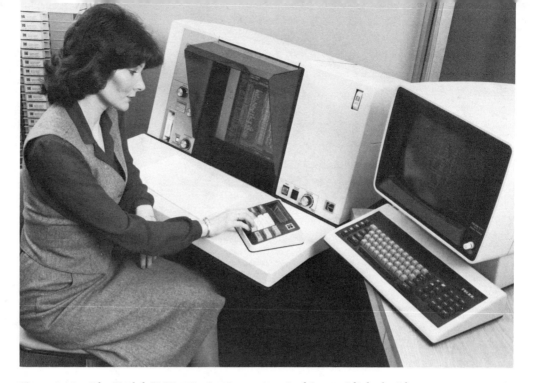

Figure 9.18. The Kodak IMT-150 microimage terminal (center) linked with a computer system automatically finds a specific image from among millions in a microimage file using computer assisted retrieval. Courtesy of Eastman Kodak Company.

Future Trends

The major trend of the 1980s will be the integration of technologies as organizations tie their information functions together. This integration will be due in large part to telecommunications. Telecommunications is a link among many technologies and plays a significant role in the integration of technologies. Greater industry standardization and compatibility will promote extensive integration and the expanded use of telecommunications. Electronic mail, through more and more intricate networks, moves the information farther faster and will be in wide use in the 1980s. Electronic mail systems now in use will become more sophisticated. Currently, mail is communicated in a store-and-forward mode. The user signing on to the system looks through all his messages; he may read all of the messages or only those desired. Future systems may have a more intricate system of establishing priorities and identifying mail.

As the decade progresses, satellites may become the preferred medium for telecommunications rather than telephone lines. The costs of communications with satellites should be reduced significantly. This factor alone will cause organizations to consider implementation. By the end of the 1980s users will be spending billions of dollars per year on electronic mail services and integration of equipment.

The most important elements in future electronic mail networks will be intelligent communicating versions of the office copier, phototypesetter, telephone, computers, and WP systems. Teleconferencing involves sending voices, pictures, or digital messages to one or more remote sites. Meeting rooms, auditoriums, offices, and offices at home will be equipped with the necessary audio/visual/computer facilities. Energy crises and technological innovations may make teleconferencing essential. Instead of traveling long distances for face-to-face meetings, executives will use teleconferences. In fact, the Department of Energy in Washington, D.C., already connects with its Germantown, Maryland, office by videoconferencing. The system will provide many opportunities for savings in travel costs and improved communications in that many who would not be sent to a meeting will be able to attend electronically.

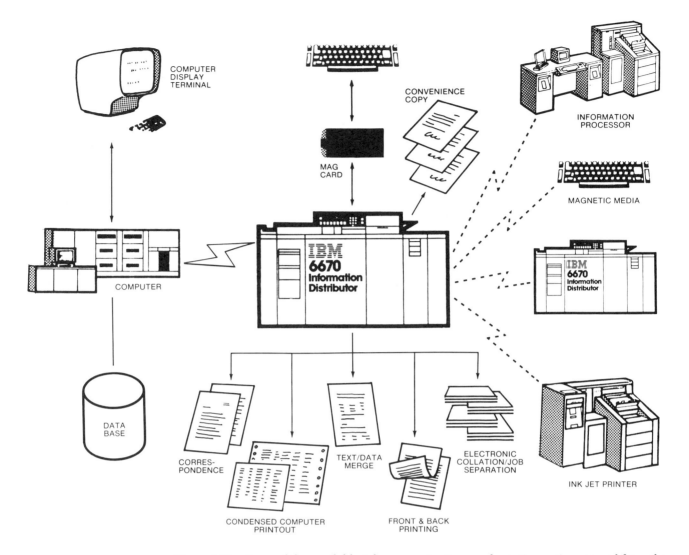

Figure 9.19. Some of the available telecommunications and printing options to and from the IBM 6670 Information Distributor. This information distributor prints with a laser, receives and transmits documents electronically, processes text and data, and can also make convenience copies. Courtesy of IBM Corporation.

Three types of teleconferencing will be available—telephone (audio-linkage through the spoken word), computer (print-based communications through keyboard terminals and store-and-forward systems), and video (both image and sound of participants). Five major studios are planned for videoconferencing and will be available in 1983.

The integration of all technologies will blur the boundaries between the technologies and allow for the continuing convergence of image, voice, text, micrographic, and data technologies.

Summary

Distribution is the mailing, delivering, transmitting, and filing of a document. Since distribution accounts for 74 percent of the time cycle of a document, it may be the most important phase of WP. The two major categories of distribution are physical distribution and electronic distribution. Physical distribution is the delivering or mailing and manual filing of a document. Electronic distribution is the electronic mailing or delivering of a document via telephone or satellite transmission and the electronic filing of the document.

Mail, both U.S. and internal, is time-consuming and increasing in cost. Private carriers provide one alternative.

Manual filing and retention of documents involve the classifying, indexing, filing, and preserving of documents.

Electronic distribution is the electronic transmission of documents via telephone lines, microwaves, hardwired cables, or satellites. Electronic distribution also serves to integrate WP, DP, phototypesetting, voice, OCR, and intelligent copier technologies.

The four major methods of telecommunications are TWX/Telex, facsimile, terminal-to-terminal, and terminal-to-computer. Key factors in telecommunications are equipment compatibility, cost of transmission, and equipment features necessary to accomplish the organization's telecommunications goals.

TWX/Telex are teletypewriter networks used by Western Union. They are relatively slow and the quality of the document received is somewhat poor, but the established network is an important advantage.

Facsimile is the transmission of documents such as charts, graphs, drawings, and pictures, as well as signed and other documents, over telephone lines and satellite.

Terminal-to-terminal telecommunications is the electronic transmission of a document from one communicating WP unit, computer terminal, intelligent copier, or OCR to another. In addition to speed and accuracy, it produces a quality document.

Terminal-to-computer telecommunications is the process of telecommunicating from a communicating WP work station, intelligent copier, or terminal to a computer. Three modes to transmit data are simplex, half-duplex, and full-duplex. Time-shared computer services enable those companies which do not have a computer to use the power of one on a time and space charge basis.

Electronic roadmaps called networks are being developed for telecommunications within and across time zones.

Micrographics is the process of recording and storing permanent records on film in miniaturized form. The three types of microforms are microfilm, microfiche, and aperture cards. Significant improvements are being made in records management capabilities because of computer output microfilm (COM), WP output microfilm (WPOM), computer assisted retrieval (CAR), and computer input microfilm (CIM).

Key Terms

Acoustic coupler
Aperture card
Asynchronous
Automatic answer
Batched
Baud
Baudot
Bisynchronous
Bit
Block of characters
Byte
Compatibility of equipment
Computer-assisted retrieval (CAR)
Correspondence code
Courier service
Data access arrangement (DAA)
Distribution
Duplex

Electronic data transfer
Electronic distribution
Electronic document distribution
Electronic filing
Electronic mail
Extended binary coded decimal internal code (EBCDIC)
Facsimile
Half-duplex
Integration
Internal carrier
Interorganizational network
Intraorganizational network
Manual filing
Message switching
Micrographics
Modem
Multidrop line

Multipoint line
Network
Parity check
Physical distribution
Point-to-point
Private carrier
Protocol
Satellite
Satellite Business Systems (SBS)
Simplex
Structured network
Synchronization technique
Synchronous
Systems Network Architecture (SNA)
Teleprocessing
Terminal-to-computer
Terminal-to-terminal
TWX/Telex
Value added

Completion
1. Telecommunications is also called _____, _____, and _____.
2. The two major benefits of telecommunications are _____ and _____.
3. The name of the telephone connecting device used in telecommunicating a document using facsimile is _____.
4. Point-to-point telecommunications is also called _____.
5. The most important consideration in designing a point-to-point telecommunications network is _____.
6. The modem converts digital coding to _____ in order for the message to be sent over the telephone wires.
7. If an organization cannot afford its own computer, it may choose to contract with a _____.
8. _____ is the telecommunications network used between branch locations of an organization using point-to-point telecommunications.
9. Aperture cards hold _____ images.
10. COM is the acronym for _____ and is used for cost-effective storage for data not often updated.
11. The two categories of distribution are _____ and _____.
12. The major problems associated with mail are _____ and _____.
13. The distribution phase consumes _____ percent of the time cycle of a document.
14. Two alternatives to the U.S. mail are _____ and _____.
15. Internal mail accounts for _____ percent of all mail.

Short Answer
1. Name two disadvantages of internal carriers.
2. Name two advantages of electronic mail.
3. Name three examples of private carriers.
4. Name the most expensive form of mail delivery.
5. Name two problems associated with manual filing.

Exercises

Exercise 9.1. Read two articles in WP journals about networks that have been established by organizations for their communications. Write a one-page summary and describe organizational advantages.

Exercise 9.2. Visit an organization that uses a network. Discuss the benefits of the network to the organization, who in the organization participates, any difficulties that have been encountered, and the physical technique of document transmission. What equipment is used? Who performs the actual transmissions? When are documents transmitted? What are the geographic locations?

Case Problem

Turner, Ltd., has recently expanded its operations to include Texas, California, Minnesota, and Louisiana. Mr. Hughes, the president, is concerned about the availability of information to all offices as well as the capability to telecommunicate documents to offices in distant cities for clients. Since it is a WP/telecommunications service center used by many organizations, it is important to have the capability to transmit documents, charts, engineering drawings, and so forth quickly and accurately.

Mr. Hughes expects that many new executive policies will have to be made and disseminated since the organization is in a growth mode. WP systems with CRTs and diskette media are now used for WP. A computer is used for backup storage of permanent documents.

What methods can be used for simple transfer of keyboarded documents? Will additional equipment need to be installed for this? What are your recommendations for telecommunications equipment and network design?

Part IV   Arnco, Incorporated

****

USER'S PROCEDURES MANUAL

Table of Contents

1. General Information

1.1 Purpose and Function

Arnco, Inc., is an administrative support and word/information processing service utilizing word processing, reprographics, and telecommunications equipment to process the written communications of its clients. We are open and staffed for your convenience from 8:00 A.M. to 11:00 P.M. Monday through Saturday. The dial-in dictation service operates 24 hours a day. Please call on us for assistance with any secretarial, clerical, or telephone answering tasks, or with production, duplication, phototypesetting, and telecommunications of any written communications.

The input for these communications may be rough draft, handwritten, dictated via the telephone dictation system, or typed for OCR. As Arnco, Inc., keyboards the documents, they are stored on magnetic media. Once this has been done, only the revised material will be retyped, not the entire document. Arnco, Inc., has a filing system for storing the magnetic media for easy retrieval.

The following services are offered by Arnco, Inc.:

1. Production of professional typewritten or phototypeset documents.
2. Fast revision of stored documents.
3. Alphabetical and numerical file sorting and manipulation.
4. Repetitive correspondence.
5. Editing-proofreading.
6. Transcription of taped material.
7. Dictation from any telephone in the world.
8. Multiple, low-cost duplicating.
9. Telecommunications to offices anywhere in the world (with appropriate equipment).
10. Retention of all documents on magnetic media and computer backup storage.
11. Free pickup and delivery.
12. Courier service within a 50-mile radius of the office.
13. Mail service—U.S., international.
14. Telephone answering service.
15. Miscellaneous clerical duties.

1.2 Staff

The owner and president of Arnco, Inc., sells Arnco, Inc., administrative support and word/information processing services to new clients, maintains a positive rapport with existing clients, and, with the assistance of the supervisor, expands and updates services and equipment. The supervisor functions as a controlling agent for the work done, setting priorities and coordinating equipment and staff capabilities with the users' needs. The supervisor makes the final check on all documents, in order to ensure completeness.

The editor-proofreader proofreads all documents processed by Arnco, Inc. The editor-proofreader is responsible for the consistency of format and accuracy of each document, including spelling, capitalization, and punctuation. When requested to do so by the user, the editor-proofreader is also responsible for word usage and grammar of the document.

The word processing specialists keyboard, program, format, print, and telecommunicate documents, using sophisticated word processing and dictation equipment. A permanent backup filing system is maintained on a time-shared computer service contracted by Arnco, Inc.

The duplicating specialist is responsible for reproducing copies as specified by the client. This job includes making decisions regarding the appropriate process for quality, quantity, and cost effectiveness in the time available. Auxiliary services such as phototypesetting, binding, collating, and stapling are also provided by the duplicating specialist. The duplicating specialist maintains supplies and orders special paper and other supply requests.

The distribution specialist delivers completed documents to clients, mails them through U.S. or international mails, or provides courier service to the clients within a 50-mile radius of the office.

The receptionist greets all clients and directs them to the supervisor if they are bringing in new work or to the appropriate word processing specialist, duplicating specialist, editor-proofreader, or distribution specialist if they are inquiring about a document in progress. In addition, several of our clients contract with Arnco, Inc., for telephone coverage after hours or when no one is in their office; the receptionist is responsible for answering these calls on a computerized switchboard. All telephone messages are entered on administrative terminals located at the receptionist's and clients' desks. These messages can be quickly accessed from the administrative terminal upon a client's return to the office. This system provides personalized and accurate telephone service. The receptionist also performs miscellaneous clerical duties for clients and Arnco, Inc. These client services are contracted and billed individually depending on the task. Arnco, Inc., clerical services include ordering of supplies and placing of service calls.

The accounting clerk bills all clients for services rendered, pays all Arnco, Inc., invoices, calculates and writes all payroll checks, and prepares data for the CPA who completes all state and federal tax forms.

1.3 Equipment

Arnco, Inc., has the following equipment:

1. Centralized dictation system.
2. Word/information processing systems.
3. Intelligent copier.
4. Phototypesetting system.
5. Telecommunications.
6. Time-share computer service.

1.4 Supplies

Arnco, Inc., will supply the following:

1. 8½ in. × 11 in. 20 lb. white bond for all reports and manuscripts.
2. 8½ in. × 14 in. 20 lb. green bond for all rough drafts.
3. 8½ in. × 14 in. 20 lb. white bond.
4. Number 10 plain white envelopes.
5. Numbered pleadings paper.

Arnco, Inc.'s, clients supply all other stationery, such as company letterhead, envelopes, continuous-form paper, and so forth. Consulting services are available for letterhead design, and other stationery needs. Arnco, Inc., equipment capabilities for paper range from 16 lb. to 90 lb. and sizes of 5½ in. to 14 in. in width, 5½ in. to 24 in. in length.

1.5 Work Flow

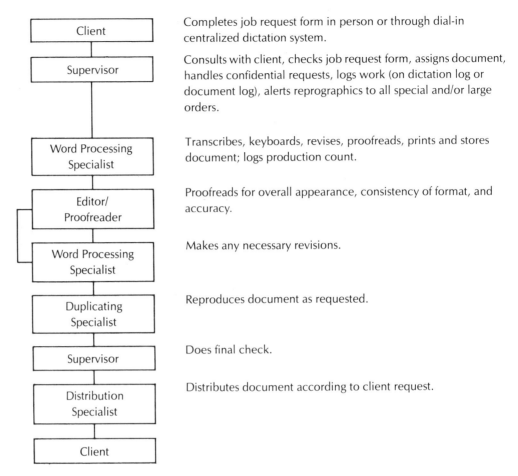

Client	Completes job request form in person or through dial-in centralized dictation system.
Supervisor	Consults with client, checks job request form, assigns document, handles confidential requests, logs work (on dictation log or document log), alerts reprographics to all special and/or large orders.
Word Processing Specialist	Transcribes, keyboards, revises, proofreads, prints and stores document; logs production count.
Editor/ Proofreader	Proofreads for overall appearance, consistency of format, and accuracy.
Word Processing Specialist	Makes any necessary revisions.
Duplicating Specialist	Reproduces document as requested.
Supervisor	Does final check.
Distribution Specialist	Distributes document according to client request.
Client	

Figure 1. Work Flow.

1.6 Job Request Form

A job request form (Figure 2) is initiated for each work assignment by the supervisor, either through consultation with the client or through instructions on dictated material. If you have special format requirements, the supervisor will be happy to discuss them with you.

If you will need the document on special paper or in a particular format, please let us know so that the initial setup will be appropriate.

1.7 Document Priorities

Requests are processed in this order:

1. Rush requests.
2. Revisions.
3. Routine requests. All routine requests are processed according to date and time required on a first-come, first-served basis. Special needs should be discussed with the supervisor as far in advance as possible.

1.7.1 Overtime. All overtime must be scheduled by the supervisor.

1.7.2 Rush Requests. All rushes will be given priority if possible. If a client's deadline cannot be met, the supervisor will contact the client for direction. An

Submitted: Date _____ Time _____ **Log Number** _____

Requested: Date _____ Time _____

Client: _____

Company Contact: _____ **Phone** _____ **Extension** _____

Special Instructions: _____

INPUT		FORMAT		EQUIPMENT		DISTRIBUTION	
Dictation	___	Left margin	___	Information processor	___	Client	___
Longhand	___	Right margin	___	Text editor	___	Express mail	___
Copytype	___	First line	___	OCR	___	Facsimile	___
OCR	___	Last line	___	Phototypesetter	___	U.S. Mail	___
Original	___	Line spacing	___	Typeface	___	Courier	___
Revision	___	Type style	___	Type size	___	Telecommunicate	___
Number of author		Adjust	___				
revisions	___	Justify	___	**MEDIA**		**BILLING**	
				Card number	___	Completed lines	___
STATIONERY		**DUPLICATING PROCESS**		Disk number	___	Completed pages	___
Letterhead	___	Number of originals	___	Job name	___	Editing	___
Envelopes	___	Number of copies	___			Duplicating	___
Furnished by client	___	Collate	___	**DESCRIPTION OF**		Processing time	___
Color paper (specify)	___	Staple	___	**WORK**		Turnaround time	___
8½″ × 11″ bond	___	Bind	___	Draft	___	Word processing	___
8½″ × 14″ bond	___	Three-hole punch	___	Final	___	Temporary storage	___
Paper weight	___	Carbons	___	Memo	___	Permanent storage	___
Other ___		Photocopier	___	Letter	___		
		Offset	___	Envelopes	___	**COPIES**	
EDITING		Spirit duplicator	___	Rep. correspondence	___	White: Word processing	
Punctuation	___	Mimeograph	___	Text	___	Yellow: Client	
Grammar	___	Printer	___	Forms	___	Pink: Duplicating	
Word usage	___			Statistical	___		
Format	___			File/sort	___		
All	___			Document assembly	___		
Proofread only	___						

Figure 2. Job Request Form.

additional charge of 10 percent will be added to all rush requests of five pages or less, 20 percent to requests six pages and over.

1.7.3 Revision.   All revision requests are completed on a first-come, first-served basis. Revisions resulting from Arnco, Inc., error will be given the same priority as rush work and will be reprocessed without charge.

1.8 Turnaround, Pickup, and Delivery Time

You can expect a turnaround time of four hours for documents to be produced by word processing that are one to five pages in length. Turnaround time on longer documents should be discussed with the supervisor. If you are working on a long document that you will be submitting in parts to ensure faster completion time, please make the supervisor aware of this to ensure consistency throughout the document.

A general guideline of turnaround time for duplicated documents is as follows:

Number of Originals	Copies Requested	Turnaround Time
1–5	1–100	Up to 1 hour
6–25	1–100	1–4 hours
26–75	1–100	1–8 hours
76–200	1–100	1–16 hours
Binding	1–100	1–24 hours
Graphics (each)		8+ hours
Photocomposition		16+ hours

The distribution specialist picks up and delivers documents on a scheduled basis at 8:00 A.M. and 2:00 P.M.

Scheduled transmission times for telecommunicating documents are 8:00 A.M., 12:00 noon, 5:15 P.M., and 11:30 P.M. Unless otherwise specified, documents will be transmitted at 11:30 P.M. when least expensive telephone rates apply. A rush transmission can be made if necessary.

1.9 Word Processing Applications

Word processing systems produce high-quality documents uniform in appearance. Many different types of documents especially appeal to the capabilities of the system. Some of these are:

1.9.1 Revisions. When a document is originally typed at Arnco, Inc., it is stored on magnetic media. Since the paper copy is used to mark revisions, it is important that the client use the latest and most exact copy.

Since the only retyping necessary is the actual revisions, clients will save considerable time in reproofing the document. The word/information processing system can move material within a page or from one page to another, insert and delete material, change margins and type styles, or adjust page length, all without retyping.

When revising, please observe the following procedures:

1. Mark the hard copy with a red pen or pencil to show insertions, deletions, and moved text. Use proofreading marks shown in Figure 3. Do not use liquid correction fluid. Do not cut and paste. Rearranged material can be completed easier and faster with marked copy.

2. If you have multiple inserts, please number them and show the number at the location of insertions.

3. If you have questions, please work with us to facilitate timesaving techniques for fast revisions.

1.9.2 Repetitive Correspondence. Many businesspeople have found that they create many of their documents from previously existing documents or that they often send a similar letter or memo to a number of people. These are both ideal word processing applications as the text is stored and need not be retyped. The portion of the document to be reused is simply copied in the new document.

1.9.3 Complex Documents. Time spent retyping complex text such as statistics, equations, and logs can be significantly reduced using word processing. This is especially true for text which includes Greek, mathematical, or technical symbols or a variety of type styles.

1.9.4 File/Sort, Alphabetically and Numerically. The word/information processing equipment allows any list to be typed once, but produced in part or total in a variety of ways—zip code order, alphabetically, numerically, by geographical region. The information may be updated by insertions, deletions, or changes. The files can be used to output labels, reports, envelopes, and lists. These files or lists can be merged with other text to create letters and reports.

1.10 Editing-Proofreading

An editor-proofreader is available for consultation in the writing of documents. He/she is qualified to improve grammar, style, and consistency. Every document is proofread for errors in typing, consistency, format, spelling, and punctuation.

Mark	Explanation	Example	Revised Copy
$\wedge$	Insert	if $\wedge$ is	if it is
✐	Delete	if it is	it is
stet	Leave as originally written	*stet* if it is	if it is
✐	Delete character	go too it	go to it
◯	Spell out	to ⓌⓅ	to word processing
/	Use lower case	to Ǥo	to go
⌐	Move left	⌐This is	This is
⌐	Move right	⌐ This is	This is
≡	Caps	doctor Jones	Doctor Jones
∼	Transpose	si impossible	is impossible
⊙	Period	soon⊙He	soon. He
⋏	Comma	after the meeting⋏he	after the meeting, he
⋏	Semicolon	Proofread carefully⋏ errors are costly.	Proofread carefully; errors are costly.
⓪	Colon	Note the following⓪	Note the following:
✓	Apostrophe	Word processings benefits	Word processing's benefits
⋏	Dash	Word processing⋏a cost effective	Word processing--a cost effective
✓	Add superscript	x y	x^2y
	Add subscript	$CO_2$is	CO_2 is
‖	Align vertically	‖He will ‖ tomorrow	He will tomorrow
=	Align horizontally	He will tomorrow	He will tomorrow
⌗	Make new paragraph	soon⌗He will	soon. He will
no ⌗	No paragraph	*no* ⌗ office costs. Data can be	office costs. Data can be
___	Underscore	Go home!	Go home!
⊐⊏	Center	⊐Data⊏	Data
ss	Single space	The document is *ss* complete	The document is complete
ds	Double space	*ds* The document is complete	The document is complete
ts	Triple space	*ts* The document is complete	The document is complete
⌒	Close up	wo⌒rd	word
/⌗	Insert space	word/processing	word processing

Figure 3. Editing/Proofreading Marks.

1.11 Type Styles

A variety of type styles and sizes is available in typewritten and phototypeset copy. Phototypesetting allows for many different type sizes and typefaces. Please take advantage of the opportunities of this service for brochures, reports, and promotional materials.

1.12 Confidential or Classified Documents

All security or confidential requests will be processed, produced, and distributed by the supervisor personally. There is no admittance to confidential files by anyone other than the supervisor or owner/president.

1.13 OCR

There may be some documents better or easier typed in rough draft in a client's office and sent to Arnco, Inc., to be finished and produced. Documents keyboarded with an OCR recognizable type font in the client's office will be completed much more quickly since Arnco, Inc., will not have to keyboard them initially. This method of input is excellent for rush or special documents.

Documents can then be scanned to make any necessary revisions, printed, and stored on magnetic media. Documents that we do not keyboard on a single-element typewriter using an OCR recognizable type font are those with equations. Documents with equations are keyboarded directly on the word processing system.

1.13.1 Typing for OCR. To ensure good results, follow these rules for typewriter setup:

1. Use an OCR recognizable type font.
2. Use a good quality carbon ribbon.
3. Move the multiple copy lever on the typewriter to the *A* position.
4. Set the impression control lever for even character impressions with no broken or tailing characters.
5. Do not change the vertical line spacing while typing a page. Do not move the platen manually once you have begun typing the page.
6. Do not change the pitch while typing a page.
7. Use 16 lb. to 24 lb. smooth, flawless solid color bond or copier paper, without a watermark. To determine whether paper has a watermark, hold one sheet up to a strong light. A visible brand name or symbol is the watermark.
8. Use ½ in. left and right margins and 1 in. top and bottom margins.
9. Arnco, Inc.'s, OCR reader/scanner does not underline. Edit all copy for underlining so that it will be done on the word processing system.

1.13.2 Corrections Using OCR. A less than symbol (<) or a vertical bar (|) are the two typewriter symbols used for deletions. The vertical bar is used to overstrike a character to delete the character under it. For example, *thaǿn* will be read by the OCR reader/scanner as *than*.

Less than symbols (<) are used to delete the preceding character, word, or line. One symbol (<) deletes the previous character; two symbols (< <) delete the previous word; three symbols (< < <) delete the entire line. A line drawn carefully with a No. 2 black lead pencil can be used to delete all unwanted characters; the crossed out characters will be dropped as the OCR reader/scanner reads the page of type.

1.13.3 Editing on OCR. After the page is removed from the typewriter, make editing marks, insertions, and so forth in red felt or nylon tip pen. Any notes for the revision on the word processing system should be written in the top, bottom, or side margins.

1.13.4 Scanning the Text Using the OCR Reader/Scanner. Arnco, Inc., will set the reader/scanner for the appropriate pitch, page length, and vertical spacing for the document. Using the telecommunications capabilities of the OCR reader/scanner and word processing system, we will scan the document onto the magnetic media.

1.13.5 Final Production on WP System. For all revisions that you have marked, Arnco, Inc., will access the points of revision and make all necessary insertions, deletions, and changes. Arnco, Inc., will proofread and print a final copy of the document according to client specifications. It will be stored on the client's diskette for future reference.

1.14 Media Storage and Retention

Arnco, Inc., offers a media storage and retention service that reduces or eliminates the clients' needs for extensive manual filing systems. Any documents electronically stored are accessible to clients for copies or revision Monday through Saturday, 8:00 A.M. to 11:00 P.M.

1.14.1 Temporary Storage. All documents are recorded and stored on magnetic media (card, diskette, or cassette) for a period of five days. After the fifth day, the media is recycled. Any client may request an extended storage of media by checking permanent storage on the job request form.

1.14.2 Permanent Storage. Documents stored permanently by client request will be retained on diskette and backed up by storage on our computer. In order to keep storage service charges at a minimum, the Arnco, Inc., supervisor will contact clients once each quarter to verify the clients' desires for continued storage.

1.15 Duplicating

1.15.1 Available Methods of Reproduction. Any document keyboarded is automatically printed out with two carbon copies. In addition to the carbon process, which can make five legible copies, Arnco, Inc., provides the following duplicating processes.

1. *Photocopying.* This is the highest quality method of duplicating with the least expenditure of manpower. It is also the most expensive. Arnco Inc., equipment has the capability to duplex, staple, collate, and copy on 8½ in. × 11 in. and 8½ in. × 14 in. paper ranging from 16 lb. to 70 lb. weights in black print only. This is an excellent method for fast turnaround, high quality, collation, and documents with multiple originals.

2. *Offset.* This is an especially cost effective process for high-volume, high-quality copies. The equipment has the capability to duplex on a variety of sizes (3 in. × 5 in. to 8½ in. × 14 in.) of paper from 20 lb. to 110 lb. weight. It is an excellent method given a turnaround time of at least six hours. Colored ink on colored paper gives some variety to promotional documents.

3. *Spirit.* This is an inexpensive, medium-quality process for low-volume (25 to 200 copies) requests. This method is most frequently used for informal, in-house

documents. The equipment has the capacity for 8½ in. × 11 in. and 8½ in. × 14 in. 16 lb. to 20 lb. paper with red, green, blue, black, and purple masters.

4. *Mimeograph.* This is an inexpensive process for medium-quality, high-volume (25 to 3,000) copies. This is a method often used for in-house, informal communications. The equipment has the capacity for 3 in. × 5 in. to 8½ in. × 14 in. 16 lb. to 70 lb. paper with ink in primary colors.

1.15.2 Choosing a Method of Reproduction. The method of duplicating will generally be specified by the client. If not, the supervisor will consult the client to make a decision based on turnaround time required, quality and volume desired, and cost.

1.15.3 Photocomposition. Arnco, Inc., provides phototypesetting of documents. The ability to choose from a variety of type faces and sizes as well as to use italics within the text is appealing to clients. Arnco, Inc., uses a combination method of producing documents using photocomposition; the word processing specialist keyboards the text and the duplicating specialist converts it to phototypesetting.

The type faces and sizes from which a client may choose are shown in Figure 4.

1.15.4 Binding. Arnco, Inc., uses the following methods to bind documents.

Figure 4. Type Sizes and Styles.

Americana	Avant Garde Demi Bold Condensed
Americana Italic	**Avant Garde Bold**
Americana Bold	**Avant Garde Bold Condensed**
Americana Extra Bold	Baskerville
American Typewriter Light	*Baskerville Italic*
American Typewriter Light Condensed	**Baskerville Bold**
American Typewriter Medium	***Baskerville Bold Italic***
American Typewriter Medium Condensed	Bauhaus Light
American Typewriter Bold	Bauhaus Medium
American Typewriter Bold Condensed	Bauhaus Demi Bold
Antique Olive Light	**Bauhaus Bold**
Antique Olive	Benguiat Book
Antique Olive Italic	*Benguiat Book Italic*
Antique Olive Bold	Benguiat Medium
Antique Olive Black	*Benguiat Medium Italic*
Aster	**Benguiat Bold**
Aster Italic	***Benguiat Bold Italic***
Aster Bold	Bembo
Auriga	*Bembo Italic*
Auriga Italic	**Bembo Bold**
Auriga Bold	Bodoni Book
Avant Garde Extra Light	*Bodoni Book Italic*
Avant Garde Book	**Bodoni Bold**

1. Stapling.
2. Three-hole punching and enclosing in binders.
3. Metal spiral binding.
4. Plastic spiral binding.

Stapling is done automatically and is least expensive. A maximum of 50 pages can be used.

Three-hole punching and enclosing reports and manuals in binders is a popular choice with clients. Lead time may be required for ordering binders. A variety of colors and sizes is available.

Metal spiral binding is available in a variety of styles. Lead time may also be required for ordering the binding materials.

Plastic binding is available in a variety of colors. Lead time to order the binding materials may be necessary since our supply is limited. Plastic binding is not recommended for documents exceeding 200 pages in length.

1.15.5 Chargeback Costs. The following chart lists current charges.

	Number of Originals	*Number of Copies*	*Cost per Copy*
Photocopy	1–50	1–100	$0.06
	51–150	1–10	.06
	51–150	10–50	.05
	51–150	50+	.04
	151+	1–25	.06
	151+	25+	.05
	Duplex, subtract		10%
Offset	1–2	50–100	$0.03
	1–2	100–500	.02
	1–2	500+	.015
	3+	100–500	.015
	3+	500+	.01
	Duplex, subtract		10%
	Colored ink, add		10% each color
	Card stock or		TBD
	heavier weight paper		
Spirit Duplicating	1+	25–200	$0.015
Mimeograph	1–2	25–100	$0.02
	1+	100–500	.0175
	1+	500–1,000	.015

For orders using any of the following, add:

	Colored ink	10%
	Heavier stock	TBD
	Rushes	10%
	Collating	10%
	Stapling	10%
	Three-hole punch	10%

Metal or Plastic Binding	25–50	1–100	$0.35
	25–50	100+	.30
	51–100	1–100	.50
	51–100	100+	.45
	100+	1–100	.70
	100+	100+	.65

	Size	No.	Cost
Binders	1 in.	1–25	$1.50
		25–50	1.40
		50–100	1.25
		100+	1.00
	2 in.	1–25	2.25
		25–50	2.10
		50–100	1.95
		100+	1.75
	3 in.	1–25	2.95
		25–50	2.75
		50–100	2.50
		100+	2.25

All charges are to be noted on the job request form. The accounting department will bill the client on the first of each month.

1.16 Telecommunications

1.16.1 Purpose and Function. Telecommunications is a fast, efficient method of sending and receiving documents stored on magnetic media via the telephone lines. Documents requiring immediate delivery as well as routinely scheduled intercompany mail may be best transmitted by telecommunications.

Arnco, Inc., offers the distribution service of telecommunications to its clients. Documents can be transmitted immediately to the recipient. The document can be received on magnetic media, which allows the recipient the option of revision and/or storage. The cost to the client (after equipment is installed) is only the telephone long distance charge (if any) and a small service charge.

1.16.2 Cost Savings. Generally, transmitting a document by telecommunications is economical when prompt or immediate delivery is desired. Comparative costs of distribution of a 20-page document sent from Orange County, California, are given below:

Destination	U.S. MAIL			TELECOMMUNICATIONS		
	First Class	Express	Special Delivery	Day	Evening	Night
Los Angeles, CA	$ .71	$9.35	$2.81	$1.14	$ .81	$ .48
San Francisco, CA	.71	9.35	2.81	2.42	1.71	.96
Dallas, TX	.71	9.35	2.81	2.40	1.46	.97
Chicago, IL	.71	9.35	2.81	2.40	1.46	.97
Boston, MA	.71	9.35	2.81	1.90	1.64	1.09
Rome, Italy (air)	3.20		5.30	7.69	5.78	4.62
Madrid, Spain (air)	3.20		5.30	7.69	5.78	4.62

1.16.3 Time Savings. Considerable time is saved by telecommunicating a document. The following is a table showing time comparisons for a 20 page document sent from Orange County, California.

| | U.S. MAIL | | | TELECOMMUNICATIONS |
Destination	First Class	Special Delivery	Express	
Los Angeles, CA	1 Day	Next a.m.	Overnite	5 min.
San Francisco, CA	2 Days	1 Day	Overnite	5 min.
Dallas, TX	3 Days	2 Days	Overnite	5 min.
Chicago, IL	3 Days	2 Days	Overnite	5 min.
Boston, MA	3 Days	2 Days	Overnite	5 min.
Rome, Italy	7–10 Days	5–8 Days		5 min.
Madrid, Spain	7–10 Days	5–8 Days		5 min.

1.16.4 Time Zones. You must be aware of time differences (Figure 5) when telecommunicating.

1.16.5 Priority. Rush documents are transmitted immediately and take priority over other work in process. Documents which can be scheduled for transmission on a regular basis are scheduled at 11:30 P.M., when least expensive telephone rates apply. Other scheduled transmission times are 8:00 A.M., 12:00 noon, and 5:15 P.M.

Some documents require transmission on a regularly recurring basis. Most recurrent documents are due at the receiving location within a specified time frame. For example, an expediting report due the first Monday of every month could be transmitted at 11:30 P.M. Friday evening to assure a Monday delivery.

Figure 5. U.S. Time Zones.

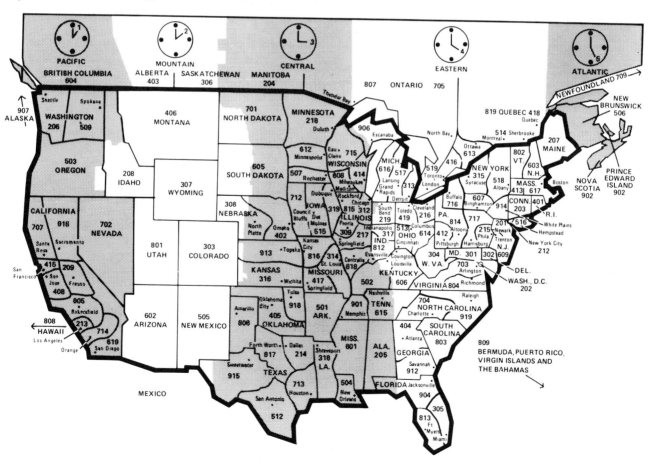

A telecommunications log (Figure 6) and a telecommunications calendar (Figure 7) are maintained by the word processing specialist responsible for telecommunications. The calendar is for scheduling documents which recur on a regular basis and require daily review. The telecommunications log is to track documents sent and received.

1.16.6 Protocol. Arnco, Inc., can communicate with the following compatible equipment with dial-up terminals:

    a. 300 bits per second, asynchronous.
    b. 1200 bits per second, bisynchronous.
    c. 2400 bits per second, bisynchronous.

1.16.7 Unattended Transmission. After 11:00 P.M. the communicating equipment is left in the unattended mode, so that messages may be received. Telecommunicated documents sent to clients will be immediately delivered after 8 a.m.

1.16.8 Verification of Transmission. An automatic verification of all documents sent and received is retained by the word processing specialist for statistical compilation and verification of transmission.

1.16.9 Adding the Telecommunications Option. For a client's recipients to add the telecommunications option, the following criteria must be met:

    a. Compatible equipment and modem with communications capability.
    b. A dedicated telephone line.
    c. Personnel trained in communication techniques.
    d. Procedures for successful transmission.

For ease in sending and receiving, all clients complete for Arnco files the resident telecommunications equipment form (Figure 8) for all their sending and receiving locations. This form enables the Arnco WP communications specialist to complete all transmissions quickly and accurately.

1.16.10 Security. The supervisor sends and receives all documents designated by the client as confidential.

In addition, each client location is given an identification password to ensure information is sent to and received by the proper location. By client request, absolute confidentiality of a document can be ensured with a prearranged transmission time and one-time identification password.

2. Guide to Effective Dictation

To increase office productivity, all Arnco, Inc., clients and managers are encouraged to use the centralized dictation equipment. Two categories of written correspondence are dictated and transcribed:

    1. Original dictation—documents original in content, such as letters, memos, and reports.
    2. Prerecorded or database text—documents stored on magnetic media, numbered and identified in the client's database binder.

2.1 Preparing to Dictate

Decide on your objective before beginning to dictate. Organize your thoughts in outline form on paper or jot notes in the margins of documents.

TELECOMMUNICATIONS LOG

DATE	SEND	RECEIVE	TO	FROM	DESCRIPTION	TIME TRANSMITTED	NO. PAGES

Figure 6. Telecommunications Log.

Figure 7. Telecommunications Calendar.

SUN	MON	TUES	WED	THURS	FRI	SAT
	1 Project status report	2	3	4	5 Payroll	6
7	8 Project status report	9	10	11	12	13
14	15 Project status report	16	17	18	19 Payroll	20
21	22 Project status report	23	24	25	26	27
28	29 Project status report	30	31		Payroll	

RESIDENT TELECOMMUNICATIONS EQUIPMENT

Company Name and Address: ______________________
____
____

Telephone Number: ______________________

Type of Equipment Used for Commo: ______________________

Speed: ____________ Modem: ____________

Commo Provisions: Auto Answer: ______ Half Speed: ______

WP Commo Specialist: ______ Hours: ____________

Type Style (S): ________ Pitch (P): ________

Comments: ______________________
____
____
____

Figure 8. Resident Telecommunications Equipment.

2.2 Organizing Materials

Have everything within reach before you begin. Do you have letters you are answering, the address for a new customer, a business card for a difficult name, all related documents, and so forth?

2.3 Accessing Dictation from Centralized Equipment

The centralized dictation unit number is 553-9300. Dial this number and you will hear a tone. The equipment is ready to use. Speak clearly and directly into the phone.

2.4 Dictation Instructions

1. Identify yourself by name, firm, and title.
2. Give your telephone number and extension.
3. Specify the type of material you are dictating, for example, letter, memo, report, notes and whether it is confidential.
4. Specify draft or final copy.
5. Specify priority. If you are dictating several items, specify order of priority. For all rushes, call the Arnco, Inc., supervisor first to ensure immediate turnaround of your document.
6. Specify format, stationery, copies, envelopes, spacing, and other general requirements.
7. Specify mode of distribution and list the names and addresses of persons to receive copies of the document.

8. As you dictate, spell out names, uncommon terms, words that sound alike, technical terms, and other words that might be misunderstood.

9. Dictate paragraphs and unusual punctuation, closing, enclosures, and recipients of carbon copies.

10. Specify retention instructions for input and output media.

11. Include the following for a repetitive letter:
   a. The number of recipients to whom the letter will go.
   b. The letter, using *variable* wherever variable information is to be inserted.
   c. Carbon copies, if any.
   d. The list of variable names and addresses.

12. Include the following for a document using standard paragraphs or database text:
   a. Identification of stored text and/or the numbers of stored paragraphs or pages.
   b. Way in which the stored text will be sequenced with new text, if any.
   c. New text.

13. Spell out troublesome words, such as:

a while	(noun), a short time	elicit	bring forth
awhile	(adverb), for a while	illicit	not legal
accept	receive	eminent	prominent
except	exclude	imminent	impending
advice	opinion	it's	it is
advise	counsel	its	possessive of *it*
affect	to change	principal	main person, sum of money
effect	(noun), a result		
	(verb), to bring home	principle	code of conduct
all ready	completely ready	stationery	paper
already	beforehand	stationary	not moving
ascent	rising	their	possessive pronoun
assent	agree	they're	they are
ensure	make certain	there	a place
insure	provide insurance	weather	climate
corps	troops	whether	introducing an alternative
corpse	dead body	who's	who is
council	assembly	whose	possessive of *who*
counsel	advise	your	possessive pronoun
disburse	pay	you're	you are
disperse	send out		

14. Specify the end of the dictation.

2.5 Accessing Dictation Equipment Using Pushbutton Telephones

The following buttons on the pushbutton telephone are used with the centralized dictation system:

1   to begin dictation again after a pause.

2   for continuous listening.

3 to back up tape about ten words; a continuous hold will return the tape to the beginning of your dictation, and the machine will then automatically replay dictation.

4 to pause, either during dictation or during playback.

\# to indicate the end of dictation, before you hang up.

Major corrections are made by backing up tape and replaying (see above). When the correction point is reached, touch *4* to stop and then *1* to dictate the correction. If you wish to insert several additional words, sentence(s), or paragraph(s), there are two ways to do so:

1. Access the point of correction, add new material, and redictate the remainder of the document.
2. Add the new material at the end of your dictation with instructions as to where the material will go. The word processing specialist will rearrange the material for you.

2.6 Accessing Dictation Equipment Using Dial Telephones

When you dial the direct line to the dictation equipment, a one-second beep tone indicates connection for dictation. With dial telephones the system cannot pause, review, or listen. Just call in, dictate, and hang up. If you cannot complete dictation for any reason, before hanging up dictate instructions for incomplete dictation and finish later.

If you wish to insert several additional words, sentence(s), or paragraph(s), there are two ways to do so:

1. Dictate it at any point during your dictation, being sure to specify it as an insertion and where it is to be inserted.
2. Dictate it at the end of your dictation, but specify it as an insertion with the appropriate place for insertion.

In either case, the word processing specialist will rearrange the material for you.

2.7 Technical Reference Section

2.7.1 Phonetic Alphabet. For clarity of dictation, the following phonetic alphabet is suggested:

A, Alpha
B, Bravo
C, Charlie
D, Delta
E, Echo
F, Foxtrot
G, Gulf
H, Hotel
I, India
J, Juliette
K, Kilo
L, Lima
M, Mike

N, November
O, Oscar
P, Papa
Q, Quebec
R, Romeo
S, Sierra
T, Tango
U, Uniform
V, Victor
W, Whiskey
X, X-ray
Y, Yankee
Z, Zulu

2.7.2 Greek Alphabet.

Letter	Caps	Lower Case	Handwritten		Letter	Caps	Lower Case	Handwritten	
Alpha	A	α	A	α	Nu	N	ν	N	γ
Beta	B	β	B	β	Xi	Ξ	ξ	Ξ	ξ
Gamma	Γ	γ	Γ	γ	Omicron	O	o	O	o
Delta	Δ	δ	Δ	δ	Pi	Π	π	Π	π
Epsilon	E	ϵ	$\mathcal{E}$	ϵ	Rho	P	ϱ	P	$\wp$
Zeta	Z	ζ	Z	ζ	Sigma	Σ	σ	Σ	σ
Eta	H	η	H	η	Tau	T	τ	T	τ
Theta	Θ	θ	$\odot$	ϑ	Upsilon	Υ	υ	Υ	ν
Iota	I	ι	I	ι	Phi	Φ	ϕ	ϕ	φ
Kappa	K	$\varkappa$	K	κ	Chi	X	χ	X	χ
Lambda	Λ	λ	Λ	λ	Psi	Ψ	ψ	Ψ	ψ
Mu	M	μ	M	μ	Omega	Ω	ω	Ω	ω

2.7.3 Signs and Symbols.

+	plus		$\times$ or $\bullet$	multiply by
−	minus		!	factorial
$\pm$	plus or minus (tolerance)		Å	Angstrom
=	equal to		$\cdot\,\partial$	partial derivative (variation, differential)
$\neq$	not equal to			
$\equiv$	identical with		∞	infinity
$\not\equiv$	not identical with		$\int$	integral
$\sim$	approximately (adjective) difference (verb)		f	function
$\approx$	approximately equal to		( )	parentheses
$\simeq$	congruent to		[ ]	brackets
>	greater than		{ }	braces
<	less than		< >	angle enclosures
$\geq$ or $\gtreqqless$	equal to or greater than		Δ	increment
$\leq$ or $\lesseqqgtr$	equal to or less than		∇	divergence of gradient (nabla)
:	is to (ratio)		—	macron (over letter)
$\rightarrow$	approaches limit of		$\cdot$	first derivative of letter over which it appears
$\propto$	varies as (proportionality)		$'$	prime
$\sqrt{}$	radical (square root)		$\therefore$	therefore
Σ	sum		$\perp$	perpendicular

2.7.4 Elements and Symbols.

actinium	Ac	gold	Au	promethium	Pm
aluminum	Al	hafnium	Hf	protactinium	Pa
americium	Am	helium	He	radium	Ra
antimony	Sb	holmium	Ho	radon	Rn
argon	Ar	hydrogen	H	rhenium	Re
arsenic	As	indium	In	rhodium	Rh
astatine	At	iodine	I	rubidium	Rb
barium	Ba	iridium	Ir	ruthenium	Ru
berkelium	Bk	iron	Fe	samarium	Sm
beryllium	Be	krypton	Kr	scandium	Sc
bismuth	Bi	lanthanum	La	selenium	Se
boron	B	lead	Pb	silicon	Si
bromine	Br	lithium	Li	silver	Ag
cadmium	Cd	lutetium	Lu	sodium	Na
calcium	Ca	magnesium	Mg	strontium	Sr
californium	Cf	manganese	Mn	sulfur	S
carbon	C	mendelevium	Md	tantalum	Ta
cerium	Ce	mercury	Hg	technetium	Tc
cesium	Cs	molybdenum	Mo	tellurium	Te
chlorine	Cl	neodymium	Nd	terbium	Tb
chromium	Cr	neon	Ne	thallium	Tl
cobalt	Co	neptunium	Np	thorium	Th
columbium (see	Cb	nickel	Ni	thulium	Tm
niobium)		niobium	Nb	tin	Sn
copper	Cu	(columbium)		titanium	Ti
curium	Cm	nitrogen	N	tungsten	W
dysprosium	Dy	nobelium	No	(wolfram)	
einsteinium	Es	osmium	Os	uranium	U
erbium	Er	oxygen	O	vanadium	V
europium	Eu	palladium	Pd	xenon	Xe
fermium	Fm	phosphorus	P	ytterbium	Yb
fluorine	F	platinum	Pt	yttrium	Y
francium	Fr	plutonium	Pu	zinc	Zn
gadolinium	Gd	polonium	Po	zirconium	Zr
gallium	Ga	potassium	K		
germanium	Ge	praseodymium	Pr		

2.7.5 Examples of Technical Abbreviations. Abbreviations of units of measurement, time, and quantity are referred to frequently. These expressions are abbreviated when used with a numeral, but they are written out if used in a general sense without a numeral. Unit abbreviations are never pluralized.

absolute	abs	centigram	cg
acceleration due to gravity	g	centiliter	cl
		centimeter	cm
Addendum	Add.	centimeter-gram-second (system)	cgs
air horsepower	air hp		
alternating current	ac, AC	centimeter per second	cm/sec
altitude	alt	centimeters of mercury	cm Hg
ampere	amp	centipoise	cp
ampere-hour	amp-hr	circa (about)	ca
and others	et al.	coefficient	coef
Angstrom unit	Å	cologarithm	colog
ante meridiem (before noon)	a.m.	conductivity	mho
		confer (compare)	cf
antilogarithm	antilog	cosecant	csc
approximate	approx	cosecant (hyperbolic)	csch
atomic mass units	amu	cosine	cos
atomic number	at. no.	cosine (hyperbolic)	cosh
atomic percent	at. %	cosine of the amplitude, an elliptic function	cn
atomic weight	at. wt		
atmosphere	atm	cotangent	cot
average	avg	cotangent (hyperbolic)	coth
		coulomb	coul
bar	spell out	counter electromotive force	cemf
barn	b		
barrel	bbl	counts per second	counts/sec
billion electron volts	Bev	counts per minute	counts/min
board feet (feet board measure)	fbm	cubic centimeter	cm³, cc
		cubic centimeter per coulomb	cm³/coul
body-centered cubic	bcc		
boiling point	bp, BP	cubic decimeter	dm³
brake horsepower	bhp	cubic foot	ft³
brake mean effective pressure	bmep	cubic feet per day	ft³/day
		cubic feet per minute	ft³/min, cfm
Brinell hardness number	Bhn		
		cubic feet per second	ft³/sec
British thermal unit per square foot per hour	Btu/ft²-hr	cubic hectometer	hm³
		cubic inch	in.³
British thermal unit per pound	Btu/lb	cubic meter	m³
		cubic hectometer	hm³
		cubic inch	in.³
calorie	cal	cubic meter	m³
candlepower	cp	cubic micron	μ^3
centerline	CL or ₵	cubic millimeter	mm³
center of impact	CI	cubic yard	yd³
center of mass	CM	curie	Ci
center of pressure	CP	cycle	spell out
center-to-center	C-C	cycles per minute	cpm

cycles per second (see Hertz)	cps	Figure	Fig.
		flux (see neutrons)	
		foot-candle	ft-c
debyé	spell out	foot-Lambert	ft-L
decibel	db	foot-pound	ft-lb
decibels (referred to 1 mw)	dbm	foot-pound-second (system)	fps
degree (angle)	deg	for example	e. g.
degree absolute (Kelvin)	°K	freezing point	fp, FP
degree Baumé	°B	frequency modulation	FM
degree centigrade (Celsius)	°C	friction horsepower	fhp
		fusion point	fnp, FNP
degree Fahrenheit	°F		
degree Rankine	°R		
degree Réaumur	°Ré	gallon	gal
diameter	diam	gallons per hour	gph
direct current	dc, DC	gallons per minute	gpm
dose (see neutrons)		gallons per second	gps
double amplitude	DA	Geiger-Mueller	G-M
dram	dr	grain	gr
drawing number	dwg No.	gram	gm
dyne	d	gram-calorie	g-cal
		gram-molecular volume	gmv
		gram-molecule	g-mol
edition, editor	Ed.	gram per liter	g/l
effective horsepower	ehp	gram per cubic centimeter	g/cm^3
electromagnetic units	emu		
electromotive force	emf	grams per cubic centimeter per second	g/cm^3-sec
electromotive interference	emi		
electrons per square centimeter	e/cm^2	gravity	g
		gravitation	G
electron volts	ev	greatest common divisor	gcd
electrostatic units	esu	greatest common factor	gcf
entropy unit	eu	gross	gr
Equation	Eq.	gross weight	gr wt
erg second	erg sec		
error function	erf	haversine	hav
et alibi, et alii (and others)	et al.	hectare	ha
		henry	h
et cetera (and other things)	etc.	hectometer	hm
		Hertz (cycle per second)	Hz
exempli grata (for example)	e. g.	horsepower	hp
		horsepower-hour	hp-hr
exponential	exp	hour	hr
		hundredweight (112 lb)	cwt
face-centered cubic	fcc	hydrogen ion concentration	pH
farad	f		
fermi (=10^{-13} cm)	F		
feet, foot	ft	ibidem (in same place)	ibid.
feet board measure	fbm	id est (that is)	i. e.
feet per minute	ft/min	inch	in.
feet per second	ft/sec	inches of mercury	in. Hg

inches per second	in./sec	lumen	lu
inch-pound	in.-lb	lumen-hour	lu-hr
indicated horsepower	ihp	lumens per watt	lu/w
indicated horsepower-hour	ihp-hr	conductivity (see ohm)	mho
inside diameter	ID	Mach number	M
		magnetomotive force	mmf
joule	j	mass	m
		maximum	max.
kilocalorie	kcal	mean effective pressure	mep
kilocycles	kc	mean free path	mfp
kilo-electron volt	kev	measure for wire diameter (1/1000 in.)	mil
kilogauss	kgauss		
kilogram	kg	cost factor (1/1000 dollar)	mill
kilogram-calorie	kg-cal		
kilogram-meter	kg-m	mega (prefix meaning million)	M
kilograms per cubic meter	kg/m³		
		megacycle	Mc
kilograms per second	kg/sec	megacycle per second	Mc/sec
kilogram-weight	kg-wt	megavolt	Mv
kilojoule	kj	megavolt-ampere	Mva
kiloliter	kl	megawatt	Mw
kilomegacycles	kMc	megawatt-days	Mwd
kilometer	km	megawatt-days per central ton	Mwd/CT
kilometers per second	km/sec		
kilo-ohm	kΩ	megawatt-days per metric ton uranium	Mwd/MTU
kiloton	kt		
kilovar	kvar	megawatt-days per ton	Mwd/T
kilovolt	kv	megawatt-days, thermal	Mwdt
kilovolt-ampere	kva	megawatt-days, thermal per ton	Mwdt/T
kilovolts peak	kvp		
kilowatt	kw	megawatt, electrical	Mwe
kilowatt, electrical	kwe	megawatt-hours	Mwhr, Mwh
kilowatt-hour	kwhr, kwh		
kilowatt-hour, electrical	kwhe	megawatt-hours, thermal	Mwht
kilowatt, mechanical	kwm	megawatt-seconds	Mws
kilowatt, thermal	kwt	megawatt, thermal	Mwt
kinetic energy	Ke	megohm	MΩ
1000 lb/sq. in.	ksi	melting point	mp, MP
		meter	m
lambert	L	meter-kilogram	m-kg
least common divisor	lcd	meter-kilogram-second	mks
least common multiple	lcm	microampere	μa
lethal dose (subscript indicates percent)	LD_{50}	microampere-hour	μahr
		microangstrom	μÅ
limit	lim	microcuries per milliliter	μc/ml
liquid oxygen	LOX	microfarad	μf
liter	l	microgram	μg
loco citato (in place cited)	loc. cit.	microhenry	μh
		microinch	μin.
logarithm (common)	log	micromicrofarad	$\mu\mu$f
logarithm (natural)	ln	micromicron	$\mu\mu$

micromole	μmol	ohm (resistance)	Ω
micron	μ	ohm-centimeter	Ω-cm
micron-ohm-centimeter	μ-ohm-cm	on center	OC
microsecond	μsec	opere citato (in work cited)	op.cit.
microvolt	μv		
microwatt	μw	ounce	oz
mile	mi	ounce-foot	oz-ft
miles per hour	mph	ounce-inch	oz-in.
milliampere	ma	outside diameter	OD
milliangstrom	mÅ	oxidizer-to-fuel ratio	o/f
millibar, millibarn	mb		
millicurie	mCi	page	p
millicycle	mc	paper	P
millicycles per second	mcs	parts per million	ppm
millifarad	mf	percent per degree centigrade	%/°C
milligram	mg		
milligram-hour	mg-hr	percent per kilowatt	%/kw
millihenry	mh	percent per second	%/sec
millilambert	mL	post meridiem (after noon)	p.m.
milliliter	ml		
milli-mass-units	mMu	pound	lb
millimeter	mm	pound-foot (torque)	lb-ft
millimicron	mμ	pound-inch (torque)	lb-in.
millimole	m mol	pounds per brake horsepower-hour	lb/bhp-hr
milliohm	mΩ		
million electron volts	Mev	pounds per cubic foot	lb/ft^3
million gallons per day	Mgd	pounds per day	lb/day, ppd
million volts	Mv		
millirem per hour	mrem/hr	pounds per hour	lb/hr
milliroentgen	mr	pounds per horsepower	lb/hp
millisecond	msec	pounds of mass per hour (torque)	lb-mass/hr
millivolt	mv		
milliwatt	mw	pounds per square foot	lb/ft^2, psf
minimum	min.	pounds per square inch	lb/in.^{2}, psi
minute	min	pounds per square inch absolute	psia
molar (concentration)	M		
molecule, molecular	mol	pounds per square inch differential	psid
molecular weight	mol wt		
mole percent	mol %	pounds per square inch gage	psig
month	mo		
		power factor	pf
namely	viz	Prandtl number	Pr
nautical mile	n.mi	probable error	PE
Negative	Neg.	pro tempore (temporarily)	pro tem
neutrons per square centimeter	n/cm^2		
neutrons per unit volume $\times$ velocity (or flux)	nv	reactive kilovolt-ampere	kvar
		reactive volt-ampere	var
neutrons per unit volume $\times$ velocity $\times$ time (or dose)	nvt	Reference	Ref.
		revision	Rev.
		relative humidity	RH
number (with a figure)	No.	revolutions per minute	rpm

revolutions per second	rps	standard cubic feet per minute	scfm
roentgen	r	standard temperature and pressure	STP
roentgen absorbed dose	rad		
roentgen equivalent man	rem	Supplement	Supp.
roentgen equivalent physical	rep		
root mean square	rms	tangent	tan
rydberg	ry	temperature	temp
		that is (id est)	i.e.
sack	sk	ton	T
second, secant	sec		
Section	Sec.		
shaft horsepower	shp	unit of pressure (1333.2 bars)	torr
sine	sin		
sine of the amplitude, an elliptic function	sn	ultrahigh frequency	uhf
specific gravity	sp g	versus	vs
specific heat	sp ht	volt	v
specific volume	sp vol	volt-alternating current	v-ac
spherical candle power	scp	volt-ampere	va
square centimeter	cm²	volt-ampere reactive	var
square foot	ft²	volt-direct current	v-dc
square hectometer	hm²	Volume	Vol.
square inch	in.²	volume percent	vol %
square kilometer	km²		
square meter	m²		
square micron	μ^2	watt	w
square mile	mi²	watts per gram	w/gm
square millimeter	mm²	watt-hour	w-hr
square yard	yd²	watts per candle	wpc
standard cubic centimeter	scc	week	wk
		weight %	wt %
standard cubic feet	scf		
standard cubic feet per hour	scfh	yard	yd
		year	yr

Part V   Arnco, Incorporated

****

WORD PROCESSING SPECIALIST'S PROCEDURES MANUAL

Table of Contents

1. General Information

1.1 Purpose and Function

Arnco, Inc., is an independent administrative support and word processing service that uses word/information processing, duplicating, and telecommunicating equipment to process, produce, reproduce, and distribute written communications for several businesses.

Arnco, Inc.'s, major contract clients are:

Sandahl, Inc., a law firm.
Reiswig Medical Clinic, Inc.
Stewart Trust and Savings, Inc.
Carlson Engineering Company.

There are also several small independent businesses.

Arnco, Inc., strives to provide efficient and cost effective administrative support as well as word/information processing support to each of its clients. We serve as a supportive force, willing to do any job within our capacity cheerfully, efficiently, and professionally. Our services include a dial-in telephone answering service, miscellaneous clerical duties, a centralized dictation system, word processing systems with an electronic filing and storage system in a time-shared computer, intelligent copier and duplicating system, courier service, and telecommunications.

1.2 Staff Job Descriptions

1.2.1 Owner and President.   The owner and president of Arnco, Inc., is responsible for the organization and direction of the company. Specific responsibilities include:

1. Making contacts with new clients to sell Arnco, Inc., services.
2. Maintaining rapport with existing Arnco, Inc., clients.
3. Expanding services of Arnco, Inc.
4. Updating equipment and systems for the organization.

1.2.2 Supervisor.   The supervisor is responsible for coordinating the work flow, assuring quality control, and meeting deadlines. Specific responsibilities include:

1. Handling customer relations.
2. Maintaining forms control.
3. Coordinating job requests with clients.
4. Delegating assignments.
5. Maintaining the work log.
6. Assuring quality control on final documents.
7. Processing and producing all confidential requests.
8. Forwarding completed job request forms to accounting clerk for billing.
9. Updating the system.
10. Recruiting, selecting, training, and evaluating staff.

1.2.3 Editor-Proofreader.   The editor-proofreader is responsible for the accuracy and quality control of all documents. Specific responsibilities include:

1. Editing all documents for readability, consistency of format, spelling, capitalization, and punctuation before they are keyboarded.
2. Proofreading all documents for spelling, pagination, capitalization, punctuation, and overall appearance after they have been processed.

3. Ensuring that all documents concur with Arnco, Inc.'s, and clients' standards and procedures.
4. Acting as consultant to users when editing assistance is desired.
5. Serving as backup for the supervisor in the case of absence.

1.2.4 Word Processing Specialist.   The word processing specialist processes WP job requests. Specific responsibilities include:

1. Keyboarding, revising, and storing documents from handwritten, typed, or dictated form onto magnetic media.
2. Formatting appropriately.
3. Proofreading all documents for consistency of format, punctuation, spelling, capitalization, and typographical errors.
4. Maintaining production logs for monthly productivity reports.
5. Telecommunicating documents.
6. Maintaining magnetic media and computer backup files.

1.2.5 Duplicating Specialist.   The duplicating specialist completes reprographic requests for the center. Specific responsibilities include:

1. Determining the most cost effective methods of reproduction while assuring appropriate quality for all documents to be duplicated.
2. Operating and maintaining reprographics equipment.
3. Converting documents stored on magnetic media to phototypeset documents.
4. Duplicating documents.
5. Binding, stapling, and collating documents.
6. Completing job request forms for duplicating costs for client billing.
7. Maintaining reprographic supplies inventory.

1.2.6 Distribution Specialist.   The distribution specialist is responsible for distributing completed job requests as directed by clients. Specific responsibilities include:

1. Picking up job requests and delivering completed job requests from client locations twice daily, at 8:00 A.M. and 2:00 P.M.
2. Delivering rush completed job requests to client locations.
3. Operating facsimile to send and/or receive documents.
4. Mailing documents through U.S. mails or private carriers.
5. Providing courier service within a 50-mile radius of our office.

1.2.7 Receptionist.   The receptionist provides much of the image of Arnco, Inc. Specific responsibilities include:

1. Greeting clients and other visitors and directing them to the appropriate person.
2. Answering Arnco, Inc., telephones.
3. Answering client telephones after hours and when client is out of the office; entering all client telephone messages on the administrative terminal message switching system.
4. Performing miscellaneous clerical tasks requested by clients.
5. Ordering and shelving supplies.
6. Placing and monitoring service calls.

1.2.8 Accounting Clerk.   The accounting clerk processes all accounts receivable and payable as well as all other accounting tasks required by Arnco, Inc. Specific responsibilities include:

1. Billing clients for services rendered.
2. Maintaining client payment records.
3. Depositing incoming checks.
4. Verifying and paying invoices for Arnco, Inc.
5. Calculating, processing, and writing payroll checks for Arnco, Inc.
6. Maintaining checking account records and reconciling bank statements.
7. Preparing and maintaining all accounting data required by the CPA to complete all state and federal tax returns.
8. Calculating productivity measurements for all departments.

1.3 Supplies

All stationery, forms, paper, and letterheads are available from the supply closet. Please inform the receptionist when the supply of items becomes low.

The duplicating specialist will be responsible for maintaining paper and other duplicating and photocomposition supplies, although the receptionist actually places the order. A schedule should be maintained on the calendar with notations of when to reorder supplies. For example, if preventative maintenance on the photocopier is scheduled, a notation to order the preventative maintenance kit should be made on the calendar three weeks prior to the scheduled service. Supplies should be ordered in sufficient quantities to take advantage of price breaks. Cost effectiveness while maintaining inventory control should be the goal. Arnco will supply the following:

1. 8½ in. × 11 in. 20 lb. white bond for all reports and manuscripts.
2. 8½ in. × 14 in. 20 lb. green bond for all rough drafts.
3. 8½ in. × 14 in. 20 lb. white bond.
4. Number 10 plain white envelopes.
5. Numbered pleadings paper.

Arnco clients supply all other stationery, such as company letterhead, envelopes, continuous form paper, and so forth. Consulting services are available for letterhead design, and other stationery needs. Arnco equipment capabilities range from 16 lb. to 90 lb. and sizes of 5½ in. to 14 in. in width, 5½ in. to 24 in. in length.

1.4 Equipment Repairs

Report all inoperative equipment to the receptionist, who will place a service call. A two-part repair order with an explanation of the difficulty should be completed. The top (white) copy should be placed on the malfunctioning equipment to alert the repair service to specific difficulties and the second (pink) copy sent to the accounting clerk for accounting purposes.

2. Procedures

2.1 Job Requests

A three-part job request form (Figure 1) is completed by the supervisor in consultation with the client or by instructions on dictated media for each job processed by Arnco, Inc. The top (white) copy stays with the document, the second (yellow) copy is given to the client. The third (pink) copy is forwarded to the duplicating specialist when the document is to be duplicated.

Incoming work from clients comes in four forms: dictated text, either through the central dictation system or recorded on portable units in the field, handwritten text, copy type text, or OCR text.

Submitted: Date _____ Time _____ **Log Number** _____
Requested: Date _____ Time _____
Client: _____
Company Contact: _____ **Phone** _____ **Extension** _____
Special Instructions: _____

INPUT
Dictation _____
Longhand _____
Copytype _____
OCR _____
Original _____
Revision _____
Number of author
   revisions _____

STATIONERY
Letterhead _____
Envelopes _____
Furnished by client _____
Color paper (specify) _____
8½″ × 11″ bond _____
8½″ × 14″ bond _____
Paper weight _____
Other _____

EDITING
Punctuation _____
Grammar _____
Word usage _____
Format _____
All _____
Proofread only _____

FORMAT
Left margin _____
Right margin _____
First line _____
Last line _____
Line spacing _____
Type style _____
Adjust _____
Justify _____

DUPLICATING PROCESS
Number of originals _____
Number of copies _____
Collate _____
Staple _____
Bind _____
Three-hole punch _____
Carbons _____
Photocopier _____
Offset _____
Spirit duplicator _____
Mimeograph _____
Printer _____

EQUIPMENT
Information processor _____
Text editor _____
OCR _____
Phototypesetter _____
Typeface _____
Type size _____

MEDIA
Card number _____
Disk number _____
Job name _____

DESCRIPTION OF WORK
Draft _____
Final _____
Memo _____
Letter _____
Envelopes _____
Rep. correspondence _____
Text _____
Forms _____
Statistical _____
File/sort _____
Document assembly _____

DISTRIBUTION
Client _____
Express mail _____
Facsimile _____
U.S. Mail _____
Courier _____
Telecommunicate _____

BILLING
Completed lines _____
Completed pages _____
Editing _____
Duplicating _____
Processing time _____
Turnaround time _____
Word processing _____
Temporary storage _____
Permanent storage _____

COPIES
White: Word processing
Yellow: Client
Pink: Duplicating

Figure 1. Job Request Form.

2.2 Work Flow

All documents are processed through Arnco's service as shown in Figure 2.

2.2.1 Document Priorities. Requests are processed in this order:

1. Rush requests.
2. Revisions.
3. Routine requests. All routine requests are processed according to date and time required on a first-come, first-served basis. Special needs should be discussed with the supervisor as far in advance as possible.

2.2.2 Overtime. All overtime must be scheduled by the supervisor.

2.2.3 Rush Requests. All rushes will be given priority if possible. If a client's deadline cannot be met, the supervisor will contact the client for direction. An additional charge of 10 percent will be added to all rush requests of five pages or less, 20 percent to requests six pages and over.

2.2.4 Revision. All revision requests are completed on a first-come, first-served basis. Revisions resulting from Arnco's error will be given the same priority as rush work and will be reprocessed without charge.

2.2.5 Confidential or Classified Documents. All security or confidential requests will be processed, produced, and distributed by the word processing supervisor personally. No admittance is permitted to the confidential files by anyone other than the supervisor or owner/president.

2.2.6 OCR. Input from OCR will be processed more quickly since initial keyboarding is not required. Arnco, Inc., will furnish OCR elements for clients.

2.3 Document Log

A document log (Figure 3) is maintained by the supervisor, in order to ensure ability to ascertain status and location of any job at any time.

2.4 Productivity Log

Each word processing specialist maintains a daily productivity log (Figure 4) for all documents produced. At the end of each month the numbers of documents, lines, and pages are totaled according to type of input and submitted to the accounting clerk, who compiles totals for each specialist, for total company productivity and client billing. A line count chart, a transparent overlay superimposed on the document to count lines (Figure 5),is shown in paper form. A transparent overlay can be made from the paper copy.

2.5 Dictation Log

The dictated text on the central dictation system is logged in by the supervisor on the dictation log (Figure 6) when the system is monitored daily at 8:00 A.M., 12:00 noon,

Figure 2. Work Flow.

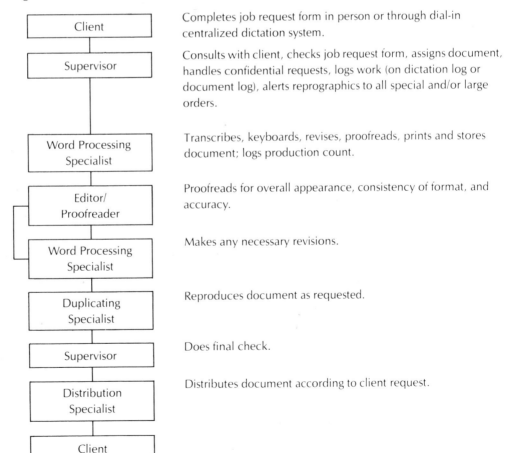

Client	Completes job request form in person or through dial-in centralized dictation system.
Supervisor	Consults with client, checks job request form, assigns document, handles confidential requests, logs work (on dictation log or document log), alerts reprographics to all special and/or large orders.
Word Processing Specialist	Transcribes, keyboards, revises, proofreads, prints and stores document; logs production count.
Editor/ Proofreader	Proofreads for overall appearance, consistency of format, and accuracy.
Word Processing Specialist	Makes any necessary revisions.
Duplicating Specialist	Reproduces document as requested.
Supervisor	Does final check.
Distribution Specialist	Distributes document according to client request.
Client	

4:00 P.M., and 11:00 P.M. Dictated media that have been recorded by the client on portable equipment and hand-delivered to Arnco, Inc., are logged on the dictation log at the time of receipt. The dictation log, maintained by the supervisor, provides a means of tracing all documents dictated by clients.

Figure 3. Document Log.

ARNCO, INC. DOCUMENT LOG

DATE REC'D	DATE REQ'D	DOCUMENT NUMBER	CLIENT	DESCRIPTION	SPECIALIST	EDIT/ PROOF	DUPLICATE	DISTRIBUTE C M F T	COMPLETE DATE	INITIAL

Figure 4. Productivity Log.

ARNCO, INC. PRODUCTIVITY LOG

LEGEND

D = Dictation   O = Original
LH = Long Hand   R = Revision
CT = Copy Type
OCR = Optical Character Recognition

DATE	LOG NUMBER	START TIME	END TIME	PRODUCTION TIME	NO. OF LINES	NO. OF PAGES	INPUT LH/D/CT/OCR	O/R

Figure 5. Line Count Chart (opposite).

Top scale (left to right): 2 3 4 5 6 7 8 9 10 11 12 13 14 15 16 17 18 19 20 21 22 23 24 25 26 27 28 29 30 31 32 33 34 35 36 37 38 39 40 41 42

Left vertical scale: 1 2 3 4 5 6 7 8 9 10 11 12 13 14 15 16 17 18 19 20 21 22 23 24 25 26 27 28 29 30 31 32 33 34 35 36 37 38 39 40 41 42 43 44 45 46 47 48 49 50 51 52 53 54

SS

1½ SP

DS

TS

Diagonal scale (upper): 1 2 3 4 5 6 7 8 9 10 11 12 13 14 15 16 17 18 19 20 — and continuing 11 12 13 14 15 16 17 18 19 20 21 22 23 24 25 26 27 28 29 30 31 32 33 34 35 36

Middle diagonal scale: 1 2 3 4 5 6 7 8 9 10 11 12 13 14 15 16 17 18 19 20 21 22 23 24 25 26 27

Horizontal mid-scales: 28 27 26 25 24 23 22 21 20 19 18 17 16 15 14 13 12 11 10 9 8 7 6 5 4 3 2 1

Lower horizontal scales: 21 20 19 18 17 16 15 14 13 12 11 10 9 8 7 6 5 4 3 2 1

Right vertical scale: 1 2 3 4 5 6 7 8 9 10 11 12 13 14 15 16 17 18

Bottom scale: 14 13 12 11 10 9 8 7 6 5 4 3 2 1

DATE RECEIVED	DATE REQUIRED	DOCUMENT NUMBER	CLIENT	DESCRIPTION	SPECIALIST	EDIT/ PROOF	DUPLICATE	DISTRIBUTE C M F T	DATE COMPLETED	INITIAL

Figure 6. Dictation Log.

2.6 Telephone Numbers for Centralized Dictation System

The telephone numbers of the centralized dictation system work on a rotating basis, beginning with (714) 553-9300 and using 553-9301, 9302, 9303, 9304, and 9305.

2.7 Originator Instructions, Dictation, and Playback

To dictate, simply depress the digits of the telephone number, pause to hear the tone, and begin to speak. The recorder will automatically begin to record. The following buttons on the *pushbutton* telephone are used with the centralized dictation system:

1 to begin dictation again after a pause.

2 for continuous listening.

3 to back up tape about ten words; a continuous hold will return the tape to the beginning of your dictation, and the machine will then automatically replay dictation.

4 to pause, either during dictation or during playback.

to indicate the end of dictation, before you hang up.

Major corrections are made by backing up tape and replaying (see above). When the correction point is reached, touch *4* to stop and then *1* to dictate the correction. If you wish to insert several additional words, sentence(s), or paragraph(s), there are two ways to do so:

1. Access the point of correction, add new material, and redictate the remainder of the document.
2. Add the new material at the end of your dictation with instructions as to where the material will go. The word processing specialist rearranges the material.

When you *dial* the direct line to the dictation equipment, a one-second beep tone indicates connection for dictation. With dial telephones the system cannot pause, review, or listen. Just call in, dictate, and hang up. If you cannot complete dictation for any reason, before hanging up dictate instructions for incomplete dictation and finish later.

If you wish to insert several additional words, sentence(s), or paragraph(s), there are two ways to do so:

1. Dictate it at any point during your dictation, being sure to specify it as an insertion and where it is to be inserted.
2. Dictate it at the end of your dictation, but specify it as an insertion with the appropriate place for insertion.

In either case, the word processing specialist rearranges the material.

2.8 Attending the Centralized Dictation Recorders

Recorders are checked daily at 8:00 A.M., 12:00 noon, 4:00 P.M., and 11:00 P.M. Always keep cassettes in the central dictation unit, adding cassettes as they are taken out of the unit for transcription.

2.9 Logging Dictated Documents

The supervisor scans each cassette for the necessary information to complete a job request form, logs the documents on the dictation log, and determines whether the document is confidential.

2.10 After-Hours Dictation

All recorders are checked at 11:00 P.M. and loaded for maximum unattended recording time.

2.11 Transcription

When possible, dictated material is transcribed as a first time final. Each specialist is supplied with transcribing equipment. Cassettes should be retained for permanent storage if the client specifies retention.

2.12 Portable Recorders

Portable recorders and cassette tapes are available to users for a loan period of up to one week. The supervisor is responsible for the loan and return of all equipment. An equipment loan request form (Figure 7) must be completed for each loan.

Figure 7. Equipment Loan Request.

```
                    EQUIPMENT  LOAN  REQUEST

      TO:     _____

                  (Client)

      Equipment/Media:  _____

      Serial No.  _____

      Date Received:  _____

      Date Returned:  _____


      Approved:  _____

                Arnco, Inc. Supervisor or Designee
```

3. Optical Character Recognition

All documents keyboarded in the client's office with an OCR type font and input to Arnco, Inc., will be completed much more quickly. In addition, Arnco, Inc., uses OCR to input many documents since it is a cost effective way to keyboard documents on a single-element typewriter. Documents can then be scanned or read onto magnetic media to make any necessary revisions, printed, and stored in final form on magnetic media. Documents that we do *not* keyboard on a single-element typewriter using an OCR type font are those with vertical line spacing changes within a page or those with equations. These are keyboarded directly on the WP system.

3.1 Typing for OCR

To ensure good results, follow these rules for typewriter setup:

1. Use an OCR recognizable type font.
2. Use a good quality carbon ribbon.
3. Move the multiple copy lever on the typewriter to the *A* position.
4. Set the impression control lever for even character impressions with no broken or tailing characters.
5. Do not change the vertical line spacing while typing a page. Do not move the platen manually once you have begun typing the page.
6. Do not change the pitch while typing a page.
7. Use 16 lb. to 24 lb. smooth, flawless solid color bond or copier paper, without a watermark. To determine whether paper has a watermark, hold one sheet up to a strong light. A visible brand name or symbol is the watermark.
8. Use ½ in. left and right margins and 1 in. top and bottom margins.
9. Arnco, Inc.'s, OCR reader/scanner does not underline. Edit all copy for underlining so that it will be done on the word processing system.

3.2 Corrections Using OCR

A less than symbol (<) or a vertical bar (|) are the two typewriter symbols used for deletions. The vertical bar is used to overstrike a character to delete the character under it. For example, *thaɸn* will be read by the OCR reader/scanner as *than*.

Less than symbols (<) are used to delete the preceding character, word, or line. One symbol (<) deletes the previous character; two symbols (< <) delete the previous word; three symbols (< < <) delete the entire line. A line drawn carefully with a no. 2 black lead pencil can be used to delete all unwanted characters; the crossed out characters will be dropped as the OCR reader/scanner reads the page of type.

3.3 Editing on OCR

After the page is removed from the typewriter, make editing marks, insertions, and so forth in red felt or nylon tip pen. Any notes for the revision on the word processing system should be written in the top, bottom, or side margins.

3.4 Scanning the Text Using the OCR Reader/Scanner

Arnco, Inc., will set the reader/scanner for the appropriate pitch, page length, and vertical spacing for the document. Using the telecommunications capabilities of the OCR reader/scanner and word processing system, we will scan the document onto the magnetic media.

3.5 Final Production on the WP System

Access the points of revision and make all necessary insertions, deletions, and changes. Proofread and print a final copy of the document. Store the document on the client's diskette for future reference. Duplicate and distribute final copies as required.

4. Keyboarding Procedures

4.1 Format Style

A representative sample of common documents used by some of Arnco's many clients is included in Section 11. The following keyboarding procedures will be followed unless otherwise specified by the client.

4.2 Paper

All documents will be produced as follows:

    a. 8½ in. × 11 in. 20 lb. bond, white, for all reports and manuscripts.
    b. 8½ in. × 11 in. 20 lb. bond, green, for all rough drafts.
    c. Number 10 envelopes, white.
    d. 8½ in. × 14 in. 20 lb. bond, white, as needed.

Continuous form paper, letterhead, printed envelopes, and other special paper are supplied by the client. The WP system's capabilities allow for weights from 16 lb. to 90 lb. and widths of 5½ in. to 14 in., lengths from 5½ in. to 24 in. Numbered pleadings paper is also available for legal clients.

4.3 First Line

Roll the paper in to the appropriate line or set up equipment with display units with the appropriate first line. The appropriate first line, of course, varies with each document.

4.4 Headers and Footers

Unless otherwise specified, all page numbers and page headings (headers) should be placed in top margin text beginning on line 3. Line 63 should be used as the first line of a footer or bottom margin text.

4.5 Type Style

All documents are keyboarded with gothic elite type, unless otherwise specified.

4.6 Margins

A six-inch line with elite spacing is used, left margin 18 and right margin 90, unless otherwise specified.

4.7 Spacing

Space twice after all ending punctuation (. ! ? :) even if it falls at the end of a line. Use required or coded spaces between words you do not want to separate onto two lines (i.e., June*5,*1933, or Mr.*Zappia or 24716*Via*Street or Post*12).

4.8 Carrier Returns in Single Spacing

Use a required or coded carrier return after all short lines. Use two single carrier returns between paragraphs and after a subheading. Use three single carrier returns after a centered heading and before and after tables within text. Rough drafts of a single-spaced document will be played back in double space for ease of editing.

4.9 Carrier Returns in One and One-Half and Double Spacing

Use a required or coded carrier return after all short lines. Use two carrier returns after a centered heading, before and after tables within text, and between blocked paragraphs. Use one carrier return between indented paragraphs and before a subheading.

4.10 Hyphens

Use required or coded hyphens for words such as father-in-law when the hyphen should not be dropped during playback.

4.11 Dashes

Dashes are typed using two consecutive required or coded hyphens with no spaces before or after.

4.12 Underscoring

Single word underscores are used when several words in the body of a document are to be underscored to ensure ease of revision. Punctuation marks, quotes, parentheses, and so forth, should *not* be underscored.

4.13 Reference Initials

The author's and word processing specialist's reference initials and/or the document identification must appear on all documents. Reference initials are followed by the card or disc identification, that is, LJA:pje/001100. Placement of reference initials and document identification depends upon the type of document and spacing within the document. On letters, reference initials are generally placed a double space below the last line in the signature block. In most other cases they are placed a double space below the last line of text.

4.14 Tabs

Use the present five-space tab grid if at all possible. If individual tabs are used, note these on the card sleeve for documents stored on magnetic cards, as well as on the file copy. Note tabs on the document format for documents stored on diskette. Note tabs on the file copy, as well.

4.15 Required Tabs

Required or coded tabs are used to set up a temporary left margin for all indented text. Required or coded tabs must be entered on the first line of an indented paragraph and canceled at the end of that paragraph by using a required or coded carrier return.

4.16 Stop Codes

Depending on your equipment, stop codes may be recorded to stop playback for variable insertion and for adjustments such as changing line spacing, line length, right margin zone, type style changes, superscripts, and subscripts. Stop codes and their purpose and location should be noted on the card sleeve for documents stored on magnetic cards. They will be visible for documents stored on diskette. Note them also on the file copy.

4.17 Adjust/No Adjust

While most documents are keyboarded and printed in adjust, for columnar or tabular information activate the no adjust mode to print a document or any portion thereof line for line as keyboarded, without changing line endings.

4.18 Decimal Tabs

In columnar typing, numbers containing decimals are keyboarded using the decimal tab feature. The tab must be set where the decimal will print.

4.19 Footnotes

Type the superscript of the footnote at the end of the word or phrase, one-half space above it.

Place the footnote on the bottom of the page on which it is first referenced. Identify it with the same superscript as that used in the text. Type footnotes single spaced, but double space between them. Type the identifying number one five-space tab in from the left margin. Start the first line immediately after the superscript with no space between; start additional lines flush with the margin. For example:

[1]Donald P. Crane, *Personnel: The Management of Human Resources,* Kent Publishing Company, Boston, Massachusetts, 1982, p. 93.

4.20 Fractions and Numbers

Keyboard fractions using the slash key rather than the fraction key; i.e., 1/4, 1-5/8.

4.21 Rough Drafts

Print all rough drafts in double space on green paper. Page numbers and titles are used for easy reference when revising. When the client wishes to allow spaces or underscores in the text for an insertion, record these spaces and underscores on the media.

4.22 Repetitive Text and Databases

Several clients have stored a database, which includes material such as paragraphs and commonly used letters. Familiarize yourself with this data for each client so that you can apply it to documents to prevent unnecessary rekeyboarding.

4.23 Line Count, Page Length

A line count of 25 is used for all pages of double-spaced copy unless there is single-spaced text within the body. A line count of 50 is used for single-spaced copy.

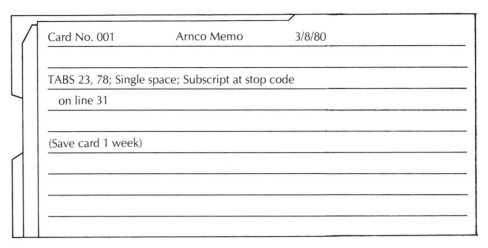

Card No. 001   Arnco Memo   3/8/80

TABS 23, 78; Single space; Subscript at stop code

  on line 31

(Save card 1 week)

Figure 8. Card Sleeve.

4.24 Card Sleeves or Jackets

Magnetic cards are stored in a card sleeve or jacket. Notations such as tabs, line spacing, and stop codes are logged in pencil on the sleeve (Figure 8). All deviations from the procedures in this manual must be noted on the sleeve.

4.25 Indices for Magnetic Diskettes

The WP system automatically creates an index. If a new document is added to a diskette, print a new index.

4.26 Document Identification on Diskette

The diskette identification code includes the client code number and the diskette number. The first three digits of the diskette identification code are the client's code; the next three digits are the diskette number based on the type of document (Figure 9).

The supervisor has assigned the following client code numbers:

001   Arnco, Inc.
002   Sandahl, Inc.
003   Reiswig Medical Clinic, Inc.
004   Carlson Engineering Company

The document portion of the diskette number is given the following numbers:

100–199	Text	500–599	Statistical
200–299	Correspondence	600–699	File/Sort
300–399	Repetitive Correspondence	700–799	Document Assembly
400–499	Forms		

A Carlson Engineering Company statistical document would be stored on diskette no. 004500 or, if diskette 004500 is full, on 004501. As diskettes are filled, the next numbers are used; in this case, 005501.

Placement of reference initials and document identification depends upon the type of document and spacing within the document. On letters, reference initials and document identification are placed a double space below the last line in the signature block or a double space below the last line of the document.

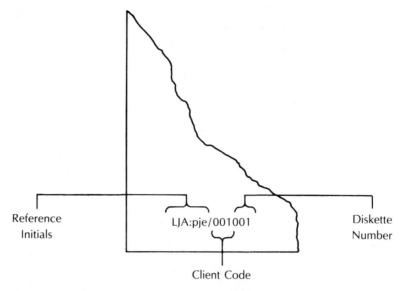

Figure 9. Diskette Identification.

4.27 Document Identification on Magnetic Cards

For multipage documents keyboarded on magnetic cards, use consecutively numbered magnetic cards. Since cards are used for temporary media storage only, include client code and card numbers in the document identification. The identification, LJA:pje/004101-7 (Figure 10), for example, indicates author's and word processing specialist's initials and a seven-page document keyboarded for Carlson Engineering. The card notation is recorded only on the last page of a multipage document. This method of identifying the magnetic card makes it easy to locate the card in the files for future revisions. If the document is to be stored permanently, it is transferred to a diskette. It is then necessary to change the document identification to reflect the diskette identification.

Placement of reference initials and document identification depends upon the type of document. On letters, reference initials are generally placed a double space below the last line in the signature block. In most other cases, they are placed a double space below the last line.

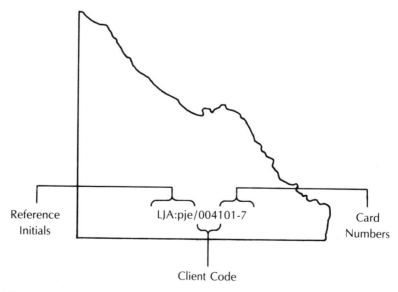

Figure 10. Magnetic Card Identification.

4.28 Quantity

All documents will be output with two carbon copies. Carbon copies are made on plain white tissue. More than five carbon copies requested by the client are handled by the duplicating specialist.

4.29 Keyboarding Equations

1. Display equations are centered horizontally and aligned vertically on the main line as well as on each level above and below the main line:

$$x \frac{dv}{dx}(y^2 + a^2)y - y^2 \frac{dy^2}{d^2x} = 0$$

2. Fractional expressions appearing in text are converted to one line:

$$\frac{x}{y} = x/y$$

3. Long equations are divided at an equals or plus or minus sign, bringing the sign down to the second line. If the equals sign is too far to the right, indent three tabs in:

```
xxx  =  xxxxxxxxxxxxxxxxxxxxxxxxxxxxxxxxxxxxxxxxxx
     =  xxxxxxxxxxxxxxxxxxxxxxxxxxxxxxxxxxxxxxxx
     +  xxxxxxxxxxxxxxxxxxxxxxxxxxxxxxxxxxxxx.
```

```
xxxxxxxxxxxxxxxxxxxxx  =  xxxxxxxxxxxxxxxxxxxxxxxx
                      +  xxxxxxxxxxxxxxxxxxxxxxxxxxxxx.
```

4. Equations in a series are aligned on the equals signs.

5. Short equations are started two tabs from left.

6. Enclosing symbols—parens ( ), brackets [ ], and braces { } — are as high as the material enclosed; and integrals ∫, summations Σ, and radicals √ as high as the material that follows but no higher:

$$\left[\frac{e^{x^2+y^2}}{2} \right] \qquad \int \frac{+ \sin x}{\log x} \, dx$$

7. Three carrier returns are used before and after display equations.

8. Exercise care in interpreting mathematical symbols. Do not confuse theta and phi, gamma and y, nu and v, rho and p, tau and t, upsilon and u, omega and w. Differentiate between script and regular letters, capitals and lower case. Compare nomenclature with preceding equations to make sure that symbols and groups coincide.

9. Equations are punctuated at the end according to sentence structure.

10. When typing equations, leave spaces for rub-ons.

    5 spaces:

    4 spaces:

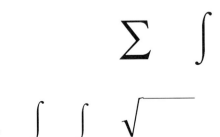

3 spaces: uppercase Greek letter; some rub-ons.

$$\Sigma \quad \int \quad \sqrt{} \quad \sqrt{} \quad \sqrt{} \quad \infty \quad (\quad (\quad \xi \quad \epsilon \quad \subseteq \quad \subset$$

2 spaces: lowercase Greek letters; most other rub-ons.

5. Quality Control —Editing-Proofreading

The quality of Arnco, Inc., documents is of the utmost importance. Although productivity is emphasized, quality can NEVER be sacrificed.

5.1 Proofreading

After producing a document, proofread it *carefully* before releasing it to the editor-proofreader. Read through once for content, then again for typographical errors and format. Your first reading will be from left to right, top to bottom. Your second reading might be from bottom to top, right to left. You may want to ask someone else to read the original as you read aloud the prepared document.

The editor-proofreader is ultimately responsible for the editing-proofreading of all documents before and after final printout. After proofreading by the editor-proofreader, the document is forwarded to the supervisor for a final check.

A good proofreader should ask the following questions:

1. Is the document's format consistent? Check horizontal spacing, vertical line spacing, widow and orphan lines, paragraph identification, page numbering, capitalization, format, and spelling.
2. Is the document correct? Check format, punctuation, capitalization, spelling, and typographical errors.
3. Have all revisions been made?
4. Have all of the client's instructions been followed and requirements met?
5. Are pages numbered sequentially and headed appropriately?
6. Are all formats noted on the card sleeve or diskette?
7. Is all pertinent information logged on the card sleeve or stored on the diskette?
8. Was the machine dictation reviewed after document was completed?
9. Were input and output media stored as required by client?

5.2 Editing-Proofreading Marks

Arnco, Inc., uses the editing-proofreading marks shown in the table on page 177. Clients and staff use the same marks. Study them for accurate production.

6. Language Arts

6.1 Troublesome Words

The words listed below have been identified as troublesome or difficult to use properly. Become familiar with the meaning or usage of each of these, so that you can use them correctly.

a while	(noun), a short time	affect	to change
awhile	(adverb), for a while	effect	(noun), a result
			(verb), to bring home
accept	receive		
except	exclude		
		all ready	completely ready
advice	opinion	already	beforehand
advise	counsel		

ascent	rising	principal	main person, sum of money
assent	agree		
ensure	make certain	principle	code of conduct
insure	provide insurance	stationery	paper
corps	troops	stationary	not moving
corpse	dead body	their	possessive pronoun
council	assembly	they're	they are
counsel	advise	there	a place
disburse	pay	weather	climate
disperse	send out	whether	introducing an alternative
elicit	bring forth	who's	who is
illicit	not legal	whose	possessive of *who*
eminent	prominent	your	possessive pronoun
imminent	impending	you're	you are
it's	it is		
its	possessive of *it*		

6.2 Word Division

It is preferable to avoid dividing words whenever possible. However, if a word falls more than five characters before or after the right margin, use the following guides for hyphenation.

6.2.1 Do Not Divide.

a. A word that is pronounced as one syllable.
   Example: shipped
b. A contraction.
   Example: you're
c. An abbreviation.
   Example: AOPA

6.2.2 Do Divide.

a. Between syllables.
   Example: let-ter
b. If you can leave at least three characters on both lines.
   Example: type-writer

6.2.3 Preferable Word Division.
Although it is acceptable to divide a word between syllables, it is preferable to divide a word:

a. Between the compounding parts of compound words.
   Example: time-table
b. After a single-letter syllable in the middle of the root word.
   Example: sepa-rate
c. After a prefix.
   Example: pre-view
d. Before a suffix.
   Example: cap-tion
e. Between two consecutive vowels with separate sounds.
   Example: gladi-ator

6.2.4 Avoid Dividing.

a. Words at the ends of two consecutive lines.
b. Last word of a paragraph.
c. Last word of a page.

6.3 Numbers

There are many rules for expressing numbers. If in doubt, check a reference manual. Always use words to express a number which begins a sentence.

6.3.1 Express in Figures.

a. Numbers above ten.
b. Time with A.M. or P.M.
c. Exact ages and years.
d. Percentages, amounts.
e. Money.

6.3.2 Express in Words.

a. Numbers from one through ten.
b. Approximate time or with o'clock.
c. Approximate ages and years.
d. Numbers in the millions.

6.4 Spelling

Correct spelling is essential. If you are in doubt, look it up. The following list presents some troublesome spelling words. Familiarize yourself with all words listed.

accidentally	eligible	occasion
accommodate	endeavor	occurred
acknowledgment	equipped	personal
acquaintance	especially	personnel
affect	exceed	principal
already	exorbitant	principle
benefited	extension	privilege
calendar	extraordinary	questionnaire
canceled	facsimile	receipt
catalog	February	rhythm
Cincinnati	fourth	recommend
conscience	incidentally	separate
conscious	judgment	similar
convenience	liquefy	stationery
definite	loose	supersede
disappoint	maintenance	transferred
effect	misspell	yield

6.5 Abbreviations

Abbreviations should be avoided in business writing; however, they are frequently used in forms and statistical typing.

6.5.1 Titles.
Abbreviate a title such as Mr., Dr., Ms., and Mrs. when followed by the full name.
Example: Dr. Thomas Leigh

Do not abbreviate these titles when they are followed by only the last name.
Example: Doctor Leigh

6.5.2 Academic Titles. Academic titles following a name are capitalized.
Example: Richard D. Jobse, Ed.D.

6.5.3 Numbers. Abbreviate number as No. when it is followed by figures. Nos. is the abbreviation for numbers.
Example: A No. 10 envelope

6.5.4 Addresses. In business correspondence, it is preferable not to abbreviate words such as street, lane, drive.
Example: 333 Third Street
Direction. Directions are generally not abbreviated.
Example: 333 East Third Street
Compound directions which follow a street address are abbreviated.
Example: 1411 Figuroa Street, N.E.

6.5.5 Time. Use abbreviations for time, A.M. and P.M., unless the word o'clock is used.
Example: 10 o'clock (acceptable), 10 A.M. (preferable)

6.6 Commonly Used Abbreviations

6.6.1 Two-Letter U.S. State and Territory, and Canadian Province Codes. According to postal policy, two-letter codes should be used on all mail.

U.S. State and Territory Codes

Alabama	AL	Montana	MT
Alaska	AK	Nebraska	NE
Arizona	AZ	Nevada	NV
Arkansas	AR	New Hampshire	NH
California	CA	New Jersey	NJ
Colorado	CO	New Mexico	NM
Connecticut	CT	New York	NY
Delaware	DE	North Carolina	NC
District of Columbia	DC	North Dakota	ND
Florida	FL	Ohio	OH
Georgia	GA	Oklahoma	OK
Guam	GU	Oregon	OR
Hawaii	HI	Pennsylvania	PA
Idaho	ID	Puerto Rico	PR
Illinois	IL	Rhode Island	RI
Indiana	IN	South Carolina	SC
Iowa	IA	South Dakota	SD
Kansas	KS	Tennessee	TN
Kentucky	KY	Texas	TX
Louisiana	LA	Utah	UT
Maine	ME	Vermont	VT
Maryland	MD	Virgin Islands	VI
Massachusetts	MA	Virginia	VA
Michigan	MI	Washington	WA
Minnesota	MN	West Virginia	WV
Mississippi	MS	Wisconsin	WI
Missouri	MO	Wyoming	WY

Alberta	AB		Nova Scotia	NS
British Columbia	BC		Ontario	ON
Labrador	LB		Prince Edward Island	PE
Manitoba	MB		Quebec	PQ
New Brunswick	NB		Saskatchewan	SK
Newfoundland	NF		Yukon Territory	YT
Northwest Territories	NT			

6.6.2 Address Abbreviations.

Alley	Al.		Park	Pk.
Avenue	Ave.		Place	Pl.
Boulevard	Blvd.		Road	Rd.
Court	Ct.		South	S.
Drive	Dr.		Southeast	S.E.
East	E.		Southwest	S.W.
Heights	Hts.		Square	Sq.
Lane	Ln.		Street	St.
North	N.		Terrace	Ter.
Northeast	N.E.		West	W.
Northwest	N.W.			

6.6.3 Commonly Used Business Abbreviations.

account	acct.		division	div.
accounts payable	a/p		each	ea.
accounts receivable	a/r		enclosure	enc.
also known as	a.k.a.		end of month	e.o.m.
amount	amt.		expense	exp.
approximately	approx.		extension	ext.
as soon as possible	asap		forward	fwd.
assistant	asst.		free on board	f.o.b.
association	assn.		for your approval	f.y.a.
attention	attn.		for your information	f.y.i.
attorney	atty.		gross	gr.
average	avg.		headquarters	hdqrs.
balance	bal.		identification	ID
bill of lading	B/L		incorporated	Inc.
bill of sale	B/S		insurance	ins.
building	bldg.		interest	int.
charge	chg.		inventory	invt.
company	co.		invoice	inv.
care of	c/o		limited	ltd.
cash on delivery	c.o.d.		manager	mgr.
commission	comm.		manufacturing	mfg.
continued	cont'd.		maximum	max.
corporation	corp.		merchandise	mdse.
credit	cr.		minimum	min.
data processing	DP		miscellaneous	misc.
debit	dr.		Misters	Messrs.
department	dept.		month	mo.
discount	disc.		number	No.

organization	org.	received	recd.
original	orig.	registered	reg.
paid	pd.	requisition	req.
post office	P.O.	signed	/S/
postscript	P.S.	secretary	sec.
president	pres.	standard	std.
profit and loss	P & L	statement	stmt.
public relations	PR	treasurer	treas.
purchase order	PO	vice president	V.P.
quarter(ly)	qtr.	word processing	WP
quantity	qty.		

6.7 Capitalization

6.7.1 Beginning Words.   Capitalize the first word of:

a. A sentence.
b. A line of poetry.
c. A item in an outline.
d. A salutation.
e. A complimentary closing.
f. A complete sentence following a colon.
g. A sentence directly quoted within another sentence.

6.7.2 Proper Nouns.   Proper nouns are words that describe a particular person, place, or thing. They are always capitalized.
Example: Houston, Texas

6.7.3 Titles.   Titles that come before a name are capitalized.
Example: Governor Brown
Titles that follow names are not capitalized, except titles of high government rank.
Example: Margaret Taylor, instructor
Jerry Brown, Governor

6.7.4 Directions.   Directions and points of the compass are not capitalized unless they represent a specific geographic area.
Example: Drive west. She is from the South.

6.7.5 Published Works.   Capitalize principal words in titles of published works such as films, plays, books and magazines, articles, and poems.
Example: The Complete Guide to Effective Dictation
Prepositions, conjunctions, and articles within such titles are capitalized only if they contain at least four letters or are either the first or last word of the title.
Example: The World Beyond Death

6.8 Quotation Marks

Periods and commas go inside the ending quotation mark. Colons and semicolons go outside the ending quotation mark. Exclamation and question marks are placed inside or outside depending on content. If they pertain only to the quoted matter, they are placed inside; if they pertain to the complete sentence, they are placed outside the ending quotation marks. Long quotations (more than three lines) are single spaced, indented five spaces from both left and right margins, and set without quotation marks.

6.9 Comma

The two main purposes of the comma are to separate elements in a sentence and to set off parenthetical thoughts.

Use a comma to separate two independent clauses joined by one of the following conjunctions: or, nor, but, and.

Example: Gloria keyboarded the document, and Jane proofread the document for her.

Use a comma to separate a dependent clause that precedes an independent clause.

Example: When he returns to his desk, Mr. Boring will be able to assist you with the order.

Note: Watch for words which often introduce a dependent clause: when, if, since, after, because, before, unless.

Use a comma to separate a dependent clause that follows an independent clause only if the dependent clause is not necessary to the overall meaning of the sentence.

Example: You may keyboard the document after you look it over.

A dependent clause that occurs within the sentence should be separated by two commas.

Example: Mr. Vanderee will return, unless he is delayed, by 3 P.M.

Place a comma after each item in a series of three or more words except for the last word.

Example: The recipe calls for carrots, eggs, and raisins.

If the words in a series are joined by *and, nor,* or *or,* do not use commas to separate them.

Example: Jane does not like carrots nor apples nor raisins.

If the abbreviation etc. ends a series within a sentence, it *must* be followed by a comma.

Example: Potatoes, corn, carrots, etc., are in the stew.

Use a comma to separate two consecutive adjectives that modify a noun.

Example: Mr. Hahn is a friendly, persuasive speaker.

Use commas to set off interruptions to a sentence.

Example: Our department, moreover, prides itself on quality control.

Use commas to set off explanatory statements which give added information, but are not essential to the meaning of the sentence.

Example: The department manager, Mr. Suggs, is away from the office this week

State names following cities are set off by commas.

Example: She went to Humboldt, Tennessee, for a month.

Dates followed by the year are set off by commas.

Example: December 25, 1968, was an important date.

Titles following names are set off by commas.

Example: Kay Keenan, Ph.D., will speak at the conference.

Use commas to set off a direct address.

Example: You must admit, Mrs. Hahn, that we did caution you.

Use a comma to indicate an omission in a sentence.

Example: Miss Day will begin her vacation on May 3, Miss Sikes, May 10.

6.10 Colon

A colon is used to indicate that something important follows.

Use a colon before a vertical listing.

Example: The reasons follow:

1. Poor planning.
2. Inadequate staff.
3. Insufficient funding.
4. Lack of interest.

Use a colon before a listing within a sentence.

Example: She ordered the following supplies: pencils, pens, pads, and paper.

6.11 Semicolon

The semicolon is used primarily to separate independent clauses and to take the place of a comma.

Use a semicolon to separate two independent clauses that are not joined by a coordinating conjunction.

Example: You ordered 126 desk sets; only 125 were delivered.

Use a semicolon to separate items in a series if any of the items in the series contain commas.

Example: The speakers are Rebecca Langley, president; Ralph Williams, comptroller; and Muriel Campbell, director.

Use a semicolon to separate two independent clauses joined by a coordinating conjunction if either of the clauses contains internal commas.

Example: When he discovered the error, Mr. Boring checked your billing; and he asked for your records.

Use a semicolon when two independent clauses are joined by a transitional expression.

Example: Illness leave is costly; nevertheless, it is an essential benefit.

Note: Watch for the following introductory expressions:

accordingly	moreover
after all	nevertheless
also	perhaps
besides	so
consequently	then
furthermore	therefore
hence	thus
however	well
indeed	yes
in fact	yet

6.12 Hyphen

Hyphens are used to join words and for word division. Because usage in hyphenation is constantly changing, always consult a current dictionary.

Use a hyphen to signify that two words have one meaning.

Example: clerk-typist
one-half
president-elect
self-reliant

Use a hyphen to join two adjectives which together precede and modify a noun.

Example: Up-to-date procedures, well-known individual

6.13 Apostrophe

The two main purposes of the apostrophe are to form contractions and possessives.

Use an apostrophe to form a one-word contraction:

Example: continued, cont'd

Use an apostrophe to form a two-word contraction:

Example: who is, who's

Use an apostrophe and s ('s) to form the possessive of a singular or plural noun that does not end in an s.

Example: The man's keys were locked in his car. Men's performances in numerical computations are often better than women's.

Use an apostrophe generally to form a possesive of a singular or plural noun ending in an s.

Example: Sylvia Symonds' grades have been consistently high. The boys' laughter filled the halls.

Use an apostrophe and s ('s) for singular nouns ending with an s sound that adds another syllable with possession.

Example: Leon Harris's appointment

7. Duplication Process

After a document is keyboarded, proofread, and printed by the WP specialist, it is forwarded to the editor-proofreader for final proofreading. After proofreading and having any necessary corrections made, the editor-proofreader gives the document to the duplicating specialist if more than five carbon copies are required. If no duplicating is required, the document is given directly to the supervisor.

A daily production log (Figure 11) is maintained by the duplicating specialist for all documents reproduced, phototypeset, and bound. At the end of each month, the production logs for each day are totaled and submitted to the accounting clerk for productivity measurement.

Figure 11. Production Log.

ARNCO, INC. PRODUCTION LOG

DATE	CLIENT	DESCRIPTION	DOC. NO.	PAGES PHOTO COPIED	PAGES OFFSET	PAGES SPIRIT	PAGES MIMEO	PAGES GRAPHICS	LINES PHOTO-TYPESET	PAGES PHOTO-TYPESET	DOCS. BOUND

The duplicating specialist notes charges for client billing on the job request form. After phototypesetting and/or duplicating the document, the job is checked for completion of all the client's requests by the supervisor.

8. Distribution Process

After the document is proofread and printed, it is either telecommunicated by the WP specialist or placed in an envelope and marked for distribution by the distribution specialist in one of the following ways:

1. Client
2. Mail: U.S., express
3. Courier service
4. Facsimile

The distribution specialist is responsible for delivery to the client, courier service within a 50-mile radius, mail, and facsimile. The word processing specialist is responsible for telecommunications.

8.1 Telecommunications

8.1.1 Purpose and Function. Telecommunications is a fast, efficient method of sending and receiving documents stored on magnetic media via the telephone lines. Documents requiring immediate delivery as well as routinely scheduled intercompany mail may be best transmitted by telecommunications.

Arnco, Inc., offers the distribution service of telecommunications to its clients. Documents can be transmitted immediately to the recipient. The document can be received on magnetic media, which allows the recipient the option of revision and/or storage. The cost to the client (after equipment is installed) is only the telephone long distance charge (if any) and a small service charge.

8.1.2 Cost Savings. Generally, transmitting a document by telecommunications is economical when prompt or immediate delivery is desired. Comparative costs of distribution of a 20-page document sent from Orange County, California, are given below:

	U.S. MAIL			TELECOMMUNICATIONS		
Destination	First Class	Express	Special Delivery	Day	Evening	Night
Los Angeles, CA	$ .71	$9.35	$2.81	$1.14	$ .81	$ .48
San Francisco, CA	.71	9.35	2.81	2.42	1.71	.96
Dallas, TX	.71	9.35	2.81	2.40	1.46	.97
Chicago, IL	.71	9.35	2.81	2.40	1.46	.97
Boston, MA	.71	9.35	2.81	1.90	1.64	1.09
Rome, Italy (air)	3.20		5.30	7.69	5.78	4.62
Madrid, Spain (air)	3.20		5.30	7.69	5.78	4.62

8.1.3 Time Savings. Considerable time is saved by telecommunicating a document. The following is a table showing time comparisons for a 20-page document sent from Orange County, California.

| Destination | U.S. MAIL | | | TELECOMMUNICATIONS |
	First Class	Special Delivery	Express	
Los Angeles, CA	1 Day	Next a.m.	Overnite	5 min.
San Francisco, CA	2 Days	1 Day	Overnite	5 min.
Dallas, TX	3 Days	2 Days	Overnite	5 min.
Chicago, IL	3 Days	2 Days	Overnite	5 min.
Boston, MA	3 Days	2 Days	Overnite	5 min.
Rome, Italy	7–10 Days	5–8 Days		5 min.
Madrid, Spain	7–10 Days	5–8 Days		5 min.

8.1.4 Time Zones. You must be aware of time differences (Figure 12) when telecommunicating.

8.1.5 Priority. Rush documents are transmitted immediately and take priority over other work in process. Documents which can be scheduled for transmission on a regular basis are scheduled at 11:30 P.M., when least expensive telephone rates apply. Other scheduled transmission times are 8:00 A.M., 12:00 noon, and 5:15 P.M.

Some documents require transmission on a regularly recurring basis. Most recurrent documents are due at the receiving location within a specified time frame. For example, an expediting report due the first Monday of every month could be transmitted at 11:30 P.M. Friday evening to assure a Monday delivery.

A telecommunications log (Figure 13) and a telecommunications calendar (Figure

8

Figure 12. U.S. Time Zones.

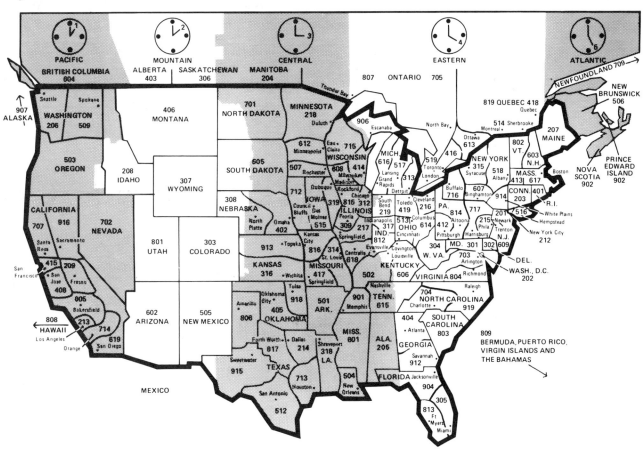

TELECOMMUNICATIONS LOG

DATE	SEND	RECEIVE	TO	FROM	DESCRIPTION	TIME TRANSMITTED	NO. PAGES

Figure 13. Telecommunications Log.

Figure 14. Telecommunications Calendar.

SUN	MON	TUES	WED	THURS	FRI	SAT
	1 Project status report	2	3	4	5 Payroll	6
7	8 Project status report	9	10	11	12	13
14	15 Project status report	16	17	18	19 Payroll	20
21	22 Project status report	23	24	25	26	27
28	29 Project status report	30	31		Payroll	

14) are maintained by the word processing specialist responsible for telecommunications. The calendar is for scheduling documents which recur on a regular basis and require daily review. The telecommunications log is to track documents sent and received.

8.1.6 Protocol. Arnco, Inc., can communicate with the following compatible equipment with dial-up terminals:

a. 300 bits per second, asynchronous.
b. 1200 bits per second, bisynchronous.
c. 2400 bits per second, bisynchronous.

8.1.7 Unattended Transmission. After 11:00 P.M. the communicating equipment is left in the unattended mode, so that messages may be received.

8.1.8 Verification of Transmission. An automatic verification of all documents sent and received is retained by the word processing specialist for statistical compilation and verification of transmission.

8.1.9 Adding the Telecommunications Option. For a client's recipients to add the telecommunications option, the following criteria must be met:

a. Compatible equipment and modem with communications capability.
b. A dedicated telephone line.
c. Personnel trained in communication techniques.
d. Procedures for successful transmission.

For ease in sending and receiving, all clients should complete for our files the resident telecommunications equipment form (Figure 15) for all their sending and receiving locations. This form will enable our WP communications specialist to complete all transmissions quickly and accurately.

8.1.10 Security. The supervisor sends and receives all documents designated by the client as confidential.

In addition, each client location is given an identification password to ensure information is sent to and received by the proper location. By client request, absolute confidentiality of a document can be ensured with a prearranged transmission time and one time identification password.

8.2 Responsibility

It is the responsibility of the *sender* to:

a. Initiate the transmission.
b. Reconnect if there is a connection problem.
c. Relay format and distribution instructions.

It is the responsibility of the *receiver* to:

a. Check to see that the document is received in its entirety.
b. Call back if transmission is unsuccessful.
c. Carry out format and distribution instructions.

8.3 Client Telephone Numbers

Listed below are the telephone numbers of Arnco, Inc., clients with telecommunications capabilities.

Name	Branch	Time Zone	Number
Arnco, Inc.	Los Angeles, CA	P	(213) 426-0161
Arnco, Inc.	Sacramento, CA	P	(916) 237-1351
Arnco, Inc.	San Diego, CA	P	(619) 348-0242
Arnco, Inc.	San Francisco, CA	P	(415) 459-2421
Brogger Construction	Indianapolis, IN	C	(317) 535-5561
Carlson Engineering	Los Angeles, CA	P	(213) 555-1111
Carlson Engineering	San Diego, CA	P	(619) 555-1376
Carlson Engineering	San Francisco, CA	P	(415) 536-1729
Stewart Trust and Savings, Inc.	Barstow, CA	P	(805) 555-1121
Stewart Trust and Savings, Inc.	Buena Park, CA	P	(714) 723-1689
Stewart Trust and Savings, Inc.	Los Angeles, CA	P	(213) 536-7211
Stewart Trust and Savings, Inc.	Montreal, Canada	E	(514) 394-6608
Sandahl, Inc.	Chicago, IL	C	(312) 565-6213
Reiswig, Medical Clinic	New York, NY	E	(212) 635-1721

8.4 Format Information

Messages, format, and distribution information are sent with documents. This permits the recipient fast, proper printing of the document.

The following information accompanies and precedes all transmissions, serving as page one of the document.

Figure 15. Resident Telecommunications Equipment.

RESIDENT TELECOMMUNICATIONS EQUIPMENT

Company Name and Address: _____

_____

_____

Telephone Number: _____

Type of Equipment Used for Commo: _____

Speed: _____   Modem: _____

Commo Provisions: Auto Answer: _____   Half Speed: _____

WP Commo Specialist: _____   Hours: _____

Type Style (S): _____   Pitch (P): _____

Comments: _____

_____

_____

_____

C: Confidential

Identifies document as classified or confidential.

D: February 1, 1983

Date—This is the date of communication not the date of the document.

T: Ms. Nancy Damron
Carlson Engineering
San Francisco, CA

To the receiving user—Supply the name, company, and location.

F: Donald M. Carlson
Carlson Engineering
Fountain Valley, CA

From the sending user—Give the name, company, and location.

S: LH
B
L
M

Type and size of stationery. LH = letterhead, B = bond, L = legal, M = memo.

P: RSH
R

Priority of the document. RSH = rush, R = routine.

CC: Bonnie Turner
Carlson Engineering
San Francisco, CA

Receiving location distributes copies as specified.

FI: Formatting Instructions

M = 18, 84		TP = 5	
T = 27, 48		P = 12	
FL = 14		TS = Gothic Elite	
LL = 60		Q = 3	
		I = text	
M = margins		P = pitch—10, 11, 12, 13.3, 15	
T = tabs		TS = type style	
FL = first line		Q = quantity	
LL = last line		I = document type—text, file,	
TP = total pages		merge file/text	

9. Magnetic Media Retention and Filing

9.1 Cards

Magnetic cards for each document to be stored temporarily are housed in the card sleeve or jacket with transmittal information noted on it and filed numerically by the number of the card and the client for whom the document was completed. Cards may be reused after five days. Any document that requires storage longer than five days must be so designated by the client within the five days and transferred to diskette. The document identification will then need to be changed to reflect diskette location.

9.2 Diskettes

Documents that require extended or permanent storage are stored on diskette. Diskettes are named and filed numerically with a six-digit number. Each client has a set of diskettes designated by client number and type of document chronologically. The document portion of the diskette number is given the following numbers:

100–199	Text	500–599	Statistical
200–299	Correspondence	600–699	File/Sort
300–399	Repetitive Correspondence	700–799	Document Assembly
400–499	Forms		

For example, Reiswig Medical Clinic's correspondence diskettes are numbered beginning with 003200 (003 is the client number; 200–299 are given to correspondence diskettes).

The document name must include client name, a brief description, and the date storage can be purged. For instance, an Arnco, Inc., repetitive sales letter with a storage request until March 1983 is labeled *Arnco Repetitive Sales Letter 3/83*. Abbreviations are permissible. Only the supervisor has the authority to purge diskettes.

9.3 Cassettes

The only cassettes used by Arnco, Inc., are input by clients using dictation equipment. Unless other directions are received, cassettes are stored for five days and then returned to the central dictation unit for reuse. If a client wishes to retain a cassette for a longer period of time, this must be specified at the time of dictation. Such a cassette is given to the supervisor for permanent retention or for distribution to the client with the completed documents.

9.4 Computer Backup Storage

Our computer is used for backup storage for the diskette file to prevent the loss of recorded text due to a damaged or misplaced diskette. All diskettes that have been created or revised are telecommunicated to the computer daily. Revised documents are stored over the former text. Due to the cost of storage on the computer, it is important that a diskette is not stored twice.

10. Technical Reference Section

10.1 Phonetic Alphabet

For clarity of dictation, the following phonetic alphabetic is suggested:

A,	Alpha	N,	November
B,	Bravo	O,	Oscar
C,	Charlie	P,	Papa
D,	Delta	Q,	Quebec
E,	Echo	R,	Romeo
F,	Foxtrot	S,	Sierra
G,	Gulf	T,	Tango
H,	Hotel	U,	Uniform
I,	India	V,	Victor
J,	Juliette	W,	Whiskey
K,	Kilo	X,	X-ray
L,	Lima	Y,	Yankee
M,	Mike	Z,	Zulu

10.2 Greek Alphabet

Letter	Caps	Lower Case	Handwritten		Letter	Caps	Lower Case	Handwritten	
Alpha	A	α	A	α	Nu	N	ν	N	γ
Beta	B	β	B	β	Xi	Ξ	ξ	Ξ	ξ
Gamma	Γ	γ	Γ	γ	Omicron	O	o	O	o
Delta	Δ	δ	Δ	δ	Pi	Π	π	Π	π
Epsilon	E	ϵ	$\mathcal{E}$	ϵ	Rho	P	ϱ	P	$\wp$
Zeta	Z	ζ	Z	ζ	Sigma	Σ	σ	Σ	σ
Eta	H	η	H	η	Tau	T	τ	T	τ
Theta	Θ	θ	$\odot$	ϑ	Upsilon	Υ	υ	Υ	ν
Iota	I	ι	$\mathcal{I}$	ι	Phi	Φ	ϕ	ϕ	φ
Kappa	K	$\varkappa$	K	κ	Chi	X	χ	$\mathcal{X}$	χ
Lambda	Λ	λ	Λ	λ	Psi	Ψ	ψ	Ψ	ψ
Mu	M	μ	M	μ	Omega	Ω	ω	Ω	ω

10.3 Signs and Symbols

+	plus		× or •	multiply by
−	minus		!	factorial
±	plus or minus (tolerance)		Å	Angstrom
=	equal to		∂	partial derivative (variation, differential)
≠	not equal to			
≡	identical with		∞	infinity
≢	not identical with		∫	integral
~	approximately (adjective) difference (verb)		f	function
			( )	parentheses
≈	approximately equal to		[ ]	brackets
≃	congruent to		{ }	braces
>	greater than		< >	angle enclosures
<	less than		Δ	increment
≥ or ≧	equal to or greater than		∇	divergence of gradient (nabla)
≤ or ≦	equal to or less than		⎯	macron (over letter)
:	is to (ratio)		•	first derivative of letter over which it appears
→	approaches limit of			
∝	varies as (proportionality)		′	prime
√	radical (square root)		∴	therefore
Σ	sum		⊥	perpendicular

10

10.4 Elements and Symbols

actinium	Ac	gold	Au	promethium	Pm
aluminum	Al	hafnium	Hf	protactinium	Pa
americium	Am	helium	He	radium	Ra
antimony	Sb	holmium	Ho	radon	Rn
argon	Ar	hydrogen	H	rhenium	Re
arsenic	As	indium	In	rhodium	Rh
astatine	At	iodine	I	rubidium	Rb
barium	Ba	iridium	Ir	ruthenium	Ru
berkelium	Bk	iron	Fe	samarium	Sm
beryllium	Be	krypton	Kr	scandium	Sc
bismuth	Bi	lanthanum	La	selenium	Se
boron	B	lead	Pb	silicon	Si
bromine	Br	lithium	Li	silver	Ag
cadmium	Cd	lutetium	Lu	sodium	Na
calcium	Ca	magnesium	Mg	strontium	Sr
californium	Cf	manganese	Mn	sulfur	S
carbon	C	mendelevium	Md	tantalum	Ta
cerium	Ce	mercury	Hg	technetium	Tc
cesium	Cs	molybdenum	Mo	tellurium	Te
chlorine	Cl	neodymium	Nd	terbium	Tb
chromium	Cr	neon	Ne	thallium	Tl
cobalt	Co	neptunium	Np	thorium	Th
columbium (see	Cb	nickel	Ni	thulium	Tm
niobium)		niobium	Nb	tin	Sn
copper	Cu	(columbium)		titanium	Ti
curium	Cm	nitrogen	N	tungsten	W
dysprosium	Dy	nobelium	No	(wolfram)	
einsteinium	Es	osmium	Os	uranium	U
erbium	Er	oxygen	O	vanadium	V
europium	Eu	palladium	Pd	xenon	Xe
fermium	Fm	phosphorus	P	ytterbium	Yb
fluorine	F	platinum	Pt	yttrium	Y
francium	Fr	plutonium	Pu	zinc	Zn
gadolinium	Gd	polonium	Po	zirconium	Zr
gallium	Ga	potassium	K		
germanium	Ge	praseodymium	Pr		

10.5 Technical Abbreviations

Units of measurement, time, and quantity are used frequently. These expressions are abbreviated when used with a numeral but written out if used in a general sense without a numeral. Unit abbreviations are never pluralized.

absolute	abs	centimeter	cm
acceleration due to gravity	g	centimeter-gram-second (system)	cgs
Addendum	Add.	centimeter per second	cm/sec
air horsepower	air hp	centimeters of mercury	cm Hg
alternating current	ac, AC	centipoise	cp
altitude	alt	circa (about)	ca
ampere	amp	coefficient	coef
ampere-hour	amp-hr	cologarithm	colog
and others	et al.	conductivity	mho
Angstrom unit	Å	confer (compare)	cf
ante meridiem (before noon)	a.m.	cosecant	csc
		cosecant (hyperbolic)	csch
antilogarithm	antilog	cosine	cos
approximate	approx	cosine (hyperbolic)	cosh
atomic mass units	amu	cosine of the amplitude, an elliptic function	cn
atomic number	at. no.		
atomic percent	at. %	cotangent	cot
atomic weight	at. wt	cotangent (hyperbolic)	coth
atmosphere	atm	coulomb	coul
average	avg	counter electromotive force	cemf
bar	spell out	counts per second	counts/sec
barn	b	counts per minute	counts/min
barrel	bbl	cubic centimeter	cm³, cc
billion electron volts	Bev	cubic centimeter per coulomb	cm³/coul
board feet (feet board measure)	fbm		
body-centered cubic	bcc	cubic decimeter	dm³
boiling point	bp, BP	cubic foot	ft³
brake horsepower	bhp	cubic feet per day	ft³/day
brake mean effective pressure	bmep	cubic feet per minute	ft³/min, cfm
Brinell hardness number	Bhn	cubic feet per second	ft³/sec
British thermal unit per square foot per hour	Btu/ft²-hr	cubic hectometer	hm³
		cubic inch	in.³
British thermal unit per pound	Btu/lb	cubic meter	m³
		cubic hectometer	hm³
		cubic inch	in.³
calorie	cal	cubic meter	m³
candlepower	cp	cubic micron	μ³
centerline	CL or Ⱡ	cubic millimeter	mm³
center of impact	CI	cubic yard	yd³
center of mass	CM	curie	Ci
center of pressure	CP	cycle	spell out
center-to-center	C-C	cycles per minute	cpm
centigram	cg	cycles per second (see Hertz)	cps
centiliter	cl		

debyé	spell out	foot-Lambert	ft-L
decibel	db	foot-pound	ft-lb
decibels (referred to 1 mw)	dbm	foot-pound-second (system)	fps
degree (angle)	deg	for example	e. g.
degree absolute (Kelvin)	°K	freezing point	fp, FP
degree Baumé	°B	frequency modulation	FM
degree centigrade (Celsius)	°C	friction horsepower	fhp
degree Fahrenheit	°F	fusion point	fnp, FNP
degree Rankine	°R		
degree Réaumur	°Ré	gallon	gal
diameter	diam	gallons per hour	gph
direct current	dc, DC	gallons per minute	gpm
dose (see neutrons)		gallons per second	gps
double amplitude	DA	Geiger-Mueller	G-M
dram	dr	grain	gr
drawing number	dwg No.	gram	gm
dyne	d	gram-calorie	g-cal
		gram-molecular volume	gmv
edition, editor	Ed.	gram-molecule	g-mol
effective horsepower	ehp	gram per liter	g/l
electromagnetic units	emu	gram per cubic centimeter	g/cm^3
electromotive force	emf		
electromotive interference	emi	grams per cubic centimeter per second	g/cm^3-sec
electrons per square centimeter	e/cm^2	gravity	g
		gravitation	G
electron volts	ev	greatest common divisor	gcd
electrostatic units	esu	greatest common factor	gcf
entropy unit	eu	gross	gr
Equation	Eq.	gross weight	gr wt
erg second	erg sec		
error function	erf	haversine	hav
et alibi, et alii (and others)	et al.	hectare	ha
		henry	h
et cetera (and other things)	etc.	hectometer	hm
		Hertz (cycle per second)	Hz
exempli grata (for example)	e. g.	horsepower	hp
		horsepower-hour	hp-hr
exponential	exp	hour	hr
		hundredweight (112 lb)	cwt
face-centered cubic	fcc	hydrogen ion concentration	pH
farad	f		
fermi ($=10^{-13}$ cm)	F		
feet, foot	ft	ibidem (in same place)	ibid.
feet board measure	fbm	id est (that is)	i. e.
feet per minute	ft/min	inch	in.
feet per second	ft/sec	inches of mercury	in. Hg
Figure	Fig.	inches per second	in./sec
flux (see neutrons)		inch-pound	in.-lb
foot-candle	ft-c	indicated horsepower	ihp

indicated horsepower-hour	ihp-hr	conductivity (see ohm)	mho
		Mach number	M
inside diameter	ID	magnetomotive force	mmf
		mass	m
joule	j	maximum	max.
		mean effective pressure	mep
kilocalorie	kcal	mean free path	mfp
kilocycles	kc	measure for wire diameter (1/1000 in.)	mil
kilo-electron volt	kev		
kilogauss	kgauss	cost factor (1/1000 dollar)	mill
kilogram	kg		
kilogram-calorie	kg-cal	mega (prefix meaning million)	M
kilogram-meter	kg-m		
kilograms per cubic meter	kg/m³	megacycle	Mc
		megacycle per second	Mc/sec
kilograms per second	kg/sec	megavolt	Mv
kilogram-weight	kg-wt	megavolt-ampere	Mva
kilojoule	kj	megawatt	Mw
kiloliter	kl	megawatt-days	Mwd
kilomegacycles	kMc	megawatt-days per central ton	Mwd/CT
kilometer	km		
kilometers per second	km/sec	megawatt-days per metric ton uranium	Mwd/MTU
kilo-ohm	kΩ		
kiloton	kt	megawatt-days per ton	Mwd/T
kilovar	kvar	megawatt-days, thermal	Mwdt
kilovolt	kv	megawatt-days, thermal per ton	Mwdt/T
kilovolt-ampere	kva		
kilovolts peak	kvp	megawatt, electrical	Mwe
kilowatt	kw	megawatt-hours	Mwhr, Mwh
kilowatt, electrical	kwe		
kilowatt-hour	kwhr, kwh	megawatt-hours, thermal	Mwht
kilowatt-hour, electrical	kwhe	megawatt-seconds	Mws
kilowatt, mechanical	kwm	megawatt, thermal	Mwt
kilowatt, thermal	kwt	megohm	MΩ
kinetic energy	Ke	melting point	mp, MP
1000 lb/sq. in.	ksi	meter	m
		meter-kilogram	m-kg
lambert	L	meter-kilogram-second	mks
least common divisor	lcd	microampere	μa
least common multiple	lcm	microampere-hour	μahr
lethal dose (subscript indicates percent)	LD₅₀	microangstrom	μÅ
		microcuries per milliliter	μc/ml
limit	lim	microfarad	μf
liquid oxygen	LOX	microgram	μg
liter	l	microhenry	μh
loco citato (in place cited)	loc. cit.	microinch	μin.
		micromicrofarad	μμf
logarithm (common)	log	micromicron	μμ
logarithm (natural)	ln	micromole	μmol
lumen	lu	micron	μ
lumen-hour	lu-hr	micron-ohm-centimeter	μ-ohm-cm
lumens per watt	lu/w	microsecond	μsec

10

microvolt	μv	opere citato (in work cited)	op.cit.
microwatt	μw		
mile	mi	ounce	oz
miles per hour	mph	ounce-foot	oz-ft
milliampere	ma	ounce-inch	oz-in.
milliangstrom	mÅ	outside diameter	OD
millibar, millibarn	mb	oxidizer-to-fuel ratio	o/f
millicurie	mCi		
millicycle	mc	page	p
millicycles per second	mcs	paper	P
millifarad	mf	parts per million	ppm
milligram	mg	percent per degree centigrade	%/°C
milligram-hour	mg-hr		
millihenry	mh	percent per kilowatt	%/kw
millilambert	mL	percent per second	%/sec
milliliter	ml	post meridiem (after noon)	p.m.
milli-mass-units	mMu		
millimeter	mm	pound	lb
millimicron	mμ	pound-foot (torque)	lb-ft
millimole	m mol	pound-inch (torque)	lb-in.
milliohm	mΩ	pounds per brake horsepower-hour	lb/bhp-hr
million electron volts	Mev		
million gallons per day	Mgd	pounds per cubic foot	lb/ft^3
million volts	Mv	pounds per day	lb/day, ppd
millirem per hour	mrem/hr		
milliroentgen	mr	pounds per hour	lb/hr
millisecond	msec	pounds per horsepower	lb/hp
millivolt	mv	pounds of mass per hour (torque)	lb-mass/hr
milliwatt	mw		
minimum	min.	pounds per square foot	lb/ft^2, psf
minute	min	pounds per square inch	lb/in.^{2}, psi
molar (concentration)	M	pounds per square inch absolute	psia
molecule, molecular	mol		
molecular weight	mol wt	pounds per square inch differential	psid
mole percent	mol %		
month	mo	pounds per square inch gage	psig
namely	viz	power factor	pf
nautical mile	n.mi	Prandtl number	Pr
Negative	Neg.	probable error	PE
neutrons per square centimeter	n/cm^2	pro tempore (temporarily)	pro tem
neutrons per unit volume × velocity (or flux)	nv		
		reactive kilovolt-ampere	kvar
neutrons per unit volume × velocity × time (or dose)	nvt	reactive volt-ampere	var
		Reference	Ref.
		revision	Rev.
number (with a figure)	No.	relative humidity	RH
		revolutions per minute	rpm
ohm (resistance)	Ω	revolutions per second	rps
ohm-centimeter	Ω-cm	roentgen	r
on center	OC	roentgen absorbed dose	rad

roentgen equivalent man	rem	standard cubic feet per minute	scfm
roentgen equivalent physical	rep	standard temperature and pressure	STP
root mean square	rms	Supplement	Supp.
rydberg	ry		
		tangent	tan
sack	sk	temperature	temp
second, secant	sec	that is (id est)	i.e.
Section	Sec.	ton	T
shaft horsepower	shp		
sine	sin	unit of pressure (1333.2 bars)	torr
sine of the amplitude, an elliptic function	sn	ultrahigh frequency	uhf
specific gravity	sp g		
specific heat	sp ht	versus	vs
specific volume	sp vol	volt	v
spherical candle power	scp	volt-alternating current	v-ac
square centimeter	cm^2	volt-ampere	va
square foot	ft^2	volt-ampere reactive	var
square hectometer	hm^2	volt-direct current	v-dc
square inch	$in.^2$	Volume	Vol.
square kilometer	km^2	volume percent	vol %
square meter	m^2		
square micron	μ^2	watt	w
square mile	mi^2	watts per gram	w/gm
square millimeter	mm^2	watt-hour	w-hr
square yard	yd^2	watts per candle	wpc
standard cubic centimeter	scc	week	wk
		weight %	wt %
standard cubic feet	scf		
standard cubic feet per hour	scfh	yard	yd
		year	yr

11. Style Guides— Examples of Formats

Arnco, Inc., has established standard formats for a variety of documents. Unless a client requests a specific format, all word processing specialists will follow the Arnco, Inc., standard formats. Clients who have specific formats are Carlson Engineering Company; Reiswig Medical Clinic, Inc.; and, Sandahl, Inc.

Formats are shown for most kinds of documents—correspondence, text, files. In addition, common documents are included showing the style and formatting preferred by some of our general business clients who use Arnco, Inc., formats, such as Stewart Trust and Savings, Inc. Refer to the other sections of this manual for specifics such as margins, type style, and other keyboarding procedures not specified on client format examples.

The printed line numbers at the left margin of the formats are to assist you in determining the number of carrier returns needed.

Format all documents according to the client's or Arnco's standards as closely as possible. If you have questions, ask before proceeding.

The following procedures are used to determine how to format a document:

1. Format document according to client and document type. The table of contents of this manual will help you find the types of documents and client formats quickly.
2. If the client does not have a particular format, use the Arnco style guide and format.
3. If the Arnco style guide does not contain an example, format the document using your best judgment. Select a document that seems similar and follow its format as closely as possible.

11.1
Arnco, Inc.

****

General Business Formats

11.1.1 <u>Letter</u>.

Arnco, Inc.
215 Warrenton Street
Fountain Valley, CA 92708
(714) 838-4221

14   July 30, 1982
15
16
17
18
19   Mrs. Ann Blackwell
20   1493 Ankert Drive
21   Seattle, WA   76124
22
23   Dear Mrs. Blackwell:
24
25   Re: Application for Employment
26
27   Your application for employment has been forwarded to us from our
28   Portland office. Your qualifications are of the type more commonly
29   used in our Research and Development Laboratory in Houston. Since you
30   expressed a willingness to relocate--and the Portland staff knew of an
31   opening--they suggested we communicate with you.
32
33   The position is that of Word Processing Senior Specialist. We consider
34   this to be an opportunity with both responsibility and potential. A
35   qualified candidate must be proficient on all facets of the INX electronic
36   typing system. In addition, a comprehensive knowledge of the English
37   language is required; this includes grammar, punctuation, capitalization,
38   and spelling. An accurate typing speed of 60 words per minute is
39   preferred. Accuracy is more important than speed, particularly with
40   transcription of machine-dictated documents. An understanding of
41   basic proofreading marks is very helpful, as is the ability to interpret
42   written and oral instructions.
43
44   If these qualifications are among those you feel you may have, we would
45   like to hear from you. If you have never visited Houston, you will
46   find it to be a friendly, yet cosmopolitan, city. We will be happy to
47   interview you within the next ten days. If you have an interest in
48   our Research and Development Laboratory, please contact us.
49
50   Very truly yours,
51
52
53
54
55   Dan J. Carter
56   Employment Manager
57
58   DJC:pje/001200
59
60
61
62
63
64
65
66

Donna Diluna
2378 Via San Rafael
Laguna Hills, CA 92653

CONFIDENTIAL

SPECIAL DELIVERY

Mr. Thomas Stamper
Craig, Holson, and Dunham, Inc.
900 Broadway Boulevard
Los Angeles, CA 90017

11.1.2 Envelope Format--OCR Postal Preference.

DONNA DILUNA
2378 VIA SAN RAGAEL
LAGUNA HILLS CA 92653

CONFIDENTIAL

SPECIAL DELIVERY

MR THOMAS STAMPER
ATT BILLING DEPARTMENT
400 EAST BOWL AVENUE
LOS ANGELES CA 90024

11

11.1.3 <u>Memorandum</u>.

ARNCO, INC.

<u>M E M O R A N D U M</u>

TO: MR. TERRY MOORE

FROM: CLAUDIA EGKAN

DATE: February 26, 1983

SUBJECT: Security Procedures

The new security procedures become effective the first of next month.
I am concerned that they be comprehensive and communicated to all
staff.

Please let me know the decisions made on the following issues:

  1. What hours will exempt and nonexempt staff be permitted entrance
      after hours?

  2. What identification system of employment verification will be used?

  3. Which parking lots should be used after hours?

Thanks very much.

CE:pje/001201

11.1.4 <u>Agenda</u>.

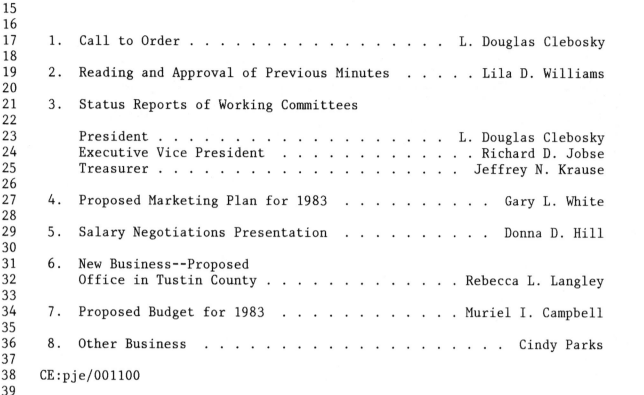

ARNCO, INC.

Monthly Board of Directors' Meeting

July 8, 1982

AGENDA

1. Call to Order . . . . L. Douglas Clebosky

2. Reading and Approval of Previous Minutes . . . . . Lila D. Williams

3. Status Reports of Working Committees

    President . . . . L. Douglas Clebosky
    Executive Vice President . . . . Richard D. Jobse
    Treasurer . . . . Jeffrey N. Krause

4. Proposed Marketing Plan for 1983 . . . . Gary L. White

5. Salary Negotiations Presentation . . . . Donna D. Hill

6. New Business--Proposed
    Office in Tustin County . . . . Rebecca L. Langley

7. Proposed Budget for 1983 . . . . Muriel I. Campbell

8. Other Business . . . . Cindy Parks

CE:pje/001100

11.1.5 <u>Minutes</u>.

ARNCO, INC.

<u>M</u> I <u>N</u> U <u>T</u> E <u>S</u>   <u>O</u> F   <u>S</u> T <u>A</u> F <u>F</u>   <u>M</u> E <u>E</u> T I <u>N</u> G

July 11, 1982

In Attendance: Bill Dowd
                  Hal Duty
                  Pat Greives
                  Barbara Horton
                  Marta Maruca
                  Alice Rossi

<u>Four-Day Work Week</u> - The possibility of implementing a 40-hour, 4-day work week was discussed. Bill Dowd volunteered to gather further information from other businesses using this system.

<u>Problem Solving</u> - There were no problems presented at this week's session.

<u>Telecommunications Procedures</u> - It was decided that a manual would be created and copies distributed to each. A committee consisting of Bill Dowd, Alice Rossi, and Marta Maruca was formed to write the manual.

<u>Update on Procedures Manual</u> - Alice Rossi presented the updated procedures on diskette identification.

<u>User of the Month</u> - It was unanimously decided that Phyllis Barnes would be the User of the Month because of her increased use of the central dictation system.

<u>Vacation Schedule</u> - Those in attendance were asked to submit their vacation requests before the beginning of the month.

<u>Adjournment</u> - There being no new business, the meeting was adjourned.

                                        Submitted by,

                                        Barbara Horton
                                        Assistant Supervisor

BH:pje/001101

Distribution: Kim Damron   Barbara Horton
                 Bill Dowd   Marta Maruca
                 Hal Duty   Alice Rossi
                 Pat Grieves   Elizabeth Scarborough

11.1.6 <u>Statistical Document.</u>

ARNCO, INC.

MARKETING DEPARTMENT EMPLOYEES

<u>NAME</u>	EMPLOYEE <u>NUMBER</u>	GRADE <u>CLASSIFICATION</u>
Bernice Wilkes	13792	5-7
Wilma Louis	14260	5-7
Denise Dolittle	15760	5-8
Thelma Pool	16321	1-1
Faith Goldberg	17231	2-4
Richard Martin	16321	5-2
Robert Franco	17232	6-4
Stefani Sandahl	17332	9-1

GRA:tc/001500

11.1.7 File.

ARNCO, INC. CLIENT FILE

ID	TITLE	FIRST NAME	MI	LAST NAME	STREET ADDRESS	CITY	STATE	ZIP	ACCT.#	TELEPHONE
1	Mr.	Harvey	H.	Stamper	8961 Blossom Avenue	Garden Grove	CA	92650	10732	(714) 539-926(
2	Mr.	Walter		Miller	276 El Presidente	San Clemente	CA	98307	12733	(714) 492-250
3	Mrs.	Ethel	T.	Cassady	100 East First Street	Irvine	CA	92715	13864	(714) 538-170(
4	Mrs.	Anna		Landau	263 Esplanade	Irvine	CA	92715	12832	(714) 549-112
5	Mrs.	Janet		Toppia	273 West Thunderbird	Laguna Hills	CA	92653	14762	(714) 553-637
6	Mr.	Larry	E.	Switzer	801 Egan Place	El Toro	CA	92653	15321	(714) 578-812
7	Mrs.	Joyce		Darem	2732 Joyzelle Lane	Garden Grove	CA	92641	15050	(714) 539-530(
8	Ms.	Stefani		Sandahl	24716 Rafael Circle	Laguna Hills	CA	92653	16030	(714) 554-979
9	Mr.	Robert	W.	Dobro	8951 Orion Way	El Toro	CA	92608	16130	(714) 839-741
10	Ms.	Marci		Anderson	8721 Beachside Lane	Huntington Beach	CA	96803	11321	(714) 563-583
11	Mr.	Harold	S.	Blackwell	3416 Lassen Lane	Costa Mesa	CA	93211	15619	(714) 830-564
12	Mr.	John	P.	Glover	9211 Robindell Drive	Mission	CA	94611	14892	(714) 559-930
13	Mrs.	Melba	A.	Murphy	1422 Heights Boulevard	Fountain	CA	94899	13319	(714) 494-490
14	Mr.	David	T.	Murphy	914 Charles Avenue	Edinal	CA	94633	11911	(714) 494-691
15	Ms.	Bridget	Y.	Arredondo	816 Omar Lane	Langley	CA			

LLD:pb/001600

11.1.8 <u>Manuscript/Report.</u>

PRESENT POSTAL PREFERENCE

Typing Addresses for OCR

Because the postal service uses optical character recognition (OCR), the
address of an envelope must be typed in a prescribed format. All lines
of the address on a No. 10 envelope should be blocked, single spaced,
12 lines down from the top, and 4 inches from the left edge of the
envelope. All lines on a No. 6 envelope should also be blocked, single
spaced, 12 lines down from the top, and 2½ inches from the left of the
envelope.

<u>All</u> items should be capitalized, and <u>no</u> punctuation is typed. The
entire address is scanned by the OCR. The use of the two-letter state
code and ZIP for automatic sorting is imperative. Two spaces should
separate the state and ZIP code.

The address format is:

                    Top line: name of recipient
                    Next line: information/attention line
                    Line above last: delivery address
                    Last line: post office, state, ZIP code

No other printing (delivery notations, mailing notations) may be placed
below the first line of the address. Notations such as "Confidential"
or "Personal" should be typed two lines below the return address and
three spaces from the left edge of the envelope in all capitals.

The attention line should be typed as the second line of the address.

Mailing notations are placed just below the postage area.

                        MRS LAURIE PARTRIDGE
                        PO BOX 6901
                        LOS ANGELES CA   90001

                        SCOTT ALEXANDER ASSOCIATES
                        ATT MANAGER
                        24716 SEASON LANE SUITE 2
                        HUNTINGTON CA   92734

JA:pje/001102

11.1.9 <u>Resume</u>.

RESUME

Lorraine Miller

24716 Via San Rafael
Laguna Hills, CA 92653
(714) 555-8593

<u>EMPLOYMENT OBJECTIVE</u>

　　Word processing specialist in a legal firm

<u>EDUCATION</u>

　　Graduate, Math-Science Major, Rancho Alamitos High School,
　　Garden Grove, CA (1968)

　　Successfully completed various secretarial courses at Citrus
　　College in Azusa, CA, and Saddleback College in Mission Viejo, CA.
　　Emphasis on legal secretarial training. 3.9 GPA with 82 quarter
　　units completed 1976-1979.

<u>EXPERIENCE</u>

　　12/79 - Present:　Secretary-Student Aid, Saddleback College,
　　　　　　　　　　　　　Mission Viejo, CA
　　10/79 - 12/79　　Typist, Oceanographic Studies Institute,
　　　　　　　　　　　　　Dana Point, CA
　　　7/77 - 10/77　　Polisher, Mojave Silver Company, Phoenix, AZ
　　　3/76 - 7/77　　Cashier and then Department Manager,
　　　　　　　　　　　　　Reace's Variety Store, Grove, CA
　　　2/75 - 3/76　　Cashier-Office Clerk, Tunell's Clothing Store,
　　　　　　　　　　　　　Huntington Beach, CA

<u>SKILLS</u>

　　Typing (70 wpm accurately)
　　Shorthand (130 wpm for 5 minutes)
　　Filing
　　Operation of most office machines including:
　　　　Cash register
　　　　10-key (by touch)
　　　　Electronic printing calculator
　　　　Full-key
　　　　Dictation equipment
　　　　Duplicating machines
　　　　Word processing equipment

```
 2
 3
 4
 5
 6
 7   Lorraine Miller
 8   Resume
 9   Page 2
10
11
12   ACHIEVEMENTS
13
14        Scholarship award, 1978, from Legal Secretaries' Association
15          of Harris County
16        First place in Mount Hope Tennis Tournament, 1977
17
18
19   PERSONAL
20
21        Health--Excellent
22        Marital Status--Single
23        Hobbies--Tennis, sewing, dirt-bike riding
24
25
26   REFERENCES
27
28        Mr. Kenneth Appleman, District Manager, Tunell's Clothing Store
29          Huntington Beach, CA   (714) 555-5432
30        Mrs. Ann LaRue, Instructor, Citrus College, 24999 Citrus Avenue,
31          Azusa, CA   (213) 555-5678
32
33   LM:pje/001103
34
35
36
37
38
39
40
41
42
43
44
45
46
47
48
49
50
51
52
53
54
55
56
57
58
59
60
61
62
63
64
65
66
```

11.2
Sandahl, Inc.

****

Legal Formats

11.2.1 Memorandum.

SANDAHL, INCORPORATED

M E M O R A N D U M

TO: All Attorneys   DATE: July 10, 1982

FROM: Fred H. Bremer

RE: In-House Lecture

Please note the following lecture:

DATE: July 21, 1982

TIME: 3:00 P.M.

PLACE: Conference Room

SUBJECT: New probate procedures

SPEAKER: Jean E. Gonzales

Plan to attend, please.

FHB:pje/002200

11.2.2 <u>Letter.</u>

S A N D A H L
I N C O R P O R A T E D

July 8, 1982

Office Enterprise
16526 Lassen Street
Fountain Valley, CA   92708

Gentlemen:

Re: Our client: Carol Carver
     Date of Accident: 9/7/80

This firm has been retained to represent the above-named
individual with respect to injuries sustained in the
accident on the date shown. It is our understanding that
our client was employed by you on the date of the accident
and as a result of injuries sustained has missed time from
work. Even though the accident was in no way connected with
her employment, we need information to proceed with this
action. Please provide us with a written statement verifying
our client's status of employment on the date of the accident,
as well as the following pertinent information:

   1.   Title of position held, position description,
        nature of duties performed, and the rate of pay on
        the date of the accident.

   2.   Date the client was first employed by you.

   3.   Number of days or hours missed from work as a
        result of the accident and wages lost directly
        related to the accident.

   4.   Date the employee returned to work following the
        accident, or, if employee has not returned to
        work, the date of resignation or the date on which
        you formally terminated the employee.

   5.   Whether the employee was, or would have been,
        entitled to any raise, promotion, transfer, or
        other benefits during the period of absence which
        the employee did not receive.

Office Enterprise
Page 2
July 8, 1982

I have enclosed an Authorization for Release of Employment
Records signed by our client. We ask your prompt response
to the information requested. Obviously, the financial
implications of this action as well as the psychological
well-being of our client are at stake. If you are unable to
send us the information within 30 days, please telephone me
immediately.

                              Sincerely,

                              Jeffrey N. Krause
                              Attorney-at-Law

JNK:pje/002201

Enclosure

11.2.3 <u>Minutes</u>.

OFFICE ENTERPRISES

ANNUAL SHAREHOLDERS' MEETING

The annual meeting of the shareholders of this corporation

was held on July 30, 1982, at 5692 Harbor Boulevard, Costa

Mesa, CA 92611.

All of the shareholders holding the outstanding and issued

capital stock of the corporation entitled to vote were

present at the meeting. The President, B. J. Steinke,

presided over the meeting. The Secretary, Ann Blackwell,

took the minutes.

The minutes of the last shareholders' meeting and of the

meetings of the Directors of the past year were read and

approved. All of the acts of the Directors, as set forth

in said minutes, were ratified and approved.

The meeting then proceeded to the election of Directors, to

hold office for the term of one year or until their

successors shall be elected and shall qualify. On motion

duly made, seconded, and unanimously carried, the following

Directors were elected: Roy J. John, Harry L. Harris, and

Jesse L. Williams.

There being no further business to come before the meeting, the meeting adjourned.

_____

Ann Blackwell, Secretary

We hereby waive notice of and consent to the time and place of this meeting of the shareholders and approve the above and foregoing minutes of this meeting on (keyboard today's date).

_____

Judith Cooper, Shareholder

_____

Jay D. Damron, Shareholder

_____

Richard D. Jobse, Shareholder

_____

John P. Aufhammer, Shareholder

LT:pje/002100

11

11.2.4 <u>Will</u>.

LAST WILL AND TESTAMENT

OF

GREGORY LEON SMITH

I, GREGORY LEON SMITH, residing at 24716 Via San Miguel, City of Laguna Hills, County of Orange, State of California, do hereby declare this to be my Last Will and Testament, hereby revoking any and all other wills and codicils by me at any time heretofore made.

FIRST: I direct that my just debts, funeral, and administration expenses be paid as soon after my death as may be practicable.

SECOND: I give, devise, and bequeath all of the rest, residue, and remainder of my estate, real and personal and wherever situated, to my wife, DIXIE LYNN SMITH, or if she predeceases me, to my issue.

THIRD: I appoint my wife, DIXIE LYNN SMITH, to be guardian to the person and property of my minor child. If she predeceases me, I appoint my mother, BEVERLY SMITH, to be guardian to my minor child and direct that neither of them shall be required to furnish any bond in any jurisdiction.

FOURTH: I appoint my wife, DIXIE LYNN SMITH, to be Executrix of my will. If she predeceases me, fails to qualify, or ceases to act as such, I appoint my father, CARL SMITH, as Executor. No person named herein as Executor or

Executrix shall be required to furnish any bond in any jurisdiction.

FIFTH: Should any part, clause, provision, or condition of this will be held to be void, invalid, or inoperative, then I direct that such invalidity shall not affect any other clause, provision, or condition hereof; but the remainder of this will shall be effective as though such clause, provision, or condition had not been contained herein.

SIXTH: This, my Last Will and Testament, I am making and executing in duplicate, one of said copies to be retained by my wife, DIXIE LYNN SMITH, and the other to be retained by my father, CARL SMITH, and I desire that either of said instruments be submitted for probate as my Last Will and Testament without the other.   That there may be no presumption of revocation of this Will by me in the event the copy of same retained by my wife cannot be found after my death, the production of either copy of this Will shall be prima facie evidence that said will was in full force and effect at the time of my death, unless a will is produced and executed by me at a date second hereto.

IN WITNESS WHEREOF, I have hereunto set my hand on this Twenty-Seventh day of June, 1982.

_____

GREGORY LEON SMITH

THE FOREGOING INSTRUMENT, consisting of three

pages, including the page signed by the witnesses, was on

the date hereof, by the said GREGORY LEON SMITH, subscribed,

published, and declared to be his Last Will and Testament,

in the presence of us, and each of us, who at his request

and in his presence, and in the presence of each other, have

signed the same as witnesses hereto.

_____RESIDING AT_____

                                           _____

_____RESIDING AT_____

                                           _____

_____RESIDING AT_____

                                           _____

pje/002101

11.2.5 <u>Pleading</u>.

HUGHES, HANS, & HARRIS
  Ronald H. Hughes
1311 North Lake Drive
Fountain Valley, CA 92708

(714) 839-3525

Attorney for defendant
Rock Of Ages Insurance Company

SUPERIOR COURT OF THE STATE OF CALIFORNIA

FOR THE COUNTY OF LOS ANGELES

JAMES RICHARDS,
 	
        Plaintiff
 	
  vs.
 	
ROCK OF AGES INS. CO.,
et al.
 	
       Defendant
	No. SAB 4937
	
	OPPOSITION OF DEFENDANT ROCK OF AGES INSURANCE COMPANY TO FILING OF SUPPLEMENTAL COMPLAINT
	
	Date: January 18, 1982
	Time: 9:00 a.m.
	Place: Department "C"

I

INTRODUCTION

Defendant Rock of Ages Insurance ("Rock of Ages") opposes that portion of the plaintiff's motion which seeks leave of court to file a supplemental complaint. Opposition to the filing of the proposed supplemental complaint is based on the grounds that, although it alleges that the original plaintiff has died since the filing of the original Complaint, it continues to present claims for emotional distress which cannot, as a matter of law, survive the death of the plaintiff.

/////

/////

/////

11.2.6 Client Information Form.

SANDAHL, INC.

CLIENT INFORMATION

Please Print   Date: _____

( ) Individual   ( ) Partnership   ( ) Corporation

  1. Name: _____

      Address: _____

      Telephone: Res. (   ) _____ Ofc. (   ) _____ Ext. _____

  2. Employer: _____

      Department: _____

      Address: _____

      Telephone: (   ) _____ Ext: _____

  3. Spouse's Name: _____

      Employer: _____

      Address: _____

      Telephone: (   ) _____ Ext: _____

  4. Personal and Emergency Data

      S.S. No.: _____ Driver's License No.: _____

      Date of Birth: _____

      Nearest Relative: _____ Relationship: _____

      Address: _____

      Telephone: Res. (   ) _____ Ofc. (   ) _____

  5. Referred by: _____

CREDIT POLICY: You will be billed monthly.
                 Full payment is due within 30 days of billing.

002400

11.3
Reiswig Medical Clinic, Inc.
****

Medical Formats

11.3.1 <u>Memorandum</u>.

REISWIG MEDICAL CLINIC, INC.

M E M O R A N D U M

July 4, 1982

TO: ALL STAFF

FROM: DAVID H. HANS, CHIEF OF STAFF

SUBJECT: IN-SERVICE TRAINING

This will introduce Ms. Denise Dodds, Director of our newly formed
In-Service Training Staff Development Office. She will be contacting
you soon to determine your needs and desires for additional training.
I appreciate your cooperation with this effort to continue to provide
the highest caliber of medical service.

DHH:pje/003200

1422 Heights Blvd.   Fountain Valley, CA 92714
(714) 838-4000

14   March 1, 1982
15
16
17
18
19   Joseph H. Cooper, M.D., Inc.
20   27852 Puerta Real, Suite 120
21   Mission Viejo, CA 92691
22
23   Dear Joe:
24
25   Re: Judi Sikes
26
27   Your patient, Judi Sikes, was seen on February 18, 1982, for evaluation
28   of a heart murmur. She has a history of hypertension which dates back
29   to March, 1978, and probably for several years prior to that. She is
30   asymptomatic from a cardiac standpoint, with the exception of some
31   mild dyspnea on exertion when climbing hills or while golfing. She
32   has occasional palpitations, described as really hard heartbeats,
33   without associated dizziness. Past cardiac history is negative for
34   rheumatic fever, although she had an episode of "typhoid fever and
35   pneumonia" at age two. Review of symptoms is positive for some right
36   shoulder and right hand aching.
37
38   On physical examination her blood pressure was 190/90, left arm sitting,
39   and 170/90, right arm sitting. Her BP fell to 149/84 in the left arm
40   standing, without associated symptoms. She had xanthelasma, probably
41   of both eyelids, and Grade I Keith-Wagner funduscopic changes, with an
42   AV ratio of less than one-half, increased arteriolar light reflex, and
43   2+ AV nicking. Carotid upstrokes were brisk without bruits. The
44   lungs were clear, and the cardiovascular exam demonstrated a PMI in the
45   fifth intercostal space, midclavicular line; S-1 and S-2 were normal.
46   There was an LV lift or double apical impulse in the left lateral
47   decubitus and a prominent nonejection click at the apex followed by a
48   murmur, best heard in the left lateral decubitus, which moved earlier
49   and increased in intensity with Valsalva. There was no change in the
50   murmur with isometrics, no diastolic murmur, and no S-3. The rest of
51   the exam was unremarkable. An EKG was normal, and the echocardiogram
52   from Houston Hospital dated 12/19/81 showed a slow mitral valve E to F
53   slope, consistent with a filling abnormality, for example, hypertension
54   or IHSS. There was a suggestion of a thick interventricular septum,
55   although the study was really TSO.
56
57   Judi Sikes appears to have a mitral valve prolapse or click murmur
58   syndrome. I doubt IHSS. The possibility of xanthelasma can be
59   evaluated with lipid profile and fasting. The patient was instructed
60   to return in two weeks for reevaluation and for a blood pressure check.
61

63

Dr. J. H. Cooper
Page 2
March 1,1982

Inderal could be added, for example, at 10 q.i.d., to control BP. It
would be strictly indicated for control of symptoms of prolapse, for
example, palpitations, chest pain, or dyspnea. Consideration could be
given to a 24-hour Holter monitor if the palpitations increase in
severity or frequency. The patient has been instructed to follow SBE
prophylaxis.

Thank you very much for sending this pleasant lady for consultation.

Sincerely,

David Reiswig, M.D.

DR:pje/003201

11

11.3.3 <u>Case History</u>.

REISWIG MEDICAL CLINIC, INC.

HISTORY

Barrett, Lonnie Jean   February 15, 1982
Albert H. Reiswig, M.D.

<u>CHIEF COMPLAINT</u>:   Prolapse and bleeding after each bowel movement for
                     the past 3-4 months.

<u>PRESENT ILLNESS</u>:   This 68-year-old white female says she usually has
                     three bowel movements a day in small amounts, and
                     there has been a recent change in the frequency,
                     size, and type of bowel movement she has been having.
                     She is also having some pain and irritation in this
                     area. She has had no previous anorectal surgery or
                     rectal infection. She denies any blood in the stool
                     itself.

<u>PAST HISTORY</u>:

    <u>ILLNESSES</u>:   The patient had polio at age 8 from which she has
                     made a remarkable recovery. Apparently, she was
                     paralyzed in both lower extremities and now has
                     adequate use of these. She has had no other serious
                     illnesses.

    <u>ALLERGIES</u>:   She denies any allergies to food or medicine.

    <u>MEDICATIONS</u>:   None.

    <u>OPERATIONS</u>:   Herniorrhaphy, 25 years ago.

    <u>SOCIAL</u>:   She does not smoke or drink. She lives with her
                     husband who is an invalid and for whom she cares.
                     She is a retired former municipal court judge.

<u>FAMILY HISTORY</u>:   One brother died of cancer of the throat; another
                     has cancer of the kidney.

<u>REVIEW OF SYSTEMS</u>:

    <u>SKIN</u>:   No rashes or jaundice.

    <u>EENT</u>:   Unremarkable.

    <u>CR</u>:   No history of chest pain, shortness of breath or
                     pedal edema. She has had some mild hypertension in
                     the past but is not under any medical supervision
                     nor is she taking any medication for this.

GI: Weight is stable. See Present Illness.

OB-GYN: Gravida II, Para II. Climacteric at age 46,
                no sequelae.

EXTREMITIES: No edema.

NEUROLOGIC: Unremarkable.

_____
Albert H. Reiswig, M.D.
Reiswig Medical Clinic, Inc.

AHR:pje/003100

11.3.4. <u>Statistical Document</u>.

REISWIG MEDICAL CLINIC, INC.

PATIENT SUMMARY

FEBRUARY	THIS MONTH	THIS MONTH LAST YEAR	THIS YEAR TO DATE	LAST YEAR TO DATE
TOTAL PATIENTS DISCHARGED	526	486	4111	4024
DAYS OF CARE TO PATIENTS DISCHARGED	3922	3611	32559	31397
AVERAGE LENGTH OF STAY	7.5	7.4	7.9	7.8
TOTAL DEATHS	32	23	234	186
Under 48 hours	6	8	60	55
Over 48 hours	26	15	174	131
Net death rate	5.0	3.1	4.3	3.3
Postoperative deaths	3	-	12	10
Postoperative death rate	1.4	-	0.7	6
TOTAL AUTOPSIES	2	2	20	15
Gross autopsy rate	6.3	8.7	8.5	8.1
Coroner's cases	6	-	17	9
Net autopsy rate	7.7	8.7	9.2	8.5
TOTAL PATIENTS ADMITTED	505	477	4122	4035
DAYS OF CARE TO HOSPITAL PATIENTS	4043	3806	32695	31717
AVERAGE DAILY CENSUS	135.2	136	133.2	131
Maximum census any day	148	148	148	153
Minimum census any day	117	120	104	91
AVERAGE PERCENTAGE OF OCCUPANCY	87.3	87.7	86.0	84.2
OPERATIONS PERFORMED	210	217	1780	1688
CONSULTATIONS PERFORMED	284	204	1933	1611
Consultation rate	53.9	42.0	47.0	40.0
TOTAL MEDICARE PATIENTS DISCHARGED	407	381	3057	3078
Days of care to Medicare patients	3374	3132	26796	31750
Percentage of patients discharged	77.4	78.4	75.2	76.5
Average length of stay	8.3	8.2	8.8	7.9
TOTAL MEDI-CAL PATIENTS DISCHARGED	4	3	27	28
Days of care	16	39	118	182
ICU PATIENTS	62	71	596	628
Days of care	259	245	1992	2029
Days unit was filled	11	12	60	81

FEBRUARY	THIS MONTH	THIS MONTH LAST YEAR	THIS YEAR TO DATE	LAST YEAR TO DATE
CCU PATIENTS	82	96	634	653
Days of care	274	289	2305	2320
Days unit was filled	6	18	88	93
DOU PATIENTS	80	79	693	723
Days of care	329	330	2751	2797
Days unit was filled	20	22	167	172

DR:pb/003500

11.3.5 <u>Report</u>.

UNIVERSITY COMMUNITY HOSPITAL
27114 AVENUE de PUERTA REAL
EL TORO, CA 92691
(714) 586-3000/586-4000

Date: 4/22/82   REPORT OF OPERATION

Preoperative Diagnosis: Mallory-Weiss tear.

Postoperative Diagnosis: Same.

Procedure: Esophagogastroduodenoscopy.

Surgeon: David Reiswig, M.D.
Asst. Surgeon: Harold W. Blackwell, M.D.
Anesthesia: Richard C. Crews, M.D.

INDICATIONS: Status post upper G.I. bleed. Reevaluation
done because of persistent anemia and previous incomplete upper endoscopy.

PROCEDURE: The patient was premedicated with Valium,
2.5 mg, slow IV push. The throat was anesthetized with Cetacaine spray.
The Olympus 11 mm Q-scope was introduced into the esophagus and advanced
under direct visual control. The proximal and middle esophagus, not
seen on previous endoscopy because of severe bleeding, were well
visualized. They appeared quite normal. No varices, erosions, and
ulcerations were seen. The endoscope was advanced to the G.I. junction,
where a 1 cm linear ulceration was noted. This is most likely the
source of the previous bleed, that is, the Mallory-Weiss tear. The
endoscope was advanced into the stomach, and the duodenum was entered
and found to be totally normal.

The patient tolerated the procedure well, and there were no complications.

ASSESSMENT: Healing Mallory-Weiss tear.

PLAN: The patient will be continued on antacids
and discharged home for follow-up as an outpatient.

Name: Lawrence Kelly
Hospital No.: 07-24-73
Room No.: 121-A

                        _____M.D.
                        David Reiswig, M.D.

cc: Dr. Jon Reiswig

DR:pb/003101

11.4
Carlson Engineering Company

****

Engineering/Technical Formats

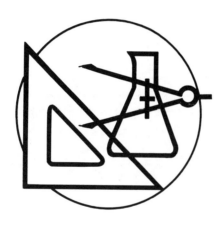

11.4.1 <u>Memorandum</u>.

CARLSON ENGINEERING COMPANY

<u>MEMORANDUM</u>

TO: OCEANOGRAPHIC STAFF

FROM: DR. JIM SHOWERMAN

DATE: September 24, 1982

RE: UPCOMING MEETING

The next Oceanographic Department meeting will be held on Tuesday,
October 29, at 11:00 a.m. Everyone is expected to attend.

You will recall that there are important decisions that must be
reached concerning some of our research projects. I have prepared
the following item with some comments for the meeting:

$$E = MC^2 + K(n + 1.5)^x + \log^y \text{ project.}$$

As before, our discussion will concern the two items:

    a. $(n + 1.5)$ and the exponent
    b. $\log^y$, where,

should n be considered the integral of $\dfrac{d\ y}{d\ x}$

or should it differentiated with respect to

    $d\ln C + X(1)^1$

    where $C = \dfrac{X}{d\ln (\log e)}$

JS:pje/004200

11.4.2 Table, Statistical Document.

CARLSON ENGINEERING COMPANY

Data Involved in the Conversion of Kuster and Herverlein's Data from Moles/Liter to Moles/Kg

moles/liter Na$_2$S Initial	Wt. % Na$_2$S Final	Wt. % S Final	moles Na$_2$S/Kg of Initial Na$_2$S Sol'n	moles Na$_2$S/Kg of the Sat'd Sol'n	g.-at. S/Kg of the Sat'd. Sol'n
1.0	6.50	9.78	0.924	0.833	3.057
0.5	3.35	5.28	0.480	0.430	1.652
0.25	1.70	2.77	0.245	0.218	0.869
0.125	0.86	1.45	0.124	0.110	0.451
0.0625	0.43	0.74	0.062	0.055	0.232
0.03125	0.24	0.37	0.031	0.028	0.117
0.015625	0.11	0.19	0.016	0.014	0.058
0.007812	0.05	0.09	0.008	0.007	0.028

004500

Carlson
Engineering, Inc.

16526 Dogwood Street
Fountain Valley, CA 92708
(714) 839-1620

November 14, 1982

Pres-Tem, Inc.
1610 Orange Street
Scranton, OH   60137

Gentlemen:

Your Pres-Tem model E6B computer gauge, which we purchased last month,
was advertised to measure horsepower at 0.1 bar increments over the
full-scale range from zero to 1500 decibels with a maximum error of
0.001 percent over a 50-bar division. The gauge we received from your
company meets neither these specifications nor my requirements.

The temperature gauge your company sent has a minimum scale division
of only 0.10 pounds per square inch (0.10 PSI) with a maximum concourse
of ten (10) degrees centigrade over the full-scale range of the hypocotyl.
The pressure range that I am working in with these gauges would indicate
a minimum/maximum temperature error of no less than 0.001 kilograms.
In the carbon dioxide-water-oxygen (CO_2-H_2O-O_2) phase equilibria
studies I am conducting, this error far exceeds six (6) components
over the four (4) phase region in the carbon (C) synthesis. A
one-hundredth degree Centigrade (0.01 C) error over the pressure range
I am studying may eliminate one (1) phase that is critical. I need
this information, or the lack of it, in order to determine the origin
and extent of epithermal, mercury-sulphide ore deposits.

In addition, Mr. Burton M. Glass, our low pressure and temperature
technician, has determined that the pressure-sensitive bourdon tube
that connects the thermothrottle to the passover ring is not K-monel
but rather Inconel-X. It is probably because of this component-part
substitution that the transmission disengaged during the initial surge
of our first experiments.

As you may well understand, we are disturbed about these problems. We
chose your equipment for accuracy, fine materials, and sound workmanship.
To this date, we are disappointed.

11

1
2
3
4
5
6
7 Pres-Tem, Inc.
8 Page 2
9 November 14, 1982
10
11
12 We trust that you will rectify this. We are returning your gauges and
13 expect that they will be modified to our original specifications.
14
15 Very truly yours,
16
17
18
19
20 Roy J. John, Ph.D.
21 Chief Geophysicist
22
23 RJJ:pb/004201
24
25
26
27
28
29
30
31
32
33
34
35
36
37
38
39
40
41
42
43
44
45
46
47
48
49
50
51
52
53
54
55
56
57
58
59
60
61

63
64
65

SOLUBILITY OF METALLIC SULFIDES

IN CERTAIN AQUEOUS ORE-FORMING SOLUTIONS

by

Ronald H. Hughes

ABSTRACT

This report presents the results of a laboratory and petrographic study
of the physico-chemical processes involved in the origin of stibnite and
sulfur deposits. The solubilities of stibnite (Sb_2S_3) and orthorhombic
sulfur in alkaline sodium sulfide solutions were measured at various
temperatures and concentrations of Na_2S in order to determine the
effects on the solubilities of changing physical and chemical conditions.
The saturation curve of stibnite in the system Sb_2S_3-Na_2S-H_2O was
determined at 25°C. The saturation curves of orthorhombic sulfur in
the system S-Na_2S-H_2O were determined at 25°C and 50°C. Stibnite
precipitates from saturated solutions with increasing temperature,
dilution, and removal of sulfide ion by processes such as oxidation or
acidification. Sulfur precipitates from saturated solutions of aqueous
Na_2S with decrease of temperature in dilute solutions, dilution of
saturated solution at 25°C or evaporation of saturated solutions at 50°C,
and removal of sulfide ion by oxidation or by acidification.

The reaction of sulfur with NaOH solutions was studied at 25°C. From
this study, a theory is proposed for the formation of alkaline sulfide

solutions in nature by the reaction of sulfur with alkaline fluids. The resulting aqueous solution of Na_2S could then transport some metallic sulfides as metal-sulfide ion complexes.

Stibnite is genetically closely related to the silica minerals, quartz, chalcedony, and opaline silica, but in most cases, stibnite is later in the depositional sequence than associated iron sulfide and carbonate minerals.

Sulfur, characteristically, is the most recently deposited of the minerals commonly found in rocks mineralized at low temperatures and pressures (near or at the earth's surface).

RHH:pb/004100

11.4.5 Form.

CARLSON ENGINEERING COMPANY

Hex Value	ILSW Bit Position					Command	State
	11	12	13	14	15		
00	0	0	0	0	0	CLEAR	0
01	0	0	0	0	1	SELECTIVE RESET	0
10	1	0	0	0	0	INPUT IDLE	0
11	1	0	0	0	1	FREEWHEELING RESPONSE	1
12	1	0	0	1	0		2
13	1	0	0	1	1		3
14	1	0	1	0	0		4
15	1	0	1	0	1	MESSAGE INCOMING	5
16	1	0	1	1	0	SCS	6
17	1	0	1	1	1	EOM	7
18	1	1	0	0	0	IDLE	8
19	1	1	0	0	1	POLL/CALL RESPONSE	9
1A	1	1	0	1	0		10
1B	1	1	0	1	1		11
1C	1	1	1	0	0	PARITY ERROR	12
1D	1	1	1	0	1	EOS IDLE	13
1E	1	1	1	1	0	POLL/CALL MONITOR	14
1F	1	1	1	1	1		15

004400

11

Answers to Self-Check Questions

Chapter 1

Completion

1. A *MIS* is a method of organizing people using well-designed *procedures* and sophisticated *equipment* to assist the management in operating the business in a cost-effective way.
2. *AS* is defined as assisting management to carry out the duties of the office.
3. There are at least three ways organizations have set up the work environment of AS staff. They are *one-to-one, one-to-several,* and *several-to-several.*
4. *WP* can be defined as a systematized method of producing, copying, and distributing documents using advanced technology, sophisticated procedures, and highly skilled personnel.
5. *People* and *procedures* are as important as the automated equipment in a WP system.
6. The DP cycle has three elements. These are *input, processing,* and *output.*
7. Computer programs are also called *software.*
8. *RM* is a systematized method of indexing, storing, and retrieving permanent documents.
9. Five applications that could be performed on an administrative terminal by a manager are:
   a. Messaging between branch offices and other organizations.
   b. Calendaring for time management.
   c. Calculating.
   d. Follow-up.
   e. Accessing information.
10. Six applications performed more easily and timely on an administrative terminal by an administrative secretary are:
   a. Scheduling meetings.
   b. Calendaring.
   c. Follow-up.
   d. Messaging.

e. Communicating between branch offices and other locations.
   f. Accessing information.

Matching:

1. d
2. j
3. e
4. a
5. k
6. g
7. f
8. h
9. c
10. i

Chapter 2

Completion

1. Careers in MIS are multilevel. Besides public and private industry, the *vendors of technology and supplies* provide many challenging opportunities.
2. An *administrative secretary* is one who provides administrative assistance to an executive.
3. An *administrative support manager* is responsible for the administration, design, and overall monitoring of the AS centers.
4. In a WP center, the most complex and technical documents are assigned to the *WP technician.*
5. The *WP supervisor* monitors work flow and trains, motivates, and evaluates personnel.
6. A *marketing support representative* trains customers to use equipment for their applications.
7. A source for general information as well as job openings is the *professional organization.*
8. A *programmer trainee* does basic design and debugs elementary programs.
9. In DP, a *systems analyst* analyzes and designs information systems to solve user information needs.

10. In RM, *information specialists* work with users as they generate documents to be entered into the system.

True/False
1. F
2. F
3. F
4. T
5. T
6. F
7. F
8. T
9. T
10. T

Chapter 3

Completion
1. The executive is also called the *user* of the system.
2. The organizational design proposed by Ulrich Steinhilper for the original concept of WP is *centralized or production center*.
3. The forms of media used in the past two decades are *tape, card, diskette*.
4. Three basic reasons used to justify WP are *rising labor costs, increased paperwork*, and *creation of career paths*.
5. The four phases of WP are *input, output, copy processing*, and *distribution*.
6. The largest expenditure of time in the document cycle is in the *distribution* phase.
7. No matter how sophisticated the equipment and the procedures, without *highly trained, skilled personnel* the system will fail.
8. Procedures manuals are beneficial to both *executives* and *WP specialists*.
9. The organizational design most supportive to the executive is the *combination or specialized production*.
10. The system design with the fewest changes in personnel structure is the *decentralized or custom support system*.

Matching
1. a
2. k
3. d
4. b
5. c
6. f
7. i
8. e
9. j
10. h

Chapter 4

Completion
1. The process by which people generate their ideas for communication to others is called *input*. (*Origination* is also an acceptable answer.)
2. The person who originates the document is called an *originator*.
3. The four methods of input are *longhand, shorthand, OCR*, and *machine dictation*.
4. The most commonly used method of input is *longhand*.
5. The least expensive form of input is *machine dictation*.
6. The most expensive form of input is *shorthand*.
7. The method of input from which it is easiest to type is *machine dictation*.
8. The transcription feature that eliminates the need for adjusting the volume of dictation is the *automatic gain control*.
9. The three major categories of input equipment are *portable units, desk-top units*, and *centralized dictation units*.

Short Answer
1. An originator who outlines key points before beginning dictation usually can make sequentially logical presentations and is less likely to forget items of importance.
2. An originator who did not gather the necessary files and data before beginning to dictate might forget items of importance, state something incorrectly, or have to interrupt dictation and train of thought to get information.
3. If a dictator does not tell the transcriber the type of stationery and format to use until the end of the document, the transcriber would have to listen to the end of the document, thereby wasting time, or the document might have to be retyped if the transcriber did not listen all the way through the document but instead guessed incorrectly.
4. Results of interruptions while dictating might be items left out and loss of logical sequence.
5. It is especially important to play back the dictation before giving it to a WP specialist when you want a final product the first time. If your document is a rough draft, do not bother to take the time to play it back.
6. An administrative secretary can assist the executive in document creation by:
   a. Opening and sorting the mail.
   b. Establishing priorities for documents to be answered.
   c. Outlining or highlighting important items within each document.
   d. Attaching related files or information to documents requiring a response.
   e. Rough drafting routine correspondence.
   f. Developing standard paragraphs to be used in repetitive use.
7. It is important for an inexperienced originator to have VOR equipment on the machine to eliminate long pauses between words, phrases, or sentences.
8. Two results that may occur if the documents are not given priorities when endless loop media is used are:
   a. The document needed first may not be completed first.
   b. Deadlines may be missed.
9. If an originator forgets an instruction until partially through the dictation of a document, he or she can insert the information simply by depressing the special cueing feature immediately and giving the instruction. The WP specialist always scans to the special cueing signals before beginning to transcribe a document, so the instruction will be heard.
10. It is usually more cost effective to dictate a document

and revise the typed draft because typed copy is easier to read and since it is recorded on media, it is easy for the WP specialist to revise. The only exception to this rule may be in the creation of highly technical documents. These may be difficult to dictate and transcribe if they contain many equations.

True/False
1. False.
2. False.
3. False.
4. True.
5. False.

Chapter 5

Completion
1. *Output* is the phase of word processing in which the document is produced; that is, keyboarded, revised, and printed.
2. An individual trained to teach a WP system to a customer and assist in customer applications of equipment is called a *marketing support representative.*
3. *Electronic typewriters,* sometimes called intelligent typewriters, are an upgraded version of standard electric typewriters.
4. Standalone units are divided into two separate categories—*display* and *blind.*
5. *Shared systems* are several work stations that share one or more resources.
6. WP hardware uses *tape, cards, diskettes,* and *rigid discs* for storage.
7. If the printing device actually hits or strikes the paper, it is called an *impact* printer.
8. A print device which resembles a daisy is called a *daisy wheel* and the printer it is used on has a print speed of *25* to *60* cps.
9. The IBM 6670 Information Distributor, which uses a helium laser beam and mirrors, is called a *laser* printer.
10. A *line* printer prints a whole line at a time.

Matching
1. b
2. d
3. g
4. i
5. k
6. j
7. f
8. e
9. c
10. a

Chapter 6

Completion
1. *Transcription* is the process of keyboarding the recorded message stored on media from dictation.
2. The rate of *20* to *25* words per minute is common when typing from machine dictation, while *15* words per minute is average when typing from shorthand.
3. A manual scanning device which is inserted in the dictation equipment for marking documents is called an *index slip.*

4. Other dictation equipment has *scanning devices,* which mark documents for transcription, but are operated electronically.
5. Handling of the media is not possible with the *endless loop* system.
6. Transcription of discrete media is done using a *desktop* transcription unit.
7. Locating the place in memory or on media where revision is to be made is called *accessing.*
8. The *WP specialist* has the responsibility for making line-ending, hyphenation, and page-ending decisions.
9. A *database* is used to create a new proposal from an old one.

Short Answer
1. The seven basic categories of documents are correspondence, repetitive correspondence, text, forms, statistical documents, document assembly, and file/sort.
2. The document may be keyboarded on a WP system and printed or played out on the same machine. The document may be keyboarded on a WP system, terminal, or a work station, and printed or played out on a separate printer. The document may be keyboarded on a single element typewriter, and scanned through an OCR reader onto the media of a system for revisions and playout.
3. Because there is seldom compatibility between different kinds of WP equipment, it is not possible to interface production or printing on varying equipment. The OCR can bridge this gap by providing from one type of equipment a printout (hard copy) which can be read or scanned and recorded onto a different equipment's media.
4. A database is a library of recorded data or documents that can be used to create new documents. This cost-effective technique saves rewriting time for the author and rekeyboarding time for the WP specialist.
5. The purpose of numbering, categorizing, color-coding, or otherwise identifying the media is to provide fast and easy access and retrieval.

True/False
1. True.
2. True.
3. False.
4. True.
5. False.
6. False.
7. False.

Chapter 7

Completion
1. Procedures are guidelines for the *user* and the *WP specialist.*
2. A *procedures manual* is a must for all WP personnel when standardized procedures are needed.
3. An individual with good language and writing skills, often employed to check a document for correctness, clarity, and content, is called an *editor-proofreader.*
4. The total time that elapses between the originator's giving the document to the WP specialist and the time it is returned is called *turnaround time.*

Short Answer

1. Standardized procedures promote:
   a. Increased efficiency of personnel.
   b. Cost-effective use of equipment.
   c. Ease of training for new or temporary employees.
   d. Consistency in style and format.
   e. Sharing of work among WP personnel.
   f. Ease of revision.
2. Proofreading is necessary to ensure that a document is error-free and to see if revisions are necessary. Since the image of the organization is often projected by the written document, it is important that it be proofread carefully.
3. Some examples of when an originator is solely responsible for proofreading are:
   a. Names and addresses and other information, which are not verifiable by the WP specialist.
   b. Statistical information which would not be apparent to the WP specialist.
   c. Enclosure information.
   d. Spelling of technical or unusual terms unknown to the WP specialist.
4. The most commonly undetected errors are found:
   a. In headings and subheadings.
   b. Near the beginning and ending of lines.
   c. Near the bottoms of pages.
   d. In long, frequently appearing words.
   e. In omissions involving simple, frequently appearing words.
   f. In transpositions of letters or characters.
   g. In captions and footnotes.
   h. In proper nouns.
   i. In vertical enumerations.
   j. In number combinations.
5. Some reasons for measuring productivity are:
   a. WP equipment and personnel are justified to management.
   b. Future equipment, personnel, and procedural decisions can be made on a documented solid basis.

   c. Turnaround time can be determined.
   d. Employee performance can be measured.
   e. Chargeback costs can be determined.
6. The line count is used to determine the number of lines completed in a document.

Matching

1. b
2. d
3. f
4. h
5. i
6. g
7. e
8. c
9. a

Chapter 8

Short Answer

1. Reprographics is the process of reproducing or duplicating a document.
2. The five reprographic processes and their advantages and disadvantages are listed below.
3. A WP system can be used to prepare error-free stencil and spirit masters. Carbon copies can also be prepared quickly and easily because there is no need for correction.
4. Four important factors to be considered when choosing a reproduction process are quality, cost, time, and quantity.
5. Some advantages of the offset duplicator are high-quality document reproduction and an inexpensive cost per copy.
6. Some of the methods used for producing a phototypeset document are:
   a. Keyboard the document on a phototypesetter.
   b. Keyboard the document on a direct impression unit.
   c. Keyboard and store the document on WP media, then convert the media through an interface device to a phototypesetter.

Reprographic Process	Advantages	Disadvantages
a. Carbon copy	Economical No additional equipment required Easy to use with WP equipment Little time required	Limited number (five or six) of readable copies Medium quality
b. Photocopying	Easy to use High-quality copy Little time required	Relatively expensive
c. Offset duplicating	High-quality copy Inexpensive on a per copy basis High volume	Requires experienced operator Requires master Expensive equipment
d. Spirit duplicating	Inexpensive on a per copy basis Copy can be varied with colored masters and special effects	Medium quality Requires master Time-consuming Relatively low volume (less than 300 copies)
e. Stencil duplicating	Inexpensive on a per copy basis Colored ink and special effects available High volume	Medium quality Time-consuming

d. Keyboard and store the document on WP media, then telecommunicate it to a typesetting system.

e. Keyboard the document on a computer terminal and utilize computer software to phototypeset it.

f. Keyboard the document using an OCR recognizable font and transmit through an OCR reader/scanner to a phototypesetter.

7. Reasons for phototypesetting a document include:

a. More economical production.

b. More attractive document.

c. Ease of reading.

d. Higher comprehension rate.

e. Greater formatting capability.

8. One reason phototypesetting increases reader comprehension is that important facts and key points can be highlighted for emphasis.

9. Types of documents that lend themselves to being phototypeset include manuals, reports, brochures, contracts, proposals, certificates, forms, and promotional literature.

10. A phototypeset document is cost-effective because 40 percent more text will fit on a page, and there will be proportional savings on paper, ink, printing, collating, stapling, storage, and postage.

Completion

1. The most commonly used method of reproducing a document is the *photocopy* process.

2. *Convenience* copiers are small units designed to make one to ten copies for each original.

3. A multifunction, high-speed, high-volume copier with a logic system is an *intelligent* copier.

4. The IBM 6670 Information Distributor uses *laser* technology to print and telecommunicate.

5. The Xerox 5700 prints at a speed of up to *43 pages per minute.*

6. *Phototypesetting* is an output process of producing a document with different type sizes and type styles via an electronic system onto photographic paper or film. (*Photocomposition* is also an acceptable answer.)

7. A phototypeset page holds *40* percent more than a typewritten page.

Chapter 9

Completion

1. Telecommunications is also called *electronic document distribution, electronic mail,* and *electronic data*

transfer. (*Electronic data dissemination* is also an acceptable answer.)

2. The two major benefits of telecommunications are *speed* and *accuracy.*

3. The name of the telephone connecting device used in telecommunicating a document using facsimile is *acoustic coupler.*

4. Point-to-point telecommunications is also called *terminal-to-terminal telecommunications.*

5. The most important consideration in designing a point-to-point telecommunications network is *equipment compatibility.*

6. The modem converts digital coding to *analog coding* in order for the message to be sent over the telephone wires.

7. If an organization cannot afford its own computer, it may choose to contract with a *time-share computer service.*

8. *Intraorganization* is the telecommunications network used between branch locations of an organization using point-to-point telecommunications.

9. Aperture cards hold *one* image.

10. COM is the acronym for *computer output microfilm* and is used for cost-effective storage of data not often updated.

11. The two categories of distribution are *physical* and *electronic.*

12. The major problems associated with mail are *time* and *cost.*

13. The distribution phase consumes *74* percent of the time cycle of a document.

14. Two alternatives to the U.S. mail are *private carrier* and *courier service.*

15. Internal mail accounts for *65 to 75* percent of all mail.

Short Answer

1. Internal carriers are time-consuming and labor intensive.

2. Two advantages of electronic mail are speed and savings.

3. Three examples of private carrier are United Parcel Service, Federal Express, and air and railway freight.

4. Courier service is the most expensive form of mail delivery.

5. Problems associated with manual filing are storage space, retrieval, and labor intensity.

Glossary

Access. Locate documents or sections of documents within the memory or on the media.

Access time. The time taken by WP or DP equipment after being given an instruction to locate documents or sections of documents within the memory or on the media.

Acoustic coupler. Data communications device that converts digital information to analog form and back to digital again when transmitting documents over telephone lines or cables.

Administrative support (AS). People assigned to assist management in performing the non-typing duties of the office.

Administrative support manager. Person responsible for the administration, design, maintenance, and monitoring of the administrative support of an organization.

Administrative support staff. Personnel, including receptionists, administrative secretaries, and supervisors, who assist management in carrying out the non-typing duties of the office.

Administrative support supervisor. Person who coordinates and schedules the work flow of AS staff; also responsible for training and evaluation.

Administrative time. Time spent by WP specialist in training, staff meetings, and in talking to the originator or WP supervisor about the formatting and production of documents.

American National Standard Code for Information Interchange. See **ASCII.**

Analog. Communications term used in contrast to digital transmission, relating to a communication channel on which information is transmitted via an electrical signal or current or continuous wave which can take any limits defined by the channel, such as voice-grade channels. Digital information is converted for transmission of documents to analog using a modem.

Aperture card. Card with space for notations and one or more filmed images mounted on it.

Archiving. Transfer of text from memory or online storage to offline storage media or from operating diskette to permanent file diskette.

AS. Administrative support.

ASCII. American National Standard Code for Information Interchange; an eight level protocol code, (seven bit plus parity check), used for transmission of information by DP and WP systems.

Asynchronous. Method whereby one telecommunicating unit can call another and send information one character at a time with each character preceded by a start bit and followed by a stop bit.

Automated or **automatic typewriter.** See **Text editor.**

Automatic answer. Device by which a telecommunicating WP system can automatically receive text without an operator in attendance.

Automatic backspace. Playback key on a dictation system that allows review of the previous several words.

Automatic gain control. Feature on a dictation unit that automatically adjusts volume during dictation or transcription.

Automatic media changer. Device used with a centralized dictating system using discrete media to eject individual cassettes or discs automatically when they have been recorded.

Autotron. Device to activate a photocopier; it also counts reproduced pages.

Background printing. See **Parallel printing.**

Bandwidth. Difference between high and low frequencies of a transmission band, described in cycles per second (Hertz).

Batch. Procedure in which blocks of characters are electronically transmitted to increase productivity, reduce transmission time, and simplify operations. Also to record or print several documents.

Baud. Unit of transmission speed equal to bit per second.

Baudot. Data transmission code that is used in some teletypewriters in which five bits represent one character.

Belt. Early form of discrete media used in dictation equipment.

Bidirectional printer. Printer that prints one line left to right and the next right to left, to avoid unnecessary carriage or element movement.

Bisynchronous. Term used for the synchronous transmission of binary coded data; a block or group of characters is telecommunicated preceded by a start signal and followed by a stop signal.

Bit. Contraction of **binary digit,** the smallest unit of information recognized by a computer, in the pure binary numeration system, either of the digits 0 or 1.

Black box. Protocol translation device.

Blind terminal or **unit.** Nondisplay WP system in which keyboarded data is printed on paper.

Block of characters. Group of characters transmitted electronically; common block sizes are 128, 256, and 512.

Boiler plate. Prerecorded or stored text that may be combined to create new or repetitive documents.

BPS. Bits per second, a measure of transmission speed.

Bubble memory. Solid state, nonvolatile technology which allows a large amount of memory storage in a small area.

Buffer. Storage area into which data is read or from which data is recorded or printed; a buffer compensates for a difference or change of flow of data when data are transmitted between devices.

Byte. Equivalent to a character, in some systems a sequence of eight adjacent bits.

Camera ready. Completed copy ready for photographing.

Carbon. Reprographic process used to produce a limited number (five or six) of copies using treated tissue-like paper or mylar film.

Cassette. Magnetic tape housed in a plastic case used in dictation and early WP equipment.

Cathode ray tube (CRT). Vacuum tube which focuses electrons on a visual screen for viewing text in WP and/or DP equipment.

Centralized center. Organizational design that is task oriented for the high-volume production of documents; equipment and personnel are placed in a central location.

Centralized dictation system. Permanently installed dictation systems used in organizations with a large number of users; dictation is wired into the WP center for transcription.

Central processing unit (CPU). Unit which controls the storage, logic, and manipulation of the data on a computer and shared logic WP system; another name for mainframe.

Channel. Path along which signals are sent for transmission between points.

Character. Coded representation of a letter, digit, punctuation mark, symbol, or control function.

Chargeback system. Method of charging projects, individuals, or departments for WP or DP production time and costs.

Chip. Piece of semiconductive material containing electronic circuits used in DP and WP systems. No longer than one inch square, a chip can contain all elements of a computer's central processing unit.

Cluster. Work group configuration.

Coaxial cable. Cable consisting of one conductor within a shield of electronically insulated wire used to connect or hardwire equipment.

Common carrier. Private company, government regulated, that provides telecommunication service facilities, such as a telephone or telegraph company.

Communicating word processing equipment. WP system equipped with communications features that allow documents to be electronically transmitted to and from it.

Compatibility of equipment. Ability of WP and DP equipment to accept and process data prepared and/or transmitted by other hardware without conversion or code modification.

Computer-assisted retrieval (CAR). Computer power used to automate the indexing and location of microforms.

Computerized word processing system. Computer equipped with WP software to permit the performance of WP functions.

Computer output microfilm (COM). Creation of microforms directly from text stored in DP systems.

Computer-related WP systems. Computers with word processing capabilities through software.

Configuration. Design of WP work stations and the components of the system.

Constant information. Information that remains the same throughout repetitive correspondence.

Consultant. Expert who provides a model, assistance, or guidance in designing, implementing, and maintaining a component of a MIS environment.

Convenience copier. Photocopier generally used for only one to ten copies.

Copy processing. See **Duplicating.**

Core. Storage capacity of a computer.

Correspondence. Written communications between two or more persons, such as letters or memos.

Correspondence code. Form of protocol used by the IBM Mag Card I.

Correspondence secretary. WP specialist.

Courier service. Hand delivery of a document by commercial carrier.

CPS. Characters per second.

Cross-training. Rotation of staff to different positions so that all know all jobs or equipment in an area.

Cursor. Highlighted indicator on a display of a WP or DP system marking the position in memory.

Custom work station. Organizational design whereby an individual performs administrative secretarial duties with the aid of WP equipment; also, a design which may assign WP specialists to individual departments.

Daisy wheel. Print wheel, an interchangeable print device used on WP printers and offering faster print speeds than an element print device.

Data access arrangement (DAA). Data communications attachment connected to a telecommunications device, used to protect the public telephone network from a sudden surge of power or interference.

Database. Library of stored documents from which new and different documents can be created with a procedure to update and retrieve.

Data communications. Sending and receiving of data on telecommunication lines.

Data entry clerk. Individual who enters data on cards, magnetic tape, or disks or directly into the computer for processing.

Data processing (DP). Entry, processing, control, and storage of data using a computer.

Data set. Device containing the electrical circuitry necessary to convert signals of communicating DP and WP equipment to and from a channel or line for transmission of documents.

Data stream. Flow of information being transmitted during telecommunications.

Data transmission. See **Electronic mail.**

Debug. To check the logic of computer programs or software for logic or sequence errors.

Decentralized center. Organizational design whereby an individual performs administrative secretarial duties with the aid of WP equipment; also, a design which may assign WP specialists to individual departments.

Dedicated line. Leased telephone line for one organization's exclusive use.

Dedicated operator. Person whose primary responsibility is to operate specific equipment.

Default. Setting in DP or WP equipment that is automatically implemented if no other choice is designated.

Desk-top dictation unit. Dictation unit used to dictate and to record conferences in offices functioning in a one-to-one or dictator-to-secretary mode. Usually there are not a large number of users so that centralized equipment is not justified.

Dictating device. Microphone or telephone handset for the originator to speak into while dictating.

Dictionary. Capability to verify the spelling and phrases in a document against a number of words, both general and technical, stored in a WP system.

Digital. Binary output of DP or WP systems; modems convert digital signals into analog waves for transmission over telephone lines.

Digital counter (scanner). Device in dictation unit used to measure units of dictation and assist in accessing certain portions of a document.

Discrete media. Input media, such as cassette, belt, or disc, that is individually distinct and can be physically handled, distributed, and/or stored.

Diskette (disc). Thin circular mylar disk coated with iron oxide to provide magnetic proportions, enclosed in a protective envelope.

Display unit. See **Video display terminal.**

Distributed logic. Multiterminal system which shares peripherals, storage, and/or logic but with intelligence (logic) and processing power also in each terminal.

Distribution. Mailing, delivering, transmitting, and filing of a document, either physically or electronically.

Document assembly. Creation of documents by combining data based text with any new text desired or with variable information such as names and addresses.

Document coding system. Technique of numbering or classifying documents for access and retrieval from the media.

Dot matrix printer. Impact printer that forms each character by a grid or matrix pattern of dots.

Double density diskette. Diskette with double the amount of storage so that the capacity is twice that of a standard diskette by doubling the number of tracks per inch or doubling the serial bit density or both.

Downtime. Time during which equipment is inoperable because of malfunction.

DP. Data processing.

Dumb terminal. Work station or terminal with no built-in logic and which ceases to function if the CPU is inoperable or malfunctioning.

Dump. To transfer information from one form of WP or DP media to another.

Duplex. Copying or printing on both sides of a page; in communications, the ability to send and receive information simultaneously.

Duplication. Process of reproduction of a document.

Editor/proofreader. Individual who provides assistance in quality control of documents, i.e., consistency in format, appropriate use of grammar, capitalization, punctuation, spelling, in the creation and production of a document.

Electronic data transfer (dissemination). See **Electronic mail.**

Electronic distribution. Electronic transmission of a document via telephone lines, microwave, satellite, or hardwired cable.

Electronic document distribution. See **Electronic mail.**

Electronic filing. Process of indexing and retrieving magnetic media and microforms.

Electronic mail. Telecommunication of documents via electronic transmission by telephone, microwave, satellite, or hardwired cable.

Electronic typewriter. Electronic typing system with limited WP capabilities.

Electronic typing system. WP equipment with special correction, revision, print, telecommunications, and text/file manipulation capabilities.

Element. Interchangeable type font and print device used on many WP systems.

Endless loop. Nonremovable tape media in a sealed system which flows in a continuous circle or loop; it is erased for reuse, never handled, and remains in a closed case.

Ergonomics. Study of equipment, facilities, and furniture designs considering human factors for improving the work environment.

Ethernet. Communications network, formed by Xerox Corporation, Digital Equipment Corporation, and Intel Corporation, which will link different types and makes of office machines.

Extended Binary Coded Decimal Interchange Code (EBCDIC). Protocol or bisynchronous transmission code introduced by IBM in which there are eight bits plus parity bit for a nine level code.

Facsimile. The process used for the transmission and long distance reproduction of charts, graphs, drawings, pictures, signed documents, and other images by electronic means via telephone lines or radio or microwave communications.

Feasibility study. Study performed to show the administrative and correspondence needs of an organization.

Fiber optics printer. High-speed nonimpact printer which utilizes lasers transmitted over hair-size glass fibers to convert digital signals to charged dots on the zinc oxide sheet master of the copier; the image is then transferred to paper.

File/sort. Capability of a system to arrange, sort, and select stored data in alphabetical, numerical, or other order.

Firmware. Specific software instructions permanently placed in control memory in DP and WP equipment, not accessible by operator.

Firmware-driven. WP equipment with capabilities determined by firmware and often implemented by read only memories (ROMs) of equipment.

Flextime. Work schedule different than the usual forty-hour, five-day 8:00 a.m. to 5:00 p.m. week; for example, ten hours per day, four days per week.

Flow chart. Graphic representation of the sequence of work from beginning to end.

Fluid duplication. Reprographic process used to reproduce material; also known as spirit, liquid, or ditto duplicating.

Font. Character set including alphabetical and numerical characters, punctuation marks, and symbols; also refers to phototypesetting element.

Foreground processing. WP task that requires dedication of the system and allows no other functions to be performed, in contrast with background processing.

Format. Predetermined arrangement of text/data for output.

Forms. High-use standard document providing a frequently used type of information.

Full-duplex. Communication flow in which data is transmitted simultaneously in both directions.

Gas plasma tube. Display screen on a keyboard or work station that allows for viewing the inputting of text files or manipulation, revision, or deletion of stored text files using gas plasma or discharge technology.

Graphics. Illustrations, charts, diagrams, maps.

Half-duplex. Communications flow in which data may be transmitted in only one direction at a time.

Handshake. In communications, an exchange of predetermined signals performed by modems and/or terminals to verify the communications connection.

Hard copy. Paper form of output.

Hardware. Electrical, electronic, magnetic, and mechanical equipment used in WP or DP systems.

Hardware-driven. Equipment with features and capabilities that are activated by functions located within the equipment itself, not by software.

Hardwired. Cable connection of WP or DP systems with peripheral devices.

Headers/footers. Information printed automatically at the top/bottom of each page of a multipage document.

Highlighting. Capability of a WP system to intensify or blink characters or screen area behind characters to emphasize a character or segment for specific functions such as change or delete.

Image processing. Process of reproducing a document via reprographics to paper or micrographics to microform.

Impact printer. Print device that strikes the paper as it prints.

Indexing feature. Device on dictation unit or paper strip which shows total length of dictation, number of documents, and beginning and end of each document.

Information processing. Throughput of numbers, words, and symbols from origination through distribution.

Information specialist. Individual who works with users as they generate documents that must be produced, reproduced, permanently indexed, stored, and communicated.

Ink jet printer. High-speed nonimpact printer which electronically sprays a stream of electrostatically charged ink droplets through an electronic font in the shape of the character.

Input. Process of creating or authoring documents; entering of text or data into the WP or DP terminals.

Input/output (I/O) terminal. Equipment with both keyboarding and printing capabilities.

Inscribed media. Early dictation equipment media that is physically cut or scratched as it records, not eraseable or reuseable.

Integrated technologies. Different types of equipment tied together through telecommunications.

Integration. Ability to move information in useable form from one device to another.

Intelligent copier/printer. High-speed, high-quality, multifunction printer with logic capabilities using laser or fiber optics technologies; some offer both the photocopy and print process, as well as collating, duplexing, and telecommunicating capabilities.

Intelligent terminal. Terminal or remote device capable of performing functions using its own logic capability on input or output data.

Interactive. Online operation of technology in which an entry elicits a response.

Interface. Connecting device used to integrate systems.

Internal carrier. Internal delivery of mail within an organization.

International Information/Word Processing Association (IWP). Professional organization for information/WP management personnel and for other WP professionals.

Interorganizational network. Network of terminal-to-terminal or terminal-to-computer telecommunications between two organizations.

Intraorganizational networks. Network established for telecommunications between branch locations within organizations.

Justification. Capability of a DP or WP system to print with an even right margin.

Keypunch operator. Individual who types data on paper cards for entry into the computer.

Key word. Main word in the text used to recall certain information on a given subject area.

Labor intensive. Process that requires a great deal of work performed by people.

Laser printer. High-volume, high-speed, nonimpact printer utilizing an extremely narrow beam of electromagnetic energy in electrophotographic printing systems.

Light emitting diode (LED). Display lighting of keyboarded data on an illuminated screen.

Line count. Number of typewritten lines per page or per document.

Line printer. Impact printer that prints a line of characters at a time at a very high speed as a peripheral device to a WP or DP system typically using a drum, chain, or train of print devices.

List processing. See **Records management.**

Load. To enter a program into the system, often by inserting magnetic media.

Lockout. Security device in dictation systems which prevents eavesdropping or accessing previously dictated text by another individual.

Logging. Recording incoming and outgoing work to monitor the workflow.

Machine dictation. Process of moving the idea of the originator through the spoken word into a machine which records it on magnetic media.

Mag. Magnetic.

Magnetic card. Magnetic film card that is erasable and reuseable which holds from 50 to 100 lines of text, depending on vendor.

Magnetic media. Reusable devices such as cassettes, belts, tape, cards, and diskettes used for recording or storage of text and software in WP and DP systems.

Magnetic tape. Magnetic storage medium.

Management information system (MIS). Method of organizing people, procedures, and equipment to assist management in business operations.

Manual filing. Physical process of classifying, indexing, filing, and preserving documents.

Marketing support representative (MSR). Individual employed by the vendor to train customers to use equipment and to apply it to their environment.

Media. Device used for the recording or storing of data for dictation, computer, or WP equipment; common forms include paper tape, magnetic cards, diskettes, tapes, cassettes, and computer discs.

Megabyte. One million bytes or characters.

Memory. Device within WP and DP equipment that enables equipment to remember and recall keyboarded and stored information.

Menu. List of operator actions for performance of tasks.

Message switching. Store-and-forward form of electronic mail that receives, stores, and distributes messages to the participants of a network.

Microcassette. Miniature cassette smaller than both a minicassette and a standard cassette; it records up to 60 minutes dictation.

Microfiche. Photographed text on sheets of film which has rows of images in a grid pattern.

Microfilm. Sequentially photographed text on film in miniature form housed in cartridges or magazines, reels, and jackets.

Micrographics. Process of recording, storing, and retrieving records on film in a miniaturized form.

Microprocessor. Integrated circuit or small computer which contains the logic for manipulating and performing operations on text/data.

Mimeograph. Reprographics process for reproducing material using stencil duplicating.

Minicassette. Miniature cassette, larger than a microcassette but smaller than a standard cassette, used in dictation equipment.

Mnemonic code. WP or DP system that uses abbreviations for function commands.

Mode. Method of transmission or operation.

Modem. Device used to convert digital signals into analog signals for transmission through telephone lines and analog signals back to digital form at the other end also known as a data set.

MTST. The first WP system, Magnetic Tape Selectric Typewriter.

Multidrop line. Communications configuration that uses a single channel or common line in a polling mode to serve multiple terminals.

Multipoint line. See **Multidrop line.**

National Association for Word Processing Specialists. Professional organization for WP specialists.

Network. Electronic roadmap of a series of points linking terminals via transmission lines to connect organizations throughout the world.

Noise. Disturbance that interferes with the operation of a telecommunications system.

Nonvolatile memory. Retention of data when power of the equipment is turned off.

Odometer. Digital counter on dictation equipment.

Off-line. Operation of a peripheral device independent of other technology; i.e., WP equipment with a computer or phototypesetter.

Offload the principal. To delegate to the AS staff lower level or routine tasks often performed by the executive.

Offset duplicating. High-volume printing process based on the fact that oil and water do not mix and that impressions may be offset from a plate or master to an intermediate and then on to a page.

On-line. Operation of a WP or DP terminal directly connected to the CPU of a computer or WP system.

Optical character recognition (OCR). Process of transferring data from paper via optical reader/scanner to magnetic media for revision and/or storage.

Origination. Process of creating a document using handwriting, OCR, dictation to a secretary using shorthand or machine dictation.

Originator. Author of a document.

Output. Process used for producing the finished document on media or hard copy.

Pagination. Division of multipage documents into pages with a specified line count.

Paper tape. Paper strips with punched holes to represent characters and codes; a form of media.

Parallel operation. Completion of one function while other functions are being performed simultaneously.

Parallel printing. Printing of text while new text is being keyboarded, stored, or revised.

Parity check. Method of checking the accuracy of electronic transmission.

Peripheral equipment. Devices such as printers, phototypesetters, or media units which work with DP or WP equipment to extend the capabilities.

Photocomposition. Setting up and printing of text in different type styles and sizes via an electronic optical system onto photographic paper or film.

Photocopying. Process of photographing a document.

Phototypesetting. See **Photocomposition**.

Physical distribution. Delivering of a document by manual or physical means, such as mail, courier service, internal carrier, and manual file.

Pitch. Horizontal character spacing per inch, size of typewriter spacing and type faces; 12 pitch is elite, 10 pitch is pica; other common pitches are 13.3 and 15 characters per inch.

Point-to-computer. See **Terminal-to-computer**.

Point-to-point. See **Terminal-to-terminal**.

Polling. Communications feature that allows a system to check with other terminals or devices to see if there are messages to transmit.

Portable dictation unit. Small, lightweight, battery-operated dictation unit for use in the field.

Prerecorded. See **Boilerplate**.

Principal. See **Originator**.

Print wheel. Interchangeable print font used on many WP systems; it produces faster print speeds than an element print device.

Private carriers. Company in the business of mail delivery, an alternative to the U.S. Postal Service.

Procedures. Guidelines for the performance of tasks, documents produced, and equipment operated.

Procedures manual. Guide for executives and support staff that outlines procedures for tasks performed, documents produced, and equipment operated.

Production work station. Work station in a centralized center where there are WP specialists who deal primarily with the production of documents, many of which are routinely done.

Production log. Form on which documents are listed with pertinent information about them for the purposes of calculating productivity and tracing documents within the system.

Program. Software instructions to the computer or WP system for the operation of DP and WP equipment.

Programmer. Individual who designs, writes, and debugs program software for a computer.

Proofreader. Individual responsible for quality control of documents; checks content, spelling, typographical errors, grammar, format, and punctuation.

Proofreader's marks. Symbols used to mark corrections required in the production of a document.

Protocol. Set of conventions for electronic transmission; includes modes, speed, character length, and code.

Qualify. Electronic selection of information from stored records.

Queue. Storage areas in a shared logic WP system linked to a specific function, such as printing or archiving to line up documents waiting for that function to be performed, while the WP specialist continues with other tasks at the keyboard.

Qume print wheel. Print wheel or daisy wheel.

Random access memory (RAM). Storage capability that allows documents to be stored randomly and retrieved by an address location or identification.

Read only memory (ROM). See **Read only storage**.

Read only storage (ROS). Used in DP and WP hardware to enable equipment to follow instructions.

Recording unit. Component in dictation unit that records the spoken word onto magnetic media.

Records management (RM). Systematized method of indexing, setting up, storing, and maintaining a retrieval system for permanent documents.

Remote device. Terminal, printer, or other device located at a distance which requires telecommunications for access.

Repetitive correspondence. Written communications that have the same or constant information going to a number of different recipients; also called form or shell letters.

Reprographics. See **Duplicating**.

Satellite. Electronic dishlike device that orbits the earth and is used to connect communications stations throughout the world via electronic beams.

Satellite Business Systems (SBS). Organization formed by IBM, Aetna Insurance Company, and Communications Satellite Corporation (COMSAT) for the purpose of establishing an integrated all-digital worldwide data communications system using satellites.

Satellite design. Organizational design wherein the WP specialist works in the physical location of a given department exclusively for that department.

Scanning device. Manual or electronic devices on transcribers that show where each document ends and where special instructions from the originator are located; electronic device on OCR that reads characters from hard copy and copies them onto media.

Scroll. Ability to move keyboarded text up and down or left and right on a video display terminal.

Sequential access. Memory (SAM) method of locating data on media in which documents are stored and searched one after another, as opposed to random access.

Shared logic. Multiterminal WP system in which each terminal shares the capabilities, storage, and peripherals of the system's central processing unit.

Shared system. WP system that has more than one work station, all of which share one or more resources, such as logic, media, and printer.

Simplex. Transmission of communications flows in one direction only.

Software. Stored set of instructions or programmed media for the operation of DP or WP hardware.

Software-driven. Equipment with features and capabilities that are activated by software such as magnetic cards or diskettes.

Specialized production. Organizational design that is a combination of centralized and decentralized systems, providing the executive with administrative and WP support in the office in addition to providing a centralized production center for long documents.

Spirit duplicating. Duplicating process using a master with aniline dye and a fast-drying alcohol to transfer the image from the master to paper.

Standalone unit. Single station, self-contained WP unit that provides keyboarding, logic, printing, and storage of data.

Standard. Level of average production of WP specialists.

Standard cassette. Discrete magnetic media; largest of three types of cassettes.

Standardized procedures. Uniform procedures and guidelines for the production and delivery of an organization's documents.

Statistical documents. Documents that contain numerical information in multicolumnar form.

Stencil duplicating (mimeograph). Duplicating process that uses an inking process and a master called a stencil to create an image on paper.

Store-and-forward. Mode of receiving messages, storing them, then sending them forward to addressee to be accessed at will.

Synchronization technique. Method of transmission.

Synchronous. See **Bisynchronous**.

Synchronous Data Link Control (SDLC). IBM communications line protocol associated with system network architecture (SNA) which provides greater transmission efficiency; it initiates, controls, monitors, and terminates information exchanges or communications lines in a full-duplex operation.

Systems analyst. Individual who analyzes and designs information systems to solve user needs.

Systems network architecture (SNA). IBM standardization between its virtual telecommunication access method (VTAM) and the network control program.

Systems operator. Individual who enters data into and operates the WP or DP system and peripheral equipment.

Telecommunications. Electronic transmission of data between WP and DP equipment via telephone lines, hardwired cables, microwaves, and satellites.

Teleconference. Electronic transmission of pictures and/or digital messages to audio visual computer-equipped facilities in different locations for the purpose of meeting and exchanging information.

Teleprocessing. Processing of documents during telecommunications transmission.

Teletypewriter (TTY). Terminal equipment manufactured by Teletype Corporation with keyboard, print, send, and receive capabilities.

Teletypewriter Exchange Service (TWX). Western Union service in which teletypewriters and other terminals using Baudot and ASCII are provided with lines to central office to access other public lines throughout the United States and Canada.

Telex. Worldwide Western Union teleprinter exchange service.

Terminal. DP or WP work station capable of input, output, and/or telecommunications.

Terminal-to-computer. Telecommunications from a WP system, intelligent copier, or terminal to a computer; also called point-to-computer.

Terminal-to-terminal. Telecommunications between two locations used when one type of WP system, that is, printer, OCR, sends to or receives information from a compatible device; also called point-to-point.

Text. General term used to describe documents such as reports, manuals, and manuscripts.

Text editor. WP work station.

Thin window. One line or partial-line CRT or gas plasma display on WP or DP equipment giving a window to see into the memory.

Throughput. Cycle of a document from origination through output, reprographics, and distribution.

Time-shared computer system. Commercially available access to a computer that is shared by two or more users on an online time and storage charge basis.

Touch-tone. Trademark of the Bell System which refers to the ten-key panel on a push-button phone.

Tracks. A measurement equivalent to one line of stored text.

Trail printing. See **Parallel printing**.

Transcribe. To keyboard dictated text.

Turnaround time. Time that elapses between the submission of a document for completion and its return to the originator.

Twin track printer. Printer with two print wheels that can print simultaneously.

TWX/Telex. Western Union teletypewriter network.

Type bar. Single character, impact print device in a basket or well, a printing mechanism; a term often applied to conventional typewriters or early WP equipment.

Unattended. Automatic features of a WP system which permit operation without anyone present.

Unbundled. Services and training programs of a WP manufacturer sold independently of the hardware.

Upgradeable. Equipment to which new capabilities can be added.

User. Originator; person who requests services of WP specialist.

Value added. Term used to describe tasks now being done due to advanced technology that were not done before.

Variable information. Information in repetitive documents that varies, such as names and addresses.

Vendor. Organization that manufactures and/or sells equipment, software, and supplies.

Vendor competitive analyst. Individual who analyzes equipment sold by other vendors to assist sales representatives in competing against such vendors.

Video display terminal (VDT). WP or computer work station which has a CRT display or gas plasma screen to allow data to be viewed as it is input, revised, or deleted.

Viewing window. One-line or partial-line CRT or gas plasma display on WP or DP equipment giving a window to see into the memory.

Voice-activated. Equipment that can function in response to spoken words.

Voice grade line or circuit. Telephone circuit used for speech communication.

Voice mail. Store-and-forward voice messaging system to automate the delivery of telephone messages.

Voice operated relay (VOR). Automatic device in the recording unit of a dictation machine that activates or deactivates the recording on the media depending upon whether or not the dictator is speaking.

Voice recognition. Voice actuated operation of WP and DP equipment.

Volatile memory. Memory on WP equipment that is lost if power is discontinued.

Winchester disc. Rigid, nonremovable, magnetic oxide coated, random access disc sealed in a filtered enclosure with the read/write heads and head actuator.

Word/information processing. Industry maturing and integrating WP and DP.

Word processing (WP). Systematized method of producing, copying, and distributing documents using technology, procedures, and trained people.

Word processing manager. Person responsible for administration, design, and overall monitoring of WP operations.

Word Processing Society. Professional organization for WP personnel.

Word processing specialist. Person skilled in the operation of a WP system; transcriber who is able to keyboard, revise, assemble, produce, and telecommunicate documents.

Word processing supervisor. Person responsible for work flow, training, and evaluation of WP staff.

Word processing technician. Senior level WP staff member in the document preparation process.

WPM. Words per minute.

Work measurement. Quantify and analyze productivity in terms of document volume, time, and cost.

WPM. Words per minute.

Index